A BEGINNER'S BOSTON

BY LAUREL ULRICH AND OTHERS

ILLUSTRATED MOSTLY BY CAROLYN PETERS

E PLURIBUS UNUM

Contents

Acknowledgments

In the fall of 1966, a group of Mormon women scraped together enough money to print a thousand copies of the first
edition of this book, hoping to sell them to friends and
neighbors to raise money for our church welfare program. An
unexpected newspaper article gave us a boost, and we were
sold out in two weeks.

Two revisions and many thousands of books later, we are
convinced there are easier ways of making money, but intro-
ducing people to Boston has gotten into our blood and we
don't know how to stop. *Beginner's Boston* has become as
much a service as a fund-rasing project. But it's been fun.
Neither Carolyn and I, nor any of those who helped us, are
paid. The proceeds go to the Cambridge Ward Relief Society,
the women's organization of the Church of Jesus Christ of
Latter-day Saints, 2 Longfellow Park, Cambridge.

As with the first edition, putting this book together was a
cooperative effort. I would particularly like to thank the
following people, "in order of appearance":

Claudia Bushman, who wrote "Learning the Language",
and Stephanie Goodson, who contributed the housing section
of "Help."

Jerry Horne, Phil Dushku, LuAnne van Uitert, Mary
Wirthlin and Alberta Baker, who gave me many good ideas
for the walking tours.

Kitty Lambert, who did the research for "Food."

Dixie Huefner, who produced most of the material in the
four chapters of the "Culture" section.

Dorothy Lyon, who wrote most of "Nature," added to "Capes & Islands" and "Sports", and taught us how to dig a clam.

Ann Romish, who updated her original chapter, "Three Ways To Have A Clambake", contributed to "Sports" and shared her enthusiasm for Nantucket.

Bonnie Horne and Marie Zabriskie, who updated "Bargains."

Jeannette Franklin, who developed the South Shore drive and helped research "A B See."

Stephanie Goodson, Gerald and Bonnie Horne, Jeannette Franklin, LuAnne van Uitert, Fred and Penny Holton, who put in many hours helping me turn a manuscript into a book.

Others who did research or helped with proofreading, paste-up, or distribution are: Sue Fagerlund, Sydney Reynolds, Sue Kohler, Janet Bice, Jean Pagnotti, Barbara Vining, Helen Rhodes, Carol Sandquist, Grethe Peterson, Valerie Anderson, Jasmine Rich, Dee Dee Williams, Ida Mugica, Tom Zabriskie, Bert van Uitert, Norman Kay, Marilyn Irish, and Kay Clay.

Carolyn Peters contributed ideas as well as art. Her enthusiasm for Boston added to the pleasure of the book for me. Karl, Melinda, and Nathan Ulrich and John, Philip, Susa, and Charles Peters illustrated the children's chapter.

Few of those listed above were born in Boston. Most of us are "beginners." Though our book has grown since the first edition, we still consider it an introduction and have deliberately kept the margins wide for your convenience in adding your own discoveries.

Laurel Ulrich

Calendar

Wake on **Sunday** to the ringing of bells. In the North End little girls in ribboned hats are hurrying to church, in Brookline the Riverside Trolley is jammed with teens doing homework for Sunday classes at the temple, and on Brattle St. in Cambridge a white-gloved policeman directs traffic past the Holy Trinity Armenian Apostolic Church. At the corner spa, comic-loving kids are trying to talk their Dad into the *Globe* or the *Herald* instead of the *New York Times*. The free samples at Morton's Bakery are almost gone. Between ten and one, the admission fee at the Museum of Fine Arts is cut in half. By afternoon, lines have begun to form at the Children's Museum and demonstrations have started at the iron works in Saugus and the textile museum in the Merrimack Valley. Nature talks at Drumlin Farm and concerts at the Gardner begin at three. By sundown, there is a stream of headlights from New Hampshire to the Cape.

Early on **Monday** morning bargain-hunting women line up at Filene's and Jordan's doors ready to pounce on the advertised specials. Building 19 in Hingham is open from nine to nine, then closed again until Saturday. Many Boston museums, galleries, historic houses, and even restaurants are closed, but the weekend crowds have disappeared from Plymouth and the ski slopes are peaceful and inviting.

Tuesday is distinguished as the day Joyce Chen serves a Mandarin-Pekingese buffet and the Museum of Fine Arts stays open free from seven to nine. It's as good as any other day for sightseeing or shopping or going to work. Isabella Stewart Gardner's palace is open, as is Abraham Browne's House in Watertown.

Wednesday is a day for clothing exchanges, Beacon Hill mansions, and the No-Name Restaurant. The department stores are open late. The Quincy Bargain Barn closes at noon. On **Thursday**, walk along Brattle St. in Cambridge, stopping to visit the Lee Nichols House. In the suburbs, pick up a weekly newspaper just off the press.

On **Friday** and **Saturday** the pushcart vendors line Haymarket Square, butchers at Faneuil Hall display their reddest beef, North End grocers sell oil by the gallon and bouquets of asparagus out of season, the department stores and supermarkets are mobbed and the theatres full. On Friday night, the Museum of Science is open at reduced rates until ten. Rush-line tickets at the Symphony go on sale Friday at noon and Saturday at six.

January brings the snow. With it comes skiing at Boston Hill, skating on the Fenway, icy sidewalks and traffic jams, and the great radio debate between oil and gas heat. Every four years the Governor is inaugurated and immediately begins cleaning up Massachusetts and quarreling with the Great and General Court. Along the coast, the beaches are wild and beautiful and, for a few hours after a snowfall, Boston sparkles.

February brings school vacation and more snow and sled-dog racing and blizzards and Chinese New Year and no-school reports and "crazy-day sales" on Washington's birthday. Off-season tourists find historical attractions open in Salem as well as Boston. The theatrical calendar is full.

March can be grey—or exasperatingly white. Sugaring-off parties, town meeting squabbles, lenten services at the Old South, and a St. Patrick's Day parade help fight depression. The Spring Flower Show is tacky by California standards but a miracle for March in these parts. If $3.75 seems steep, you can get up at five and visit the wholesale flower market instead. Toward the end of the month look for Canadian geese at Plum Island.

In **April** those famous Middlesex villages and towns launch the tourist season with rousing Patriot's Day celebra-

3

tions, but on different days. A few stalwart towns resolutely ignore the new Monday-holiday law; others bend with the times. Plimoth Plantation, Saugus Ironworks, and most houses in Concord and Lexington open for the season April 19. Early in the month you can still see sugaring in New Hampshire. Toward the end, you can watch the herring-run on the Cape. Crew races on the Charles continue into May.

May is a teasing, temperamental time of blossoms and cold rain, when the Boston Pops takes over Symphony Hall, Harvard choruses sing on the steps of Widener, and gardeners get out the Old Farmer's Almanac to check the phases of the moon. On good days, the banks of the Charles are lined with spring-struck couples. On bad days, New Englanders try to remember that Indian Summer pays them back for a cheating spring. The blossoms come in a great burst of joy—lady-slippers in the woods, apple trees in the country, lilacs at the Arboretum.

June brings more blossoms—rhododendron in front yards and in special forest preserves, mountain laurel in the Berkshires, and late in the month, wild roses on Cape Ann, Martha's Vineyard and Nantucket. The Hammond Museum in Gloucester opens. St. Peter's Fiesta draws people from everywhere to see the traditional blessing of the fleet. At the old North Bridge, the banks of the river are a sweep of green and lavender. Baseball fans flock to Fenway Park. And the kids are finally out of school.

In **July** the Boston Pops plays in Hatch Shell, the Symphony plays at Tanglewood in the Berkshires, the New England Conservatory at Castle Hill in Ipswich. Old-time bands perform on the Common and at the Pru; Cambridge Common and the Fenway rock with new sounds. Bluebloods leave their town houses for their beach houses and children splash in wading pools at Beaver Brook and in Brighton. Cape Cod and Cape Ann are filled with summer people. Campers bring clotheslines, lawn chairs, bicycles, baby carriages, radios, and all their relatives to campgrounds at the state parks. It's race week at Marblehead and summer stock season in Dennis.

August brings more of the same, plus blackberries and blueberries ripening in the woods. Every Friday at five, Plymouth residents enact the traditional pageant, "Pilgrim's Progress." There are beach buggy tours at the National Seashore, a seafood festival in New Bedford, tennis matches at the Longwood Cricket Club, and the Duster's Meeting at the Antique Auto Museum.

In **September** the Monarch butterflies land at Eastern Point in Gloucester and students from all over the world converge on Boston and Cambridge. It's time to harvest tomatoes and pick apples and wash storm windows and take one last trip to the beach.

October is a splendour of color. Tourists and deer hunters and old Dartmouth grads head for Vermont and New Hampshire. Middle-aged couples spend weekends at the Wayside Inn and look for the last of the country auctions. Dads anguish over the price of Halloween pumpkins on Rt. 2 and vow next year to plant their own. And the great Atlantic flyway is alive with birds.

November brings church bazaars and cold winds and bright-colored berries on 2000 holly trees at East Falmouth. On Thanksgiving Day high school football teams play "grudge games," turkeys roast on spits at Sturbridge Village, and Plymouth welcomes visitors with cranberry juice and free admission to historic houses.

December brings reindeer to the Common and twinkling lights to the tiny shops on Bearskin Neck. The Boston *Globe* announces its ski clinic and sends out appeals for Christmas gifts for the needy. The Handel & Haydn Society sings "The Messiah," the Boston Ballet dances "The Nutcracker," and a show at the Museum of Science planetarium tells how a new star is born. On Christmas Eve, as on each Christmas Eve for a hundred years, carolers and bellringers gather in candlelit Louisburg Square.

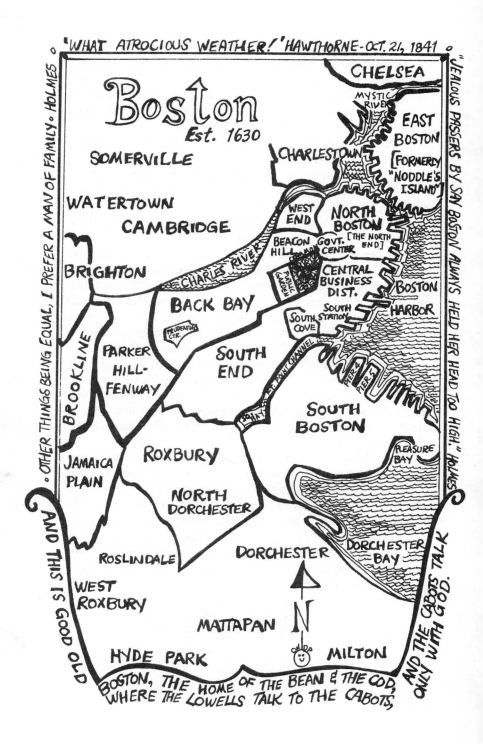

Getting Around

The geographical center of Boston is in Roxbury—at the corner of Westminster and Walnut Avenues, if one cares to be precise. Due north of the center we find the South End. This is not to be confused with South Boston, which lies directly east from the South End. North of South Boston is East Boston and south-west of that is the North End.

George Weston

Getting around in Boston isn't hard once you figure out the basic geography. Most people never do. If you want to maintain your composure, never leave home without a map. The points of the compass are irrelevant. It's more important to learn a few important landmarks, like the Common and the Charles River. Be warned, however, that the Common, like most rectangles in Boston, is an irregular polygon. The Public Garden, which joins the Common at one end, is equilateral, but then it's part of the Back Bay, one section of Boston laid out on a grid. You will find out soon enough that the Charles River divides Boston and Cambridge. Don't be surprised, however, when driving along it, to see the 52-story Prudential tower capriciously change sides. The Algonquin Indians called the Charles "Quinobequin," meaning "circular."

The cows have been unfairly blamed for Boston's crooked streets. The street system is unusual, but it's logical. School St. was once the shortest path across lots to the school, Court St. led to the court, Market St. to the market.

What is more natural than that Summer should change to Winter, that Water should parallel Milk, or that India should end at the wharf?

When lost in the suburbs it helps to know that some streets were once highways between towns. In Newton, for example, Waltham St. leads to Waltham and Brookline St. to Brookline. Both change to Newton St. at the border. Other streets change names with no apparent reason. Why Stuart suddenly becomes Kneeland is anybody's guess.

The Boston Athenaeum, domain of historians and scholars, has a number, but no name, on the door. Bostonians, says Walter Muir Whitehill, assume that anyone with serious business knows where things are. This attitude is not confined to Beacon Hill. Major cross streets throughout the city are seldom marked, the assumption being if you're on it you know its name.

If the idea of getting lost unnerves you, take a cab. **Taxis,** still called "hackney carriages" by the licensing bureau, aren't hard to find. The rates are uniform; 50¢ to get in, 10¢ for each 1/10 of a mile thereafter. Since every route is roundabout in this city, the mileage can add up, but if more than two people are going a relatively short way, a cab can be the cheapest form of transportation.

More adventuresome is the **MBTA.** Within the city it's indispensable. It helps to know that the transit planners have taken the "hub" metaphor seriously. All tracks lead downtown, making it easy and convenient to get from the suburbs into Boston, extremely difficult to get from one suburb to another. The underground lines cost 25¢, surface busses 20¢. Most downtown stations have maps on the wall. But if you intend to use the MBTA very often, you should pick up a **systems map** at the information booth at Park St., the main subway terminal. In the meantime, you can call 722-5657 for directions on getting from where you are to where you want to go. They take their time, but they answer.

MBTA MAP ON PAGE 235

A few urban dwellers, happily settled on The Hill or in Back Bay, do nicely without a car. You probably won't be so lucky. There are times when **driving** is most practical. If

you're headed downtown, however, stop and ask yourself what you'll do with your car when you get there. During business hours, street parking is impossible. Even finding a **parking garage** with space may require a bit of driving around. Check first at Boston Common underground garage off Charles St. The rates are 50¢ for the first hour, 50¢ for the second hour, and 25¢ for each additional hour up to $2.50. At the Prudential center, the Fitz-Inn garage charges 50¢ an hour with a $2.50 maximum. The Shopper's Garage near Washington St. charges 60¢ the first hour, 50¢ each additional hour, with a $2 maximum. Evening rates are often somewhat less.

You should know before you start that Boston driving has **rules** all its own. To help you get started, we've compiled a few of these. With some experience on the road you'll discover the rest.

(1) A conspicuous dent in your fender is a strategic advantage when maneuvering during rush hour.

(2) Never stop for a yellow light. You might cause a rear-end collision.

(3) Sharpen up your peripheral vision. Letting the other driver catch your eye is a sign of weakness.

(4) When the traffic light turns green, look both ways before crossing.

(5) Never park in a "no-parking" zone unless the tow zones are all full.

(6) When making a left-hand turn from the right lane, signal your intention by moving three-quarters of the way into the intersection before the light turns and waving your left hand vigorously out the window.

(7) If it becomes necessary to abandon your car in a snow storm, tie a bright-colored scarf to the antenna. It will make it much easier to find later.

(8) When you don't know what else to do, honk.

Boston belongs to the walker. If you want to love it here, skimp on subway fares and gas. Splurge on time. Walk not just to get places but to see the city. Putting feet to pavement—concrete, brick, cobblestone, granite, asphalt—you'll learn how compact, yet how enticingly, windingly diverse Boston is. Eight walking tours in the second section of the book get you started. From there it's up to you.

Learning the Language

Boston Yankees are nearly as scarce as local Indians. The city has been repeopled with waves of immigrants, first from Ireland, beginning with the great potato famines of the 1840's, and then later in the century from Italy and central Europe. In recent times, mobile Americans from Duluth, San Antonio and Seattle have entered the melting pot. Boston's "natives" are exceedingly diverse.

Describing the local tongue is complicated. Cleveland Amory refers to an actor who identified thirteen separate aristocratic or Brahmin dialects alone, without even considering the speech of the masses. Certainly the final "r" is often missing and as often reappears, with a kind of phonetic logic, in unexpected places. The same person who "opens the doeh" is likely to "have an idear." A flat "a" is in general use, and strangers asking the way to "Pack Street" should be kindly pointed to Park. Anyone saying "Pahk Street" will need no help. Paradoxically the flat "a" was considered the polite sound before the Revolution, and the broad "a" was in use by the commoner folk.

Some vocabulary is useful. New Englanders invariably carry **pocketbooks** rather than purses, **pails** rather than **buckets,** and **bags** rather than sacks. Leave your bathing suit home when you visit a **spa,** a neighborhood variety store where you might buy a bottle of **tonic;** that's soda pop, not hair oil. Local milk shakes are minus ice cream; a Western-style milk shake is a **frappe** (rhymes with map). When reading menus you should know that the red flannel in hash is beets. **Indian Pudding,** or ironically hasty pudding, is a slow-baked dessert of corn meal and milk flavored with molasses. **Scrod** is a young codfish, usually broiled. **A dropped egg** is poached, not scrambled. At the meat counter, a **fowl** is a stewing hen, not some anonymous wild bird. The locally cured corned-beef is meant to be grey; New Englanders omit the saltpeter. Cooked with vegetables it makes a **boiled dinner.**

On the road those traffic circles in the midst of intersections are called **rotaries** and driving them is an acquired talent. A **square** is usually the broadened area where two or more streets converge and shops are found; squares are not necessarily square. The Pike refers to the Massachusetts turnpike, a tollroad going west. Mass' Ave. is the common nickname for Massachusetts Avenue, originally the Concord Road marched by the redcoats. An **alewife**, as in Alewife Brook Parkway, is a variety of herring. Lakes are usually **ponds.** A **neck** is a narrow strip of land, an isthmus, or peninsula. The **esplanade** is the grassy shore of the Charles River separated from Back Bay Boston by Storrow Drive. Mainers travel "up to Boston;" their city cousins visit them **down Maine.** British visitors are amazed to find New England equivalents for the vast majority of old English towns. A few Indian names—Shawmut, Scituate, Chappaquiddick—have held on. Worcester is pronounced "wuśter," Peabody—"peé-budee," Quincy—"quiń-zee," Woburn—"wóbun."

 Knowing the local sign language makes getting around easier. A grey circle with a black "T" stands for the Massachusetts Bay Transportation Authority, the MBTA. Grey paint and subway art are giving the transit system a new look, but on some outlying streets orange paint around a pole may still mark the bus stop.

Busy intersections sometimes have Walk/Wait signs. More often a red and yellow light means pedestrians may go. **No Parking** means all those cars parked and double-parked might get tickets. **Tow Zone** means they might get towed, especially in a **snow emergency,** which on Boston's narrow streets can be anything over an inch.

Harvard University has no campus. That fenced and gated area with the Georgian buildings must be called **The Yard,** as the University of Virginia buildings are placed on The

12

Grounds. **The Coop,** pronounced with one syllable as in chicken, is a cooperative department store. **The Common** is that preserve of greenery in downtown Boston and in many other towns originally set aside for the grazing of cows.

Architecturally, a **salt box** is not a squat tower, but a two-story house with a one-story lean-to at the back,  allowing the roof line to continue at the same angle longer in the back than in the front. **A captain's walk** is the little fenced platform at the top of the mansions in seaport towns. In sadder households the same feature is called the **Widow's walk.** South Enders sit on their front **stoops,** those high steps with wrought iron railings. In other parts of the city, people chat on their **piazzas.** That handsome building on the Freedom Trail, Faneuil Hall, is pronounced "Fanyouwill" by those that know, and "Funnel" by those that really know. S. S. Pierce is pronounced "purse."

When the weather is unsettled "storm warnings are posted from Eastport to Block Island," warning ships from Maine to R. I. to stay put. What comes is a fabled **Nor'easter,** dumping quantities of snow or rain. It is permissible to wear a **Sou'wester** in a Nor'easter. **Indian Summer** refers to the warm autumn days when the Indians came out to harass the colonists before retiring for the winter.

The **weather light** on the top of the John Hancock Building gives three-hour forecasts. Blue stands for fair, flashing blue for cloudy, red for rain, flashing red for snow. Flashing red in summer means the Red Sox game is cancelled.

The great whaling days are gone, but reference is still heard to the **Nantucket sleigh ride,** the horrendous ride in a whale boat pulled by a maddened, newly harpooned whale (see Moby Dick). **Scrimshaw,** the decoration of whale bones and teeth, was turned out between Nantucket sleigh rides.

The **Watch and Ward Society,** now disbanded, was a Brahmin foundation bent upon suppressing Vice and protecting the Family Life. Besides urging the banning of books in Boston, they occasionally raided poolrooms and houses of ill fame. Boston censorship of the theatre survives. The latest uproar was over the closing of the musical "Hair."

THE FIRST RECORDED USE OF THE TERM "O.K." WAS IN A BOSTON NEWSPAPER IN 1839.

13

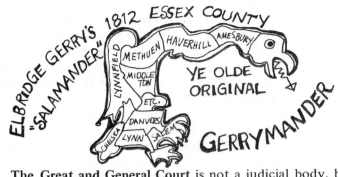

The **Great and General Court** is not a judicial body, but the formal name for the state legislature. Although Boston decided to abandon its open **town meeting** in 1822 and adopt a city-form of government, only 38 cities have followed suit. Massachusetts is left with 312 units of government retaining some form of the 17th-century pattern of community decision-making. Most towns with more than 25,000 people have opted for a representative town meeting—electing a limited number of town meeting members to legislate for the town. Most towns with less than 25,000 people have retained their open town meeting, where any registered voter may attend and vote for the policies of his choice. Articles to be considered at the town meeting must be included in the **town warrant** and may be submitted by citizens during a stipulated period in January. Elected **selectmen** administer town affairs between town meeting sessions.

Gerrymander is a national term of Massachusetts origin. In 1812, Governor Elbridge Gerry carved out such a strange electoral district it was said to ressemble a salamander. A political enemy dubbed it a gerrymander and it happened right here folks.

Oliver Wendell Holmes called Boston "the hub of the solar system." Generations of Bostonians since have not questioned his definition and show little inclination to leave the center of things. Visitors often feel the same.

14

Settling

This chapter is a medley of answers to common problems beginners face. It is primarily directed to new residents.

To tourists we have a few words of advice. If you are not yet in Boston, you may find a complete listing of **tourist accommodations** useful. Write the Convention and Visitors Bureau, Greater Boston Chamber of Commerce, 125 High St., Boston and ask for the free "Lodgings Guide." In a pinch, the YMCA is at 316 Huntington Ave. Share-a-bath singles are $6.25 a night, $31.75 a week.

Once you have a place to stay, all you need is *Beginner's Boston* and a road map. But should confusion set in, know that friendly folks will answer your questions at the **Information Center** on Boston Common (opposite West St.). It is open Mon-Fri 9-5, Sat and Sun 10-5. Closed Thanksgiving, Christmas, and New Year's Day.

HOUSING

Colonials or contemporaries, high-rise or town-houses—if you can hardly wait until daybreak to start looking, then Boston is your bag. But if housing-hunting isn't your favorite sport, you'll want to track down some clues before your personal scrutiny begins.

An excellent start is **The New Settler's Guide** which gives an introduction to 132 communities in the Greater Boston area. Descriptions of each community include the type of town and homes available, population, area, distance and driving time from Boston, tax situation, public transportation, public facilities and services, public school system, churches, organizations, recreation, medical, shopping and banking facilities. A map helps pinpoint your selection of communities. To order this year's edition write New Settler's Guide, 872 Massachusetts Ave., Cambridge, Mass. 02139. The cost by mail for Mass. residents is $2.31, for out-of-staters, $2.25.

Photographs of homes, as well as descriptions and prices, are given in the **Greater Boston House Buyer's Guide.** This monthly magazine also includes tax rates, auto insurance rates, population, transportation, schools, churches, hospitals, shopping, form of government, and pupil-teacher ratio of the communities surrounding Boston. Copies are available on the newsstands and in some supermarkets for 75¢, or for $1 by writing House Buyer's Guide of Boston, Inc., Box H, Arlington Post Office, Arlington, Mass. 02174.

House-hunting executives may wish to contact **New England Area Consultants, Inc.**, 440 Lexington St., Auburndale, Mass. 02166, for no-charge assistance in locating a home. The firm has films of the areas from Cape Cod to Nashua, N. H., and from Boston to Route 495. A computer aids in finding the type of home you desire.

The Boston Herald Traveler will send free the **Housing Classified Section** of four Sunday papers to out-of-staters. Request should be made to Paul Lannan, 300 Harrison Ave., Boston, 02118. The Boston Globe, 135 William T. Morrissey Blvd., Boston, 02125 will send current Sunday papers for 35¢ and back issues for 50¢. The Boston Sunday Advertiser, 5 Winthrop Square, Boston, 02110 will mail current and back issues for 35¢.

ANY GREMLINS WHICH MIGHT APPEAR IN THIS TEXT ARE AFFECTIONATELY DEDICATED TO THE BOSTON GLOBE.

You may wish to take the initiative by placing an ad describing your requirements in the dailies or the **Community Newspapers.** The most frequent publication date for weeklies is Thursday, but there are exceptions. Community papers are available at newsstands, drug stores and newspaper offices.

Most universities and colleges have an office listing **Off-Campus Housing** to assist students in locating rentals.

There are long waiting lists for the less expensive rentals. Many real estate agencies handle apartment and house rentals also. A brochure on **Real Estate Agencies** is available from the Greater Boston Chamber of Commerce, 125 High St., Boston, Mass. 02110. The Chamber suggests that realtors and apartment rental agencies be contacted after arrival in Boston.

Boston officially has a housing shortage. A great number of apartment units are under construction or recently completed. Intown units are more expensive that those in the suburbs. The most popular type of home in the area is the colonial (two or more stories) with many variations. There are, in less abundance, split-levels, split-entries, raised and conventional ranches (single level) and contemporaries. A "duplex" in the Northeast refers to a pair of houses joined together, while a "two-family" refers to a house with one apartment on top of the other. Brick homes are rather scarce. Homes inside the area of Route 128 where the land generally has been saturated are proportionately higher than those outside where there are still lots available for building.

Apartment-hunters should know that most landlords require one-year **leases**. These are often self-renewing unless notice is given well before the date of expiration. Read the fine print; know what you sign. **Housing regulations** in Boston and Cambridge give the landlord responsibility for adequate fire escapes, plumbing, lighting, hot water (minimum of 120 deg. F.), heat (minimum of 70 deg.), electrical outlets (two per room), screens and drains, extermination of insects and rodents, facilities for garbage and rubbish disposal. In case of violation of the housing code, you should contact the Division of Housing Inspection in Boston or the Board of Health in Cambridge.

Newcomers will soon discover Massachusetts' high real estate-personal property tax. **Local Taxes** are based on each thousand dollars of valuation. Assessors take the total valuation of property in their communities and divide it to obtain the amount to be raised. You would be wise to compare the assessment on the property with the sale price and to find out from the town assessor how recently assessments have been made. Communities are supposed to assess property at 100 per cent fair market value, but the rates range in most cases from 30 to 90 per cent. It is also important to ask what you're getting for your taxes. Some communities do not provide rubbish disposal or a sewer system; not all have public kindergarten.

If you don't find what you want the first day, keep the faith; daybreak brings new possibilities.

CARS, TAXES, AND INSURANCE

New residents must register their cars and get a Massachusetts driver's license immediately. A violation of this requirement is punishable by a fine, imprisonment or both. Before you can register your car, you must have **Liability Insurance**. When you look at the rates, you may decide you'd rather go to jail.

Full-time students or others who can prove they are **Non-Residents** needn't register their cars if their home states grant the same privilege to Massachusetts residents. A telephone call to the Registry 727-3780 should give you the facts pertaining to your state. The student must, however, file a statement with the police department in the city where his school is located. He must also obtain a decal from his school for the car's windshield.

Regardless of whether or not you are a resident, you must pay a Massachusetts **Income Tax** on any income earned in the state. Local towns collect an annual **Excise Tax** on automobiles—new or old.

Before you flee the state, be assured that Massachusetts has one insurance bargain. It is one of the few states in the country with **Savings Bank Life Insurance**. Skip the middle man and save.

VOTING

How much myth has invaded Massachusetts political history is hard to say, but people still talk about the class, regional and ethnic rivalries, the state government's distrust of Boston city government, the rural Yankees' distrust of urban masses, oldtimers' distrust of newcomers, etc. Yet Massachusetts lived through its "No Irish Need Apply" era to see Kennedys sharing political power in the state with Saltonstalls. Newcomers no longer see the old Boston, administered—even from jail—by its corrupt, colorful and seemingly indestructible mayor of yesteryear, James Michael Curley. Instead they see the "new Boston," remade both administratively and architecturally under its recent mayors, John Hynes, John Collins and Kevin White.

Whether you are a political activist or a quiet observer, you will find this competitive two-party state lively and colorful.

A potential voter must have lived in Massachusetts one year, including six months in the town or city where he intends to vote. After 30 days residency, a newcomer can vote for presidential candidates only on a special ballot. Registration and election information in your town can be obtained from the city hall.

Boston City Hall, Election Office, 1 City Hall Square, 722-4100.
Cambridge City Hall, 79 Massachusetts Ave., Cambridge, 876-6800.

MEDICAL CARE

Boston has an unusually large number of outstanding clinics. For specific problems—from hearing to psychiatry—there are excellent services available. Your doctor, medical association or nearest hospital are sources of information for these. We can only list here several of the most commonly used clinics and agencies.

Boston Emergency Physicians Service, 482-5252.
Open your Boston telephone directory and look at the list of emergency numbers in the inside cover. The Boston Emergency Physicians Service will give Boston and Brookline residents names of doctors on call when an emergency arises and they have no physician available. The Middlesex South District Medical Society also has a number listed. You might phone them for names when you are looking for a personal doctor in the area.

Massachusetts General Hospital, Storrow Drive.
In an emergency, when a doctor is not available, go directly to a reputable hospital emergency ward. If in question, the Mass. General is your best choice. As one of the world's great hospitals they have facilites for handling any medical emergency.

GENUINE
GREMLIN
⟶

Massachusetts Eye and Ear Infirmary, 243 Charles St.
For regular clinic visits they is a flat $12 fee. Beyond that you pay according to ability. In general, you'll save little on straight refractions, but for contact lenses a visit to the Eye and Ear pays. Expect a waiting list.

Poison, 232-2120.
This center is operated in cooperation with Children's Hospital. If your child swallows something you think might be dangerous phone this number for emergency instructions. Write the Poison Center, 300 Longwood Avenue, Boston 02115 for a free list of common poisons and their emergency treatment. Notice that some call for Ipecac syrup to induce vomiting. This is distributed free by the Mass. Pharmaceutical

Association through your local druggist at certain times of the year.

Children's Hospital Medical Center, 300 Longwood Ave., Boston 02115, 734-6000.
Children's is considered by many to be the mecca for pediatrics. The services are many and are billed according to ability to pay. If your child has special problems, your physician or the hospital can inform you of services available, but you wouldn't want to depend upon the hospital itself for routine care. There is a well-baby clinic at Children's.

Well-Child Clinics, phone the Health Department of the city in which you live.
Free D.P.T. shots, polio drinks, etc. are given at the Well-child Clinics, but sick children are not welcome.

Boston Lying-In Hospital, Obstetrical Clinics, 221 Longwood Ave., Boston 734-5300.
Harvard and M.I.T. cooperate with BLI in providing obstet- *WHOOPS! HARVARD & MIT NO LONGER COOPERATE WITH BLI*
rical care for university wives for about half the cost of a private physician. The disadvantages of clinics—long wait, seeing many different doctors, etc.—bother some women. Most, however, become quite attached to BLI. (So much so that quite a few return again and again!) Regular BLI Clinics admit you if your income justifies it.

Tufts Dental Clinic, 136 Harrison Ave., Boston, 426-5955.
Open Sept-May.
The Tufts Dental Clinic is inexpensive and of high quality. At present they accept no one under 12.

Red Feather Information and Referral Service, 14 Somerset St., Boston, 742-2000.
This is an excellent place to go to find out about private and public social, health, welfare, and rehabilitation organizations in the Greater Boston area. Free.

HOUSEHOLD HELP

If you are affluent, consult the yellow pages under "House Cleaning," but be warned that some agencies charge up to $40 per day, and there is often a wait. Sayeth Poor Richard: "If you want a thing well done, do it yourself." If the task is beyond you, try this list compiled by a weary mother of six:

Mt. Ida Jr. College, 777 Dedham St., Newton, Mass. 969-7000.

Girl will live with family for two year period helping with light housework and babysitting. In exchange for 2-3 hours work each afternoon and 1/2 day on Saturday, family provides full board and room plus a salary varying from $12 to $15. Phone the college and an application will be mailed to you. Usually girls live in homes in the Newton area unless special transportation is arranged.

IF ANYONE KNOWS OF AN AVAILABLE CLEANING LADY, LET THE ILLUSTRATOR OF THIS BOOK KNOW!

Radcliffe College, phone 868-7600, and ask for Radcliffe student employment.

Applications will be mailed to you. Girls live in and give 21 hours of work in exchange for full board and room. (Fewer hours of work are required if student prefers only a room).

Catholic Charitable Bureau, 10 Derne St., Boston, 523-5165. Ask for "Family Home Program".

Unwed mothers are placed in homes during pregnancy. Light housework and babysitting are expected in exchange for board and room. Applications may be obtained by telephone. The family is expected to work with a social worker.

Crittenton Hastings House of the Florence Crittenton League, 10 Perthshire Rd., Brighton, 782-7600.

Unwed mothers live-in in exchange for household help and babysitting, and $20 per week. Children in the home must not be under 9 months or over 12 years of age. Transportation must be provided for periodic check-up at the Brighton address.

CHILD CARE

Community Wives, 868-7600, ext. 2240.

This group, formerly known as Harvard Wives, lists women who wish to babysit on a weekly basis. They do not screen the sitters.

Radcliffe Student Employment Office, 868-7600, ext. 3718.

Radcliffe will post your name and needs on the employment board. Many girls' schools in the area will do likewise.

Simmons College, Placement Office, 738-2115.

They require you to register, then will give you names of Simmons students wishing to babysit. They charge a standard rate according to number of children and time of day.

Student Nurses

Some of the most sought-after baby sitters are student nurses. Unfortunately, since most do not give out names of students who wish to sit, the best way to find one is to know one. Peter Bent Brigham posts names on their bulletin board. It might be worth a trip to the nearest hospital to check theirs.

Boston Association For The Education Of Young Children, 146 Jackson St., Newton Center, 969-4531.

Phone Mrs. Morehouse between 3-5 on Monday or Friday for a list of nursery schools in your area. If she doesn't have information for your town, she can tell you who to call.

Day Care Advisory Unit, Massachusetts Dept. Of Public Health, 727-5196.

This agency will give you names of day care centers which are inspected and licensed by the state.

Pediatts, 866 Beacon St., Boston, 563-7020.
Suburban Homemaking And Maternity Agency, 3A Alton Place, Brookline, 232-7650.

These two agencies provide nurses to care for newborns—for a fee of course.

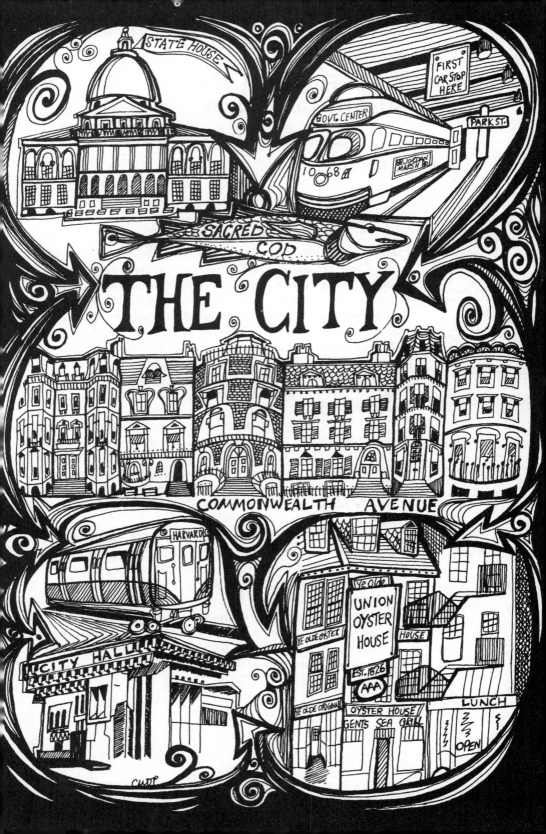

Three Hundred Years
Slightly Condensed

June 12, 1630. Governor Winthrop arrives in Salem Harbor, bringing with him the Charter of Massachusetts Bay Company. There are already individual settlements at Hull, Salem, Chelsea, Charlestown, Boston, and Portsmouth, N. H. Winthrop and his assistants move first to Charlestown, then in the autumn to Boston because the water is better. In December, Cambridge (Newtowne) is laid out. . . . A plaque in Spring Lane off Washington St. marks the site of the Great Spring near which Winthrop built his house.

JOHN WINTHROP
LIVED ON
GOVERNOR'S
ISLAND, NOW
PART OF LOGAN
AIRPORT

1636. Harvard College is founded by order of the General Court. . . . Two Cambridge walking tours document the results.

1637. Religious dissension threatens the new colony. Anne Hutchinson is excommunicated as a heretic and banished. . . . The Old Corner Bookstore (on the Freedom Trail) was built on the site of her house. A statue in her honor stands on the grounds of the State House. The states of Rhode Island and New Hampshire are also monuments to this period.

1650-70. The Massachusetts Bay Colony, with nearly 15,000 settlers under its jurisdiction, is the most powerful of the New England colonies. . . . Several houses built in mid-century are still standing. Boston's oldest dwelling, the **Paul Revere House**, dates from 1677. (see Freedom Trail) Cambridge's oldest, the **Cooper-Frost-Austin House**, 21 Linnaean St., was built in 1657. (Open Thurs 2-5 and Tues 7-9; from June-October open 2-5 on Mon as well. Admission 25¢) Both of these houses have been altered somewhat.

26

Outside shutters, for example, weren't used until around the time of the Revolution. A more complete example of a 17th-century Puritan house is the **Abraham Browne House** at 562 Main St., Watertown. Built in 1695, it has recently been restored. The weathered clapboards, nail-studded door, huge beams, and cramped stairs are all typical of the period. (Open Tues and Fri 2-5 in winter; weekdays 2-5 May-October. Admission 25¢).

IN 1720 JAMES FRANKLIN BEGAN PRINTING THE SECOND NEWSPAPER IN AMERICA, THE NEW ENGLAND COURANT WITH HIS BROTHER BENJAMIN AS APPRENTICE.

1687. Sir Edmund Andros enters Boston with 100 redcoats and is proclaimed governor of all the New England colonies. The religious as well as political dominance of the Puritans is challenged. Andros forces the congregation of the Old South Church to share its building with the Episcopalians. He personally contributes to the construction of King's Chapel. Inspired by the revolution of 1688 in Britain, the colonists overthrow him. He is imprisoned on **Castle Island.** . . . The present Old South Church and King's Chapel replaced earlier structures of the same name. Castle Island, now connected to the mainland, is reached via William J. Day Blvd. in South Boston.

1712-1754. Imposing new public buildings reflect the growing strength of the colony. . . . **Freedom trail buildings** dating from this period include the Old Corner Book Store (1712), the Old State House (1713), Old North Church (1723), Old South Church (1729), Faneuil Hall (1742), and King's Chapel (1754).

OLD SOUTH CHURCH

1766. In opposition to the "Stamp Act," Boston rowdies gather around a spreading elm in front of a local tavern and hang in effigy Andrew Oliver, distributor of stamps and brother-in-law of the acting governor. **The Liberty Tree** becomes a rallying point for the radical young Sons of Liberty under Sam Adams. . . . A marker on the side of a building on Washington St. near Essex marks the spot where it grew. It was hacked down by British troops during the occupation of Boston. Complaints from aesthetically outraged citizens felled the second Liberty Tree, a twenty-foot high aluminum replica of the first, which stood until recently on Boston Common.

REVOLUTION!

March 5, 1770. British troops, enraged by the taunts of a Boston street gang, fire into the crowd, killing five and wounding six. Crispus Attucks, a black man, is the first to fall. . . . A circle of bricks at the end of the Old State House marks the site of the **Boston Massacre**. The Crispus Attucks Monument is on Boston Common.

"BOTH REGIMENTS OR NONE, MUST GO!" SAM ADAMS MARCH 5, 1771

December 16, 1773. Fifty men under Sam Adams and John Hancock board British cargo ships and dump 342 chests of tea into the harbor. In retaliation the British close the port of Boston and establish General Gage as Governor. . . . A marker on Atlantic Ave. near Congress St. indicates the site of the **Boston Tea Party**, now filled land.

April 19, 1775. Middlesex farmers, aroused from their beds by Paul Revere, William Dawes, and Samuel Prescott, encounter British troops at Lexington Green and North Bridge in Concord. The British retreat to Boston. . . . Paul Revere's house and the Old North Church in Boston and the Minuteman National Park in Concord help visitors remember that date.

June 16, 1775. American troops under Israel Putnam dig in on Breed's Hill in Charlestown, having rejected neighboring Bunker Hill, an earlier choice. After a costly battle, the British storm the fort. The Americans retreat to the countryside. . . . **The Bunker Hill Monument** at Monument Square, Charlestown, is open daily 9-4, admission 10¢.

July 3, 1775. Washington arrives in Cambridge and takes formal command of an army of 14,500. . . . The "Washington Elm" on Cambridge Common is the traditional site.

March 17, 1776. The Americans occupy **Dorchester Heights** in South Boston under cover of cannon brought by

Henry Knox from Fort Ticonderoga on Lake Champlain. The British evacuate. The Battle of Boston is over. . . . See the monument on Telegraph Hill, South Boston, now a park. Those perky mansions with their widow's walks and ginger-bread trim came later. March 17 is a double holiday in South Boston, celebrated with a long parade and green beer in the pubs.

1795. Construction of the new State House gets under-way. Real-estate values in the neighboring pastureland start to rise. . . . Our **Beacon Hill** walking tour shows how this area developed into a magnificent residential district, now a National Historic Landmark. Another important monument of Federal architecture, is **Gore Place** at 52 Gore St., Waltham, the 20-room mansion built in 1805 as the country estate of Governor Christopher Gore. Among the most spectacular features is the "flying" staircase. Notice also the careful craftsmanship of the folding cupboard doors, the antique playthings in the nursery, and the kitchen gadgets. The grounds are beautifully landscaped. (Open April 15-November 15, Tues-Sat 10-5, Sun 2-5. Adults $1, children 50¢.)

1797. The U. S. Frigate "Constitution" is launched. During the War of 1812, she is nicknamed **"Old Ironsides"** because shot from the British Frigate "Guerrier" does not break through her sturdy oak sides. . . . Still a commissioned flagship of the U. S. Navy, she is berthed at the Boston Naval Shipyard in Charlestown. You can climb aboard any day of the year between 9:30-4. Parking and admission are free.

USS CONSTITUTION

1827. Edgar Allen Poe publishes *Tamerlane and Other Poems, By a Bostonian.* . . .Poe, "born in a trunk" while his actor parents were on tour in Boston, didn't stay around long enough to join the Saturday Club. Boston has no monument to his memory.

1831. William Lloyd Garrison begins publication in Boston of the abolitionist paper *The Liberator.* . . . You will hear echoes of Garrison on the Freedom Trail, Beacon Hill, and Back Bay walks. Read original copies of *The Liberator* at the public library or the Massachusetts Historical Society.

1836. Emerson publishes *Nature* and helps organize the Transcendental Club. . . . His home in Concord is open to the public. The Old Corner Book Store, publishing center for the flowering of New England letters, has recently been restored and is on the Freedom Trail. The Parker House, where Emerson and his famous friends met at the Saturday Club, is alive and well.

1840. The transcendental journal *The Dial* is begun with Margaret Fuller as editor. . . . The birthplace of Margaret Fuller at 71 Cherry St., Cambridge, has been a settlement house since 1902. Built in 1807, it was the most elaborate of the Federal houses in the Central Square area. Restoration is a possibility.

1847. Longfellow publishes *Evangeline*. *Hiawatha* is yet to come. . . . For a description of his Cambridge mansion, see the Brattle St. walking tour.

1850. Hawthorne publishes *The Scarlet Letter,* following it the next year with *The House of Seven Gables*. . . . He is best remembered in Concord and Salem (see Famous Towns), though he belonged to the Saturday Club and appeared occasionally at the Old Corner.

1851. Melville publishes *Moby Dick.* . . . The Whaling Museum and neighboring chapel in New Bedford recall his seafaring days. Boston can claim him through his Grandfather Melville, who participated in the Tea Party. For years the family preseved a vial of tea leaves collected from his boots that night. Holmes's poem "The Last Leaf" describes him in his outmoded tri-corner hat.

1854. Thoreau publishes *Walden*. . . . The pond is still there. See our tour of Concord.

1857. *The Atlantic Monthly* is founded with James Russell Lowell as editor. Oliver Wendell Holmes, Professor of Anatomy and Physiology at Harvard Medical School, contributes a monthly essay, "The Autocrat of the Breakfast Table". . . . Holmes' house, at 296 Beacon St. in the Back Bay, still stands. Lowell's mansion "Elmwood," now owned by Harvard, is easily seen from the traffic light at Fresh Pond Parkway and Mt. Auburn St. in Cambridge. Neither is open to the public.

"I KNOW ALL THE PEOPLE WORTH KNOWING IN AMERICA, AND I FIND NO INTELLECT COMPARABLE TO MY OWN."
MARGARET FULLER

IN 1842 CHARLES DICKENS VISITED BOSTON.

1858. Building is booming in the new **South End**. The first of the gravel dumped into the **Back Bay** marks the beginning of a new Brahmin neighborhood. . . . There are walking tours of both districts in the next chapter.

1861. Under the leadership of William Barton Rogers, thirty-seven leading citizens sign the "Original Act of Association of the Institute of Technology," creating a new kind of educational institution. In 1863, the **Massachusetts Institute of Technology** moves into an impressive new building on Boylston St. near Copley Square . . . M.I.T. moved to newly filled land in Cambridge in 1913. The Back Bay building was destroyed in 1939.

1895. The Boston Public Library is built, the last of the cultural institutions to ornament Copley Square. . . . A new addition is underway at this writing.

1903. Isabella Stewart Gardner opens her Venetian palace on The Fenway. In 1909, the Museum of Fine Arts moves to its new building nearby. . . . Both are thriving.

1916. Boston's first native-born Irish mayor, John F. ("Honey Fitz") Fitzgerald runs for U.S. Senate against incumbent Henry Cabot Lodge, Sr., the first round in a famous political battle. . . . The latest bout was in 1962 when their two grandsons, Ted Kennedy and George Lodge, fought it out for U.S. Senate. The Kennedy victory was a repeat of 1952 when JFK beat George's Dad, Henry Cabot Lodge, Jr.

May 29, 1917. John F. Kennedy is born in Brookline. . . . The National Park Service now owns the house at 83 Beals St., Brookline where he lived the first three years of his life. As the **Kennedy National Historic Site**, it is open every day, except Monday, 8:30-5. Adults 50¢. The **Kennedy Library** will be built in Cambridge on the plot of ground off Memorial Drive and Boylston St. where all those MBTA busses are now parked.

Boston Walks

FREEDOM TRAIL

> The morals of our people are much better; their manners are
> more polite and agreeable; they are purer English; our language
> is better; our taste is better; our persons are handsomer; our
> spirit is greater; our laws are wiser; our religion is superior.
>
> John Adams

To understand the spirit of Boston, walk the Freedom Trail,
the city's one official walk. All you have to do is follow the
red brick trail which starts at the Common and leads through
the downtown shopping area past the new Government
Center into the market district and across to the North End.
To see the pushcart vendors in action, walk on a Friday or
Saturday. If you're determined to see a particular building,
check the opening and closing hours carefully. For some
reason the places at the end of the trail have the shortest
hours—Paul Revere's house closes at 3:45, the Old North
Church at 4. If you get a late start you can always walk
backwards. Actually, it's no catastrophe if you don't get
inside everything. Boston's workaday streets are as educational as anything on display. Break away from your map
now and again and look at some of those people looking at
you.

   If you start about 9:30, stroll at a leisurely pace, and
don't feel compelled to read every word on the markers along
the way, you'll end up somewhere in the market district
about noon—along with all the other tourists in Boston, most
of whom will be ahead of you in the line at Durgin-Park. If
you're too starved to fight the mob, you might try the North
End. Or just snack on fruit and sweets from the sidewalk
stalls.

The numbers given below correspond to the official numbered sites on the trail. We have included a few suggestions for side trips along the way and have mapped only that portion where you're most likely to lose sight of the markers.

(1) **Boston Common** was originally laid out for the grazing of cattle. Cows still show up here during dairy week in June; reindeer appear at Christmas time. But the Common belongs to the people, as the old saying goes. Squirrel-lovers, benchsitters, students-with-a-cause are all welcome. "Playland" invites mothers to leave their children for an hour or two. But since the curfew imposed in the summer of 1969 hippies can no longer sleep here.

(2) **The State House**, designed by Bulfinch, is that gold-domed building you see on the hill. It's further described in our Beacon Hill walk.

(3) **Park Street Church**, 1809, was designed by Peter Banner, an Englishman, but the Ionic and Corinthian capitals of the steeple were by Bostonian Solomon Willard. It was the first Trinitarian church established after the Unitarian invasion of the old Puritan congregations and was known for its fiery sermons. Garrison preached his first anti-slavery address here in 1829; the song "America" was first sung here in 1831.

Open Mon-Fri 9-4:30, Sat 9-12, Sun 9-1, 4:30-9. Closed weekdays at 4 in July and August.

In (4) **Granary Burying Ground** famous and obscure Bostonians are buried. The sign on the gate tells about the famous ones. The inscription on the large "Franklin" monument was composed by Ben for his parents, but the granite marker replaced an original marble one which deteriorated. Lots of old slate stones remain, half sunken into the ground. Open every day 8-4.

As you pass, take a quick look at Bosworth Street, which ends in a flight of stairs. The old Province House once stood here.

(5) **King's Chapel** became the first Unitarian Church in America after the Revolution. Before that it was a loyalist stronghold, the first Episcopal Church in Puritan Boston. The

THERE ARE 3 MANNED LIGHTHOUSES IN BOSTON HARBOR!

AT KING'S CHAPEL, LOOK DOWN TREMONT STREET FOR A VIEW OF THE OLD NORTH CHURCH AS FRAMED BY THE NEW CITY HALL

33

building was completed in 1754. The designer, Peter Harrison, was a distinguished amateur in a day when there were few professional architects. His building is much more elaborate than the non-conformist churches of the same period. The burying ground adjoining is the oldest in Boston. Open Mon-Sun 10-4.

(6) **Site of First Public School** and **(7)** **Statue of Benjamin Franklin** are worth a look but are probably less interesting than the building behind them. Boston's old City Hall was built in 1862, one of the first French Victorian structures in Boston. Walkers in the Back Bay will recognize the style. The Louvre-type dome once held a fire-alarm.

(8) **The Old Corner Book Store**, 1712, restored recently, is the downtown subscription office of the Boston Globe as well as an historic monument. During the days of James T. Fields it was considered the "hub of the hub." Longfellow, Emerson, Hawthorne, Holmes, Whittier, Harriet Stowe and Julia Ward Howe were a few of the authors who gathered in the green-curtained corner in the back. Open Mon-Sat 9-6, Mon and Wed til 9.

(9) **Old South Meeting House**, built in 1729, was a public meeting place as well as a church. The famous meeting which led to the Boston Tea Party was held here. The

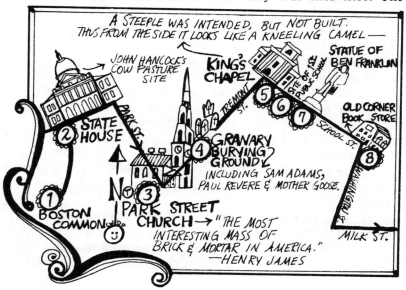

building was set aside as a memorial in 1877, soon after the congregation moved to the new Old South in Copley Square. Special services are occasionally held here, as are Harvard extension classes supported by the Old South Foundation. Open Oct 1-June 1 Mon-Sat 9-4; June 1-Oct 1, Mon-Fri 9-5, Sat 9-4. Closed holidays except July 4 and Labor Day. Adults 25¢, children under 12 free.

(10)   **Site of Franklin birthplace.** Boston hasn't forgotten Ben, even though he deserted for Philadelphia at the age of 17. A marker indicates the spot where his house once stood.

(11)   **The Old State House**, built in 1713, was known as the Town House before Massachusetts became a state. The colonial governors sat here, as did the first state governors. The exhibits and restored rooms inside are fascinating and free. Open Mon-Sat 9-4, closed Mondays, December thru April.

THE OLD STATE HOUSE HAS STEPPED GABLE ENDS; NOTICE THE LION AND THE UNICORN.

(12)   **The Boston Massacre Site** is marked by a circle of granite cobbles in the street at the end of the old State House. This area was the town marketplace in the first years of the colony. During the Revolutionary period it was still the center of town life. The stocks, pillory and whipping post were located here, as was the Cage, used to confine Sabbath breakers.

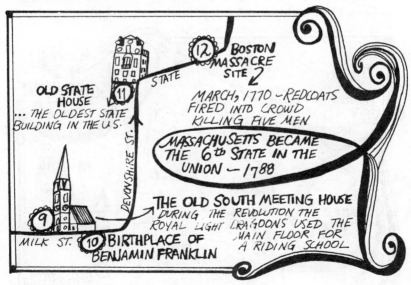

From the Old State House you can follow the red brick trail to Faneuil Hall, but in this stimulating neighborhood it's more fun to digress.

Side Trip A takes a left turn to the new Government Center. The **City Hall** and its surrounding plaza were designed by Gerhard M. Kallmann, Noel M. McKinnell, and Edward F. Knowles, who won the architectural competition held in 1962. It is an exciting building not only for itself but for the way it relates to the historic buildings around it. Walk through it to enjoy the changing views of Faneuil Hall and the Old State House. There are usually art exhibits inside.

Although individual buildings in the Government Center are by different architects, the site as a whole is based on a design by I. M. Pei. The relationship of buildings is important. Be sure to notice the old **Sears Crescent**, barely saved from the wrecker's ball and now restored. This is a new location for the giant tea-kettle which has been spouting steam in the neighborhood since 1860. The new crescent building, **Center Plaza**, encloses its end of the square visually yet allows for free movement through to the State House and old office buildings on the other side.

Sometime walk down Cambridge St. toward the West Church (described under Beacon Hill). Notice the **Boston Press Club building**, a kind of brick snail, originally built as a

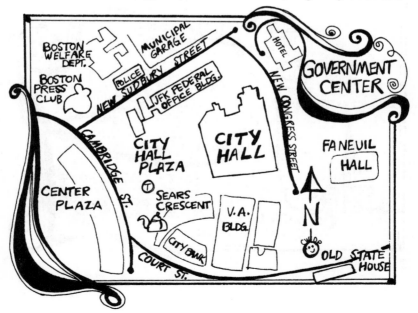

36

temporary office for a bank, then found too interesting to destroy.

Side Trip B, for people who've seen the Government Center, leads from the Old State House across to the **Stock Exchange Building**, 53 State St., built in the 1890's, a Richardsonian-Romanesque building complete with decorative ship models and undulating granite floors. Boston's small stock exchange can be seen from the third floor. Leave the Exchange Building through the Kilby St. door and go directly across the street into the parking garage. Walk through the garage, stopping to watch the huge, free-wheeling elevator transporting cars to empty slots. You'll come out into Mifflin Place, a tiny garden opening onto Broad St. Before you is the **Custom House**, Boston's first skyscraper. The original classic-revival building (1837-47) had a dome on top. The Federal government, not being subject to local ordinances restricting height, added the tower in 1915. The observation tower is open Mon-Fri 9-11:30; 1:30-4, free. Notice the peaked roof of the **Grain & Flower Exchange** building, behind the Custom House to the right. A Boston architect has his offices under the eaves. Imagine a desk in each of the little windows. Now follow Commercial St. to South Market, stopping to observe the progress of renovation at the granite **Quincy Market** buildings. You'll soon be at Faneuil Hall.

THIS IS THE CUSTOM HOUSE TOWER AS SEEN FROM A DISTANCE

THIS IS THE CUSTOM HOUSE, A GREEK-REVIVAL BUILDING, UP CLOSE

IT WAS BUILT UPON 3,000 PILES ON THE WATERFRONT FACING THE DOCKS. IT IS STILL THERE, BUT THE WATER MOVED.

37

(13) **Faneuil Hall** is used as it was originally intended—downstairs a market, upstairs a meeting hall. Originally built in 1742, it was enlarged by Bulfinch in 1806. The Ancient and Honorable Artillery Company has a museum on the top floor. It's worth stepping in if only for a look at the main room. Open Mon-Fri 9-5, Sat 9-12, Sun 1-5; Museum Mon-Fri 10-4.

From Faneuil Hall be sure to follow the red "footsteps" in the street carefully. You will be led under the expressway into Boston's famous **North End**, now an Italian section. Here you'll see strings of sausage and garlic and oregano and barrels of unknown edibles. At Easter time whole lambs and kids hang from hooks in the windows; at Christmas there are eels from a pushcart, in summer water ices and festival lights. Any time of year there are symmetrical towers of pink and green pastries, bins full of pasta and contraptions for making your own, and marvelous piles of crusty bread.

(14) **Paul Revere House** was old when the famous patriot moved there. Built in 1677, it is the oldest house in Boston. You may get an interesting tour—or a grunt—from

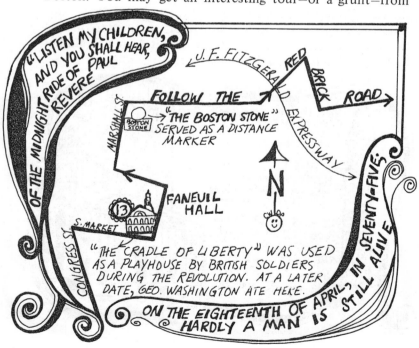

the custodian, but if you haven't seen a 17th-century house you should certainly go inside. Open Mon-Sat 9-3:45, closed holidays except April 19. Admission 25¢.

(15) **Old North Church** built in 1723, was a landmark for sailors long before it served Paul Revere. Guides inside share the lore. The adjoining mall has 13 historic bronze tablets and twice that many old men in felt hats huddled over cards or checkers. Open daily 9:30-4 (June 1-Sept 30); 10-4 (Oct 1-May 31).

If your feet are still supporting you, take Hull St. to **Copp's Hill Burying Ground**. In the 1600's the hill, then much higher, was an important gathering place as well as a cemetery. During the Revolution, the British planted their cannon on the crest for the attack on Bunker Hill and soldiers used the old gravestones for target practice. On January 24, 1793, an ox was roasted on the Hill in honor of the French Revolution. The inscriptions on the stones are fun to read, though so many graves have been tampered with no one can be sure who "lyeth here."

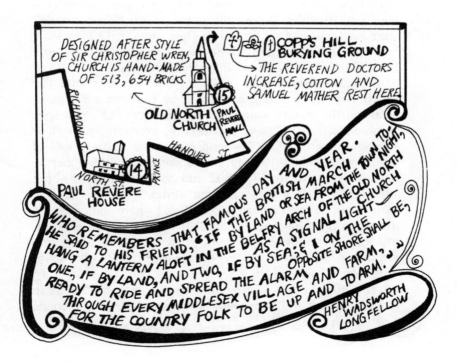

BEACON HILL

> Boston State House is the hub of the solar system. You couldn't pry that out of a Boston man if you had the tire of all creation straightened out for a crowbar.
>
> The Autocrat of the Breakfast Table

In 1795 Sam Adams and Paul Revere laid the cornerstone for a new State House to be built on John Hancock's old pasture on Beacon Hill. In the next 20 years, spurred by Charles Bulfinch, architect, town selectman, and real estate promoter, the neighborhood became an elegant new residential district. Its elegance hasn't tarnished, even though institutions and apartment dwellers have replaced some of the bluebloods. In 1963 it was declared a national historic landmark.

Throughout Beacon Hill notice footscrapers, gas lights, old carriage houses, hidden gardens, wrought-iron balconies, delicate lace curtains behind purple window panes. No matter how often you come back you'll find new ways of looking at doorways and windows, new alleyways and unexpected courts to discover. Before the peaks of the "Trimountain" were cut down by 60 feet or so (beginning in 1803) a walk on The Hill was more strenuous. On some streets, iron handrails are still useful on slippery, winter days.

(1) The State House is the logical place to begin. The exterior of the building is basically as Bulfinch designed it, although the granite wings were added later. The red bricks, painted white in 1825 and yellow later, were restored to their original color in 1928. The gold dome hasn't always looked this way. Originally painted, it was sheathed with copper by Paul Revere and Sons in 1802 and gold-leafed for the first time in 1874. It was blacked out during World War II. The main door leads through Doric Hall, where guided tours gather on open days at 11 and 2. If you can't spare an hour, at least walk to the second floor, where the Bulfinch interiors are intact. Volunteers at the Information Desk will answer questions. Open Mon-Fri 9-5.

(2) Joy Street, which runs to the left of the State House, once had three names corresponding to the social distinctions along it. Even circumspect Beacon Hill has its "other side". In the early days, the Negro district was on the downhill side of Joy. If you want to digress for a minute, follow Joy St. until you come to a sign pointing to the "North Russell Street Synagogue", which is not on North Russell St. at all, but on Smith Court. It was built in 1806 by the African Baptist Church Society. In 1832, the New England Anti-Slavery Society was founded here under the leadership of William Lloyd Garrison.

As you turn onto **(3) Mt. Vernon Street** watch for idiosyncracies in the buildings. The builder of number 50, which was once a stable, stipulated in the original deed that it could never be raised above 13 feet so he could watch his cattle grazing on the Common from his house across the street. Houses numbered 57 to 79 are set well back from the street. This results from a gentleman's agreement with the owner of number 55, Jonathan Mason, that the houses to be built would not obstruct his view of the Charles River. Mason's house was later owned by noted Beacon Hill spinster and First Family lady, Rose Standish Nichols. As the **Nichols House Museum** it is open on Wednesdays and Saturdays 1-5. Admission 25¢.

BOSTON'S FIRST HERMIT WAS REV. WILLIAM BLACKSTONE WHO LIVED ON BEACON HILL IN 1630.

(4) The Harrison Gray Otis House at 85 Mt. Vernon Street is one of three built for Otis by Bulfinch. Walter Muir Whitehill calls it "the handsomest house in Boston." However prominent Bulfinch was, his preference for detached mansions didn't prevail over the rising demand for land; most Beacon Hill houses were built in rows. Boston's streets in this period were paved with cobblestones brought from the shore, some of which remain in the driveway. The side entrance into the drive was a Bulfinch innovation. The roof rail and cupola soon became features of seaside mansions up and down the coast. The house is still a private dwelling. The **first Otis House**, on Cambridge Street on the other side of the Hill, is owned by the Society for the Preservation of New England Antiquities and is open Tues-Sat 1-4, admission $1. The **third Otis House**, at 45 Beacon Street, is owned by the American Meteorological Society.

41

(5) **Louisburg Square** is private. The cobblestoned carriage ways and fenced park are maintained by the 20 "proprietors" who meet yearly to assess themselves for the upkeep. It's pronounced "Lewisburg" by those that know. Lovely at any season, it's liveliest on Christmas Eve. The houses are no longer open to carolers as they once were, but the narrow brick streets are filled with singers and bell ringers, and candles burn at the windows in welcome to passersby.

(6) **Pinckney Street** is known for tunnels—and a great view of the river. (7) **Revere Street** has a marvelous collection of narrow courts leading off it. Barely wide enough for two walkers, each has a street sign and a row of gaslights right down the middle. Some end in gardens, some with "stage-prop" house fronts.

(8) **Charles Street** is a street of shops. The windows display Polish pots and doorknobs and salami and flowers—but mostly antiques. Browsing is fun anytime—but cheaper after hours. The Riverside Cafeteria has good pastromi and blintzes and glasses of milk in two sizes: "enough and more-than-enough."

"MARIKA'S" ON CHARLES ST. HAS ORIENTAL ANTIQUES

(9) **The Charles Street Meeting House** once stood on the shore of the Charles River. Land has a way of moving in Boston. Filling in was a continual process all through the 19th-century. The church was designed by Asher Benjamin, Bulfinch's most serious rival in those days. Actually, Benjamin was more famous for his books than his buildings. These were practical guides for the builder, who in those days was usually both carpenter and architect. Like Bulfinch, Benjamin topped his churches with domes rather than steeples. The **Old West Church** on Cambridge Street is also his. It was a branch of the public library from 1896 to 1960, when it was rescued from demolition. It is now used by a Methodist congregation.

As you turn onto (10) **Chestnut Street**, savor the unexpected view of the State House. Chestnut is known for famous people but better known for beautiful doorways, many deeply recessed in arches. The houses at 13, 15, and

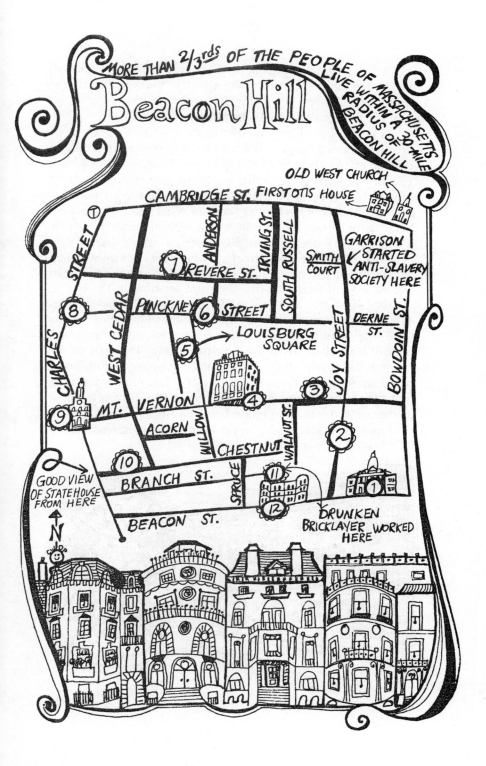

MORE THAN 2/3rds OF THE PEOPLE OF MASSACHUSETTS LIVE WITHIN A 30-MILE RADIUS OF BEACON HILL

BeaconHill

OLD WEST CHURCH
CAMBRIDGE ST. FIRST OTIS HOUSE

GARRISON STARTED ANTI-SLAVERY SOCIETY HERE

SMITH COURT

ⒶSTREET

⑦ REVERE ST.
ANDERSON
IRVING ST.
SOUTH RUSSELL

⑧
PINCKNEY ⑥ STREET
WEST CEDAR
DERNE ST.
BOWDOIN ST.
JOY STREET

⑤
LOUISBURG SQUARE

CHARLES

⑨ MT. VERNON ④ ③
ACORN
WILLOW
WALNUT ST.
②

CHESTNUT
⑩
SPRUCE
BRANCH ST. ⑪
GOOD VIEW OF STATE HOUSE FROM HERE
⑫
①

BEACON ST.
DRUNKEN BRICKLAYER WORKED HERE

N

17, attributed to Bulfinch, were once owned by Hepzibah Swan, the only woman among the Mt. Vernon Proprietors who originally developed the Hill. Her collection of antiques is in the Swan collection at the Museum of Fine Arts.

(11) Spruce Place is distinguished by the work of another famous Beacon Hill builder, the renowned drunken bricklayer. At the end of the alley you'll see a curious wall. The bricks were laid parallel to the sloping street for about four feet, at which point someone discovered the mistake and changed the course. Nobody knows what really happened. Some people say the mason was a new apprentice. Others blame his work on "an unusually potent morning dram."

(12) 39-40 Beacon Street are twin mansions now owned by the Women's City Club. Built in 1818, they have been altered several times. Notice the third window in the bay at number 40, added in the late 19th-century. The violet panes date from the early part of the century. The color results from the action of sun and time on impurities in some English glass shipped to Boston at the time. The tour of the house is fascinating but can take the better part of an hour. Every doorknob and tea set has a story. The most interesting part may turn out to be the guide, especially if she is inclined to share anecdotes of childhood on The Hill.

Open 10-4, Wednesday only. Adults 75¢, children 50¢.

BACK BAY

The Back Bay has become a "nuisance, offensive and injurious to the large and increasing population residing upon it."

Boston Health Department, 1849

Nineteenth-century technology polluted and then transformed Boston's Back Bay, once an expanse of duck-filled salt marshes and mud-flats under water at high tide. The famous big stink was caused by a population boom and the construction of railroad causeways which impeded the flow of sewage out to sea. In May 1857 the Legislature said something had to be done and authorized commissioners to fill in the bay. Once an hour, six days a week for almost forty years, thirty-five loaded gravel cars arrived from Needham nine miles away. The new area was developed according to a plan which Lewis Mumford calls "the outstanding achievement in American urban planning for the nineteenth century . . . apart from L'Enfant's plan for Washington."

(1) **Arlington Street** is the first of the alphabetical streets running from the Public Garden to Charlesbank—the one area of Boston where it's hard to get lost. The Arlington Street Church on the corner of Boylston, built in 1861, was the first church in the Back Bay. Its warm brownstone set the fashion for many houses in the new area. H. H. Richardson, who designed the dark oak pulpit and railing, later became famous for churches he built on the New Land. As you walk along Arlington Street, notice the mansard-roofed houses facing the Public Garden. They show the influence of Paris. There is no one dominant mode in the Back Bay, however. Architects and their wealthy patrons reached out to the world for exotic and individualistic ideas.

The opulent quarters of the Boston Center for Adult Education at 5 Commonwealth Ave. illustrate the tone of these streets. Not all Back Bay houses had as grand a ballroom, but even the less modest houses were, with few exceptions, built by their owners to their own specifications. There was little speculation for resale as there was in the South End.

(2) **Gibson House**, 137 Beacon St., while on the wrong side of Beacon socially, is a fascinating though decaying relic of Victorian days. It was built in 1859, one of the first of the Back Bay houses. The red-carpeted stairs, dark woodwork, and bay windows are characteristic of the period, as is the clutter of knick-knacks and bric-a-brac. It is open for guided tours 2-5 daily, except Mondays and holidays. Adults 50¢, children under 12 free.

From the first there was a social division down the middle of Beacon, the water-side decidedly the more elegant. Before Storrow Drive was built in the 1930's, the houses on the river side had unbroken access to the embankment. Most of these houses have now been cut up into apartments or converted to institutional uses. But to get an idea of the palatial early days, walk into (3) **118 Beacon Street** now owned by Fisher Junior College. You can see the ornate front entrance doors and marble stair-case with its brass railing. The college owns several houses on Beacon Street. For a complete tour, phone in advance (262-3240).

BY WALKING DOWN BEACON ST FROM BEACON HILL THROUGH THE BACK BAY, YOU CAN SEE A HISTORY OF ARCHITECTURE FROM BULFINCH TO VICTORIA & BACK TO BULFINCH REVIVAL.

The houses from **211 to 219 Beacon St.**, in the next block, illustrate another important feature of the Back Bay—the composed group. Notice how six separate houses have been designed as a whole, with matching octagonal bays and mansard towers on the end buildings, a flatter façade in the middle. The overall effect is consciously French, but in appearance only. The floor plans hew to the English pattern—six vertical town houses side by side. Most French apartments of the period were laid out horizontally, one above the other, each dwelling taking up a single expansive floor, as do the so-called "French flats" built later in another part of the Back Bay.

(4) **First Church** will be a dramatic symbol of Back Bay past and present when construction is completed. Built in 1868 and burned in 1968, it is being rebuilt by Paul Rudolph. The original tower and Berkeley Street façade have been incorporated into the new design, which includes a semi-public sunken amphitheatre on the Marlborough Street side.

46

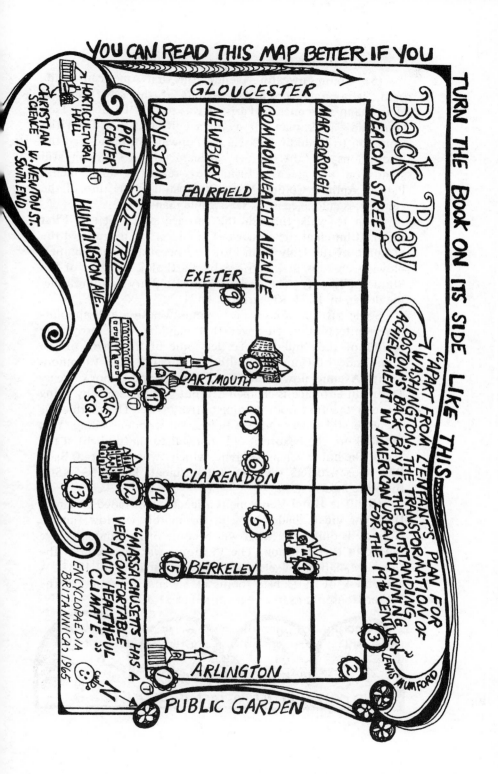

YOU CAN READ THIS MAP BETTER IF YOU

TURN THE BOOK ON ITS SIDE LIKE THIS

Back Bay

"APART FROM L'ENFANT'S PLAN FOR WASHINGTON, THE TRANSFORMATION OF BOSTON'S BACK BAY IS THE OUTSTANDING ACHIEVEMENT IN AMERICAN URBAN PLANNING FOR THE 19th CENTURY."

LEWIS MUMFORD

"MASSACHUSETTS HAS A VERY COMFORTABLE AND HEALTHFUL CLIMATE."

ENCYCLOPAEDIA BRITANNICA, 1965

GLOUCESTER

BEACON STREET

BOYLSTON

NEWBURY

COMMONWEALTH AVENUE

MARLBOROUGH

FAIRFIELD

EXETER

DARTMOUTH

CLARENDON

BERKELEY

ARLINGTON

PRU CENTER

HORTICULTURAL HALL

CHRISTIAN SCIENCE

W. NEWTON ST. TO SOUTH END

SIDE TRIP

HUNTINGTON AVE.

COPLEY SQ.

PUBLIC GARDEN

(5) **Commonwealth Avenue**, the first American boulevard, is a grand promenade. Built at the same time as Haussmann's avenues in Paris, it was part of Frederick Law Olmstead's park plan for a green belt stretching from the Common to Franklin Park via the Fenway. Stop and read the inscriptions on the statues. William Lloyd Garrison still stands on the green, refusing to "retreat a single inch." Patrick Andrew Collins, Mayor of Boston at the turn of the century, is eulogized as a "serviceable man."

Stop to walk through the carriage porch at (6) **First Baptist Church** at the corner of Clarendon St., nicknamed the "Church of the Holy Bean blowers" because of the trumpet-blowing cherubs in the frieze by Bartholdi, designer of the Statue of Liberty. The rock is native Roxbury puddingstone, the design by H. H. Richardson, 1871.

Some say the houses on Commonwealth are disappointing architecturally. However that may be, they prove the wealth of their builders. To get some of the flavor of the sunny side of Commonwealth, go into (7) **128 Commonwealth Avenue**, now owned by Chamberlayne Junior College. The main entrance is chained off, but you can see it by going through the first floor administrative office. The marble gas fireplace still works. Notice the carved wooden ceiling. You can look up the beautiful old stairwell to the skylight at the top of the house. Chamberlayne, which owns at least 20 Back Bay houses, offers tours by appointment. Phone 536-4500 for more information.

(8) **The Hotel Vendome** is a spectacle of faded elegance. Drooping green shades hang in the marble window frames. Nobody is quite sure what will become of it, although there is talk of a restoration. The Vendome was the scene of the first installation of electric lights in Boston in 1882. A guidebook of 1903 lists rooms at $5 and up; rooms at the Parker House that same year started at $1.50.

LAND CREATION IN BOSTON 1800 - 1960

(9) The Exeter Street Theatre was built as the Temple of the Working Union of Progressive Spiritualists. It is now a progressive, but proper, movie house.

Side-Trip: At Boylston Street you can digress for a look at the **Prudential** development. Who can miss it? The view from the top costs 50¢. Sturdy walkers can follow the mall through to Huntington Avenue. From there take our South End walk. Or stroll through the new **Christian Science development**. At this writing you'll see bulldozers and hard hats, but a reflecting pool and urban greenery are promised. The focus of this development is the domed Mother Church, long cramped by surrounding buildings. It is actually an extension to the older rock church which you can still see attached to it. The new buildings and the adjoining open space were designed by the firm of I. M. Pei. As you might expect, the new is carefully related to the old. The curved Sunday School building, for example, maintains the same scale as its older neighbor, **Horticultural Hall**, a building worth visiting for itself. Notice the carved swags of fruit and flowers on the exterior. Go upstairs to see the impressive library with hardwood paneling and balconies. **Symphony Hall**, across the steet, is better for listening than looking.

If you haven't been diverted from our marked route, walk along Boylston toward Copley Square, noting the new addition to **(10) The Boston Public Library**. The original building was designed by McKim, Mead, & White, 1895, as a kind of classical foil to the ornate Victorian buildings already in Copley Square (Trinity and the old Museum of Fine Arts, now gone). The new addition by Philip Johnson is very modern—but still close to the spirit of the old. Both buildings have central courtyards and granite exteriors. Boston's public library was the first major tax-supported library in the country. The new addition will have half a million books on open shelves.

49

McKim, Mead, & White are known for the pretentious city houses they built for wealthy clients in Boston and New York. Their **John F. Andrew House**, 32 Hereford St. at the corner of Commonwealth, is an example of the extravagance of Back Bay houses built toward the end of the century. A French chateau complete with a Marie Antoinette balcony brought from Paris, it consumes the end of a block. Fannie Farmer's Boston Cooking School is across the street.

LESS THAN 15% OF BACK BAY TOWNHOUSES REMAIN SINGLE - FAMILY DWELLINGS

(11) **The New Old South Church**, built in 1874, was the first building in Copley Square. When Back Bay developed and wealthy Bostonians moved to the New Land, the churches followed. Hence the *new* Old South to distinguish it from Old South on the Freedom Trail.

Henry Hobson Richardson, builder of **(12)** **Trinity Church**, was a huge man, as was Phillips Brooks, his good friend and rector of Trinity from 1869 to 1891. The Church reflects some of this largeness of body and spirit. The style, which came to be called Richardsonian Romanesque, influenced building all over the country. The rich texture and contrasting colors of the rock are somewhat obscured now by grime. To visitors accustomed to the puritan-white of most Boston churches, the interior of Trinity, with its polychrome and goldleaf decoration by John LaFarge and Augustus Saint-Gaudens, is startling—but delightful.

Walk around the building for a look at the adjoining study. The stone tracery window in the cloister was a gift to Trinity from St. Botolph's in Boston, England. The Church reflects as well as anything in Back Bay the world-embracing spirit of nineteenth century Boston. But its construction is grounded in the Back Bay marsh. To prevent rotting, the wooden piles which support it must be kept wet. In the old days, a boat was kept in the basement; when it hit bottom, the custodian knew it was time to flood. The mechanism is changed, but the water is still essential.

Visitors to morning services at Trinity receive a tour of the building.

(13) **The John Hancock Tower** is the latest round in the continuing battle of the big insurance companies for dominance in the Back Bay. The architects who designed this had a real problem—how to be more impressive than the rival Prudential tower but not too overpowering for the venerable monuments in Copley Square. Their answer was a kind of "non-building," a surrealistic skyscraper which will reflect the old buildings from a mirror-like surface. You can watch the progress from the old John Hancock tower, a good place for an overall view of the Back Bay. The observation areas are open Mon-Fri except holidays 9:30-4.

(14) **New England Life Building** has a different sort of perspective on the Back Bay, a series of historical dioramas. Go into the lobby at 501 Boylston Street for a look at the four scenes showing the Back Bay as it was in pre-historic times, as the Puritans found it, and as it was transformed in the last century. The exhibits are open free from 9-4:30 weekdays.

The walk along Newbury Street toward the public garden is one of the delights of the Back Bay. See our Browsing chapter for a guide to the shops. Or just walk along and look at the shoppers. (15) **Bonwit Teller** now inhabits the old Museum of Natural History buildings. Look for animals carved on the window keystones. Back at the Public Garden collapse on the nearest bench or relax with a ride on the Swanboats.

BONWIT TELLER WAS ONCE THE MUSEUM OF NATURAL HISTORY* * NOW THE MUSEUM OF SCIENCE ON THE CHARLES RIVER DAM

SOUTH END

He had not built, but had bought very cheap of a terrified gentleman of good extraction who discovered too late that the South End was not the thing, and who in the eagerness of his flight to the Back Bay threw in his carpets and shades for almost nothing.

Howells, *The Rise of Silas Lapham*

In the 1800's, as Beacon Hill became crowded and the downtown area commercial, Bostonians began looking for new land. Gradual filling of the coves around the narrow neck which led to Roxbury produced a new South End. Growth was rapid in the fifties. Unified blocks of pleasant row houses were laid out and it looked as though the new area would become an important—even impressive—part of Boston. Across the railroad yards were the mudflats of Back Bay. But by the 1860's they too were being filled and built upon. By the end of the century the Back Bay had become an elegant residential area and a new cultural center for the city, while the South End (for what reason—historical caprice, the panic of 1868?) had been abandoned to the poor, the solitary roomer, the masses of immigrants beginning to crowd into the city.

Today the South End is one of Boston's most exciting sections. For the walker there are contradictions at every turn—graceful bowfront houses and back yard squalor, bright corner playgrounds and skid row bars—but beneath the apparent disorder there are unmistakable signs of renaissance.

Directly opposite the Prudential tower take West Newton St. Follow it across the tracks (for years the South End has been on the wrong side). At Warren St. walk past the new vest-pocket park and turn into Pembroke.

(1) **Pembroke Street** is typical of many in the South End, with its look-alike rows of bowfront houses. Most streets were laid out by developers—for people who never moved in. Some houses have survived intact, complete with winding staircases, commodious fireplaces, and elaborate wood molding. More often they have been cut up into apartments or rooms. Pembroke St., known for its active

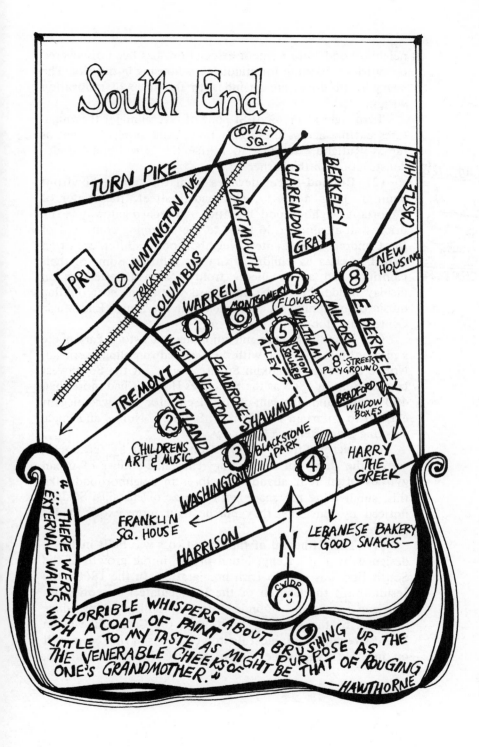

South End

COPLEY SQ.

TURN PIKE

HUNTINGTON AVE

DARTMOUTH

CLARENDON

GRAY

BERKELEY

CASTLE HILL

PRU

TRACKS

COLUMBUS

WARREN

MONTGOMERY

(FLOWERS)

NEW HOUSING

⑦

⑧

①

⑥

⑤

WALTHAM

UNION SQUARE

MILFORD

E. BERKELEY

"8" STREETS
PLAYGROUND

WEST

PEMBROKE

ALLEY

TREMONT

NEWTON

RUTLAND

SHAWMUT

BRADFORD

WINDOW
BOXES

②

CHILDRENS
ART & MUSIC

③

BLACKSTONE
PARK

④

HARRY
THE
GREEK

WASHINGTON

FRANKLIN
SQ. HOUSE

N

LEBANESE BAKERY
—GOOD SNACKS—

HARRISON

CWDP

"...THERE WERE
EXTERNAL WALLS
WITH A COAT OF PAINT
LITTLE TO MY TASTE AS MIGHT
THE VENERABLE CHEEKS OF
ONE'S GRANDMOTHER."

HORRIBLE WHISPERS ABOUT BRUSHING UP THE
A PURPOSE AS
BE THAT OF ROUGING
—HAWTHORNE

neighborhood improvement association, has been discovered by outsiders looking for middle class housing in the city. The heavy front doors are an index to the stage of renovation within.

Turn right at Tremont St., one of several major thorough-fares cutting across the South End. Walk along Tremont as far as Rutland, stopping to notice the new library under construction on the corner.

(2) **Rutland Street** deviates from the typical bowfront contour. It is a pretty, elm-shaded street, the center of important neighborhood activities. An arched gateway in the brick wall at number 36 leads to the charming courtyard of the Children's Art Center. Neighborhood children are often joined in class by children from the suburbs. Some of their paintings and a few pieces from Boston galleries are on display inside. From the courtyard you might hear tinkling music of beginning piano students in the South End Music Center next door.

(3) **Franklin Square** and adjoining Blackstone Park make a pleasant rest area even with the elevated rumbling overhead. Notice the brick "Franklin Square House" at the Southwest corner. Built in 1868 as the St. James Hotel, it had more than 400 rooms and a steam-operated elevator and was elegant enough to entertain President U. S. Grant. Nurses and single working girls often live here now.

Washington Street, cut off from sunlight by the tracks, shows the decay of impending renewal. Families of urban gypsies often rent abandoned stores in neighborhoods like this, subdividing the space with a maze of curtains. Seldom noticed by outsiders, they pursue their more exotic trades after midnight.

(4) **The Cathedral of the Holy Cross** was built in 1867, designed by P. C. Kelly. Much of the initial growth of the South End was due to Irish immigration. In the 1860's the Jesuits built the Church of the Immaculate Conception on Harrison Ave. and founded Boston College, long since removed to the suburbs. In its day, the Cathedral was an impressive departure, most Boston churches having been built on meeting-house scale. When renewal plans are complete,

54

new open space and the elimination of the elevated will give it a more appropriate setting.

The South End is composed of people from at least 40 different ethnic backgrounds. On Union Park Street you'll pass a Greek Orthodox Church. As you cross Shawmut Avenue you'll see evidence of a strong Lebanese-Syrian neighborhood. Because the streets were laid out in long blocks, cut off at either end by major arteries, neighboring streets often became separate homogeneous subcommunities—a Chinese street, a Greek street, a Syrian street side by side. In recent years neighborhood organizations united in the South End Federation of Citizens' Organizations have been a major factor in renewal.

In summer take a side trip off Shawmut to see if the window box contest is underway on Bradford Street. On Waltham Street notice the new "8 Streets" playground, a project initiated by the residents of eight neighboring streets.

(5) **Union Park** is the most prestigious of the South End streets. Notice the lavish use of wrought iron, the variety of doorways and cornices, the window gardens in the penthouses. Look for street-level doorways under the front stairs. A typical townhouse plan has two rooms to a floor. The kitchen and dining room are often on the ground floor, the parlor on the second.

"THERE IS NO ARCHITECTURE IN THE SOUTH END." IT IS A BUILDER'S SUBURB.

Over the past hundred years the elegant carriage houses and carriage ways which once lined the rear entrances of most of these homes in the South End have fallen into disuse and decay. Evidence of this can be found in the numerous alleyways. Some are fenced off, some still clearly visible. The adventuresome roamer might look down the alley that runs off Shawmut Ave. between Union Park and Upton St. to see how some residents have developed this space. In (6) **Montgomery Park**, a new breed of South Enders have pooled their energies to create a private residential park in the center of a block of houses. Look for it off Dartmouth St.

(7) **Clarendon Street** is an attractive and well-kept residential street with inviting side streets leading from it, a good basis for a leisurely stroll. At the Tremont end of Clarendon is the wholesale flower market, soon to be

removed to Albany St. on the fringes of the South End. A new park and cultural center are planned for the abandoned space.

Clarendon St. will take you directly to Copley Square, where you can pick up the Back Bay walk. Dover Street station of the elevated is at the corner of Washington Street and East Berkeley. **(8) East Berkeley Street** was until recently Dover Street. It has been Boston's skid row since Scollay Square and the West End were razed. The change of name hasn't solved the problem, but it has raised the image a bit. The new Castle Square housing development by Carl Koch was one of the first South End renewal projects to be completed and has added a new flavor to the Dover Street stew.

CHINATOWN—BAY VILLAGE

Washington St. is the modern descendant of the old road that led from colonial Boston across the tide-washed neck to the mainland. Hot dog joints, girls! girls! girls!, and the not-so-Puritan marquees of the Pilgrim and Mayflower Theatres now line the way once plagued by muggers and robbers. As you walk, look for the Essex Delicatessen. A greasy sign in the window marks the corner where the famed **Liberty Tree** once grew. Look up to see the marker set into the side of the building.

Chinese characters on the street signs tell you when you're approaching **Chinatown.** Though much smaller than the Chinese communities in New York and San Francisco, Boston's Chinatown is still one of the largest in the country. As highway construction cut into the neighborhood, many former residents moved to other sections of the city, but they return to shop. On Hudson and Oxford Streets are tiny and traditional stores. The grocery section of the **Eastern Live Poultry Company** at 48 Beach St. is much like any other Boston supermarket, except that the shelves contain canned abalone, dried mushrooms and cabbages, packaged bean thread, and Lucky Longevity Noodles imported from Hong

Kong. The produce counters have fresh bean sprouts in two sizes, fat Chinese cabbages, and piles of kohlrabi. Whole hams, barbequed ducks and spareribs, and flattened dried chickens with curving necks hang on hooks above the meat counter. Next door the freshest poultry is kept. Walk inside and meet your dinner, friendly and cackling in a wooden crate.

Tyler St. is a jumble of **restaurants** ranging in appeal from Bob Lee's aggressive waterfall front to The House of Roy's cramped basement entrance. In Chinatown the best food is sometimes found with the least atmosphere. Kim-Toy, at the corner of Beach and Tyler, is a Chinese lunch room open 24-hours a day, where you can sit in a wooden booth and eat a hamburger or an authentic noodle dish carefully prepared by Ray Chin. Traditional Chinese pastries are baked here nightly.

Tyler St. is known for history as well as food. **Sun Yat-Sen** is said to have laid plans for the Chinese revolution in a basement at number 12.

Boston's Chinese community includes third generation Bostonians as well as newcomers from the mainland or Taiwan. The children of both attend classes in Chinese language and culture weekdays after school and on Saturdays. The **Chinese Christian Church**, one of the area's most active institutions, has ambitious plans to rebuild its Tyler St. building which recently burned, and to construct a child care center and a home for elderly men who, because of Communist rule, can no longer return to the mainland to die.

THE CHINESE CHRISTIAN CHURCH WILL COOK A CHINESE DINNER IN YOUR CHURCH.

The most imposing building in Chinatown is the **Chinese Merchant's Association** at the corner of Kneeland and Hudson St., built in 1952 and ornamented with figures from Taoist tradition. The interior, not open to the public, is an exotic display of porcelain, teak, and goldleaf.

Chinese New Year (in February) is celebrated in Chinatown with percussion music, parades, dinner parties, and special exhibits. Sometime during the month outsiders are invited to a special program held at New England Life Hall. The performances start at 8 and last until midnight as the audience comes and goes. The program, usually involving

57

more than a 100 people, includes dancing, a fashion show, and a play done in Chinese with English narration at the beginning of each scene. Two of the most popular numbers are performed by the Bamboo Hut Athletic Club—Chinese Shadow Boxing, done to the beat of a drum, and a Dragon Dance, complete with a large and ferocious dragon head and swishing and slashing tail. 1970 was the year of the dog, to be followed in the 12-year lunar cycle by the mouse, ox, tiger, hare, dragon, serpent, horse, ram, monkey, and rooster. For current date and ticket information call the Chinese Christian Church, 60 Harvard St., Boston, 426-4710.

From Chinatown walk back toward the Common along Kneeland St., stopping to look for bargains under the heaps of fabric piled in dusty store windows. This area, a jangle of construction, will soon be dominated by the new buildings of the Tufts New England Medical Center. At Tremont St. turn left, walk past the Wilbur and Shubert Theatres toward the expressway. It is hard to believe that a quiet residential oasis exists in this apparently disintegrating neighborhood. But it does. Stay with Tremont until you come to Church St., then turn right to discover **Bay Village**.

Like Chinatown, this area is part of the South Cove, a section filled in during the 1830's. Many nineteenth-century workers' houses on the streets off Church St. were spontaneously renewed in the 1950's when the demand for townhouses outgrew Beacon Hill. From Church St. turn left onto **Fayette St.**, a harmonious little residential street lined with modest flat-fronted houses, each with a deeply arched entry way. A tradition says they were built by French Huguenots.

At the end of Fayette is Arlington St., which leads directly to the Public Garden and the MBTA, but you might want to spend a few more minutes exploring Bay Village. The neighborhood has a corner store or two, some rooftop gardens, a publishing house, and a cluster of movie distribution centers. **Knox St.**, a cobblestoned elbow between Melrose and Church St., is known for its restaurant at number nine. There's a number but no name on the door. When you are through exploring, Church St. will take you to Park Square.

Cambridge Walks

HARVARD YARD

> All students must refrain from wearing rich and showy clothing,
> nor must any one go out of the college-yard, unless in his gown,
> coat or cloak.
>
> Laws of Harvard College
> at Cambridge in New England

Enter Harvard Yard at Johnston Gate, stopping to read the inscription taken from the orders of the General Court of 1636 for the establishment of a 'schoale or colledge." When the first 12 students met their master in the summer of 1638, this ground contained one frame house and was called the 'college yard' to distinguish it from the cow yards adjoining. As you see it today it summarizes the growth of three centuries. There is no 17th-century building standing; the last didn't survive the neglect of the revolution when classes were moved to Concord and troops quartered in the Yard. The dominant look is red-brick and ivy. As you walk, try to tell which buildings are genuine Georgian and which part of Pres. Lowell's plan of the 1920's to unify and enclose the yard from the traffic outside.

(1) **Massachusetts Hall,** 1720, is Harvard's oldest, still used as a dormitory as it was originally. Although Harvard long ago outgrew this first campus, freshmen are still housed in the yard. Downstairs in Massachusetts Hall meets the oldest corporation in the United States, The President and Fellows of Harvard College, chartered in 1650. Harvard's oldest buildings are at the left end of the "old yard", as this

59

THIS IS MORE OR LESS A BRICK WATER TABLE

quadrangle is called. The architecturally-inclined look for the brick water table and belt courses on Hollis, the limestone lintels on Stoughton. Ordinary folk like to read the inscriptions on the corners of the buildings. Notice especially that on Holworthy.

(2) **Holden Chapel**, built in 1744, was originally meant to face the Common. The colorful pediment decoration is a 20th-century duplicate of the original on the other side.

(3) **University Hall**, is the ivy-colored granite building, designed by Charles Bulfinch in 1813, occupied by the SDS in 1969. Harvard's first stone building, it originally had a low porch across the front.

(4) **Wadsworth House**, is a sunny domestic intrusion among the red Victorian dormitories at the other end of the Old Yard. Built in 1726 as the President's residence, it is used today for alumni offices.

THE COMMONWEALTH REQUIRES THE EDUCATION OF THE PEOPLE AS A SAFE-GUARD OF ORDER & LIBERTY—

INSCRIPTION, BOSTON PUBLIC LIBRARY

(5) **Widener Library**, 1913, is the largest university library in the world. Go in and ask the guard at the door for directions to the dioramas of Harvard and Cambridge, which show the Yard as it was in 1677, 1775, and 1936. At this writing, the Gutenberg Bible is under repair. Actually it was hurt less than the guy who tried to steal it and fell through a skylight in the attempt.

(6) **Sever Hall** 1880, is one of Harvard's—and H. H. Richardson's—major monuments. It its day it was a trendsetter in keying the exterior design to interior function. Notice the brick ornamentation.

(7) **Memorial Church**, opposite Widener, is a neo-Georgian building of 1932. In June the speakers' platform is set up in the front of the steps for Cambridge's oldest surviving ritual—Harvard Commencement. The festivities begin with the arrival of the Governor of Massachusetts in a horse-drawn carriage. Leading the academic procession is the Sheriff of Middlesex County who brings the assembly to order with a tap of his pikestaff. Scattered laughter during the Latin oration identifies the few remaining Harvardians with classical learning. In the early days nobody got in unless he could read Cicero.

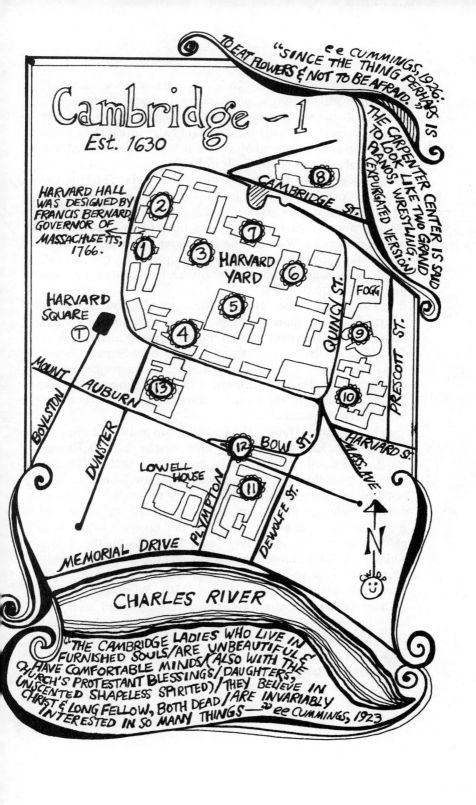

Cambridge –1

Est. 1630

ee cummings, 1926: "SINCE THE THING PERHAPS IS TO EAT FLOWERS & NOT TO BE AFRAID."

THE CARPENTER CENTER IS SAID TO LOOK LIKE TWO GRAND PIANOS, WRESTLING. (EXPURGATED VERSION)

HARVARD HALL WAS DESIGNED BY FRANCIS BERNARD, GOVERNOR OF MASSACHUSETTS, 1766.

HARVARD SQUARE Ⓣ

HARVARD YARD

CAMBRIDGE ST.

FOGG

QUINCY ST.

PRESCOTT ST.

MOUNT AUBURN

BOYLSTON

DUNSTER

BOW ST.

HARVARD ST.

MASS AVE.

LOWELL HOUSE

PLYMPTON

DEWOLFE ST.

MEMORIAL DRIVE

N

CHARLES RIVER

"THE CAMBRIDGE LADIES WHO LIVE IN FURNISHED SOULS/ARE UNBEAUTIFUL & HAVE COMFORTABLE MINDS/(ALSO WITH THE CHURCH'S PROTESTANT BLESSINGS/DAUGHTERS, UNSCENTED SHAPELESS SPIRITED)/THEY BELIEVE IN CHRIST & LONGFELLOW, BOTH DEAD/ARE INVARIABLY INTERESTED IN SO MANY THINGS—— ee CUMMINGS, 1923

(8) **Memorial Hall,** 1870, is one of the best examples in this country of Ruskin-influenced architecture. The ornate wood interior is worth seeing, if you would like to digress from our route for a minute to go inside. The white tower you can see behind Memorial is William James Hall, the behavioral sciences center built in 1963.

(9) **Carpenter Center** for the Visual Arts, 1961, is the only Le Corbusier building in the United States. If you find its unfamiliar angles and projections confusing after the red brick symmetry of the Yard, take time to look at it from several directions. Walk around and under it to Prescott St. to appreciate the way it fits into its cramped and crowded lot. Steps in the walk beside the faculty club next door will take you back to Quincy St.

CAN YOU SEE THE "GRAND PIANOS"?

(10) **Dana-Palmer House,** 1822, that yellow house on your left as you approach Mass. Ave. is used now as a guest house. In simpler days, it had a dome on top and served as the Harvard Observatory. Cross now to Bow Street. Follow Bow—past Arrow—to Mt. Auburn Street and a neighborhood dominated by Harvard Houses, residential sub-units of the college which have their own faculty associates, tutors, and extra-curricular activities.

(11) **Quincy House,** 1958, while true to the red brick of the first Harvard houses, of which nearby **Lowell House,** 1929, is a good example, was the first to break with the neo-Georgian pattern. The tower of Lowell House was inspired by Independence Hall. But for the walker the most notable thing about the buildings is the space they enclose. Walk through the gate to discover the Lowell Courts, two patches of green pleasantly remote from the bustle of Mt. Auburn St. To see more Harvard Houses, take a do-it-yourself tour from here to the river. From Boylston St. east along Memorial drive they are: Eliot (1930); Winthrop (1913), built as freshmen dormitories and later converted to house use; Leverett (1959), Harvard's first high-rise buildings; Dunster (1929); and Mather (1967), which combines a tower with lower buildings surrounding a courtyard.

(12) **Lampoon Building,** 1909, that whimsical "castle" in the center of the street, is headquarters of Harvard's

humor magazine, and of the cramped and quaint Starr Bookshop.

(13) Holyoke Center, a massive complex built in stages between 1961-1965, was designed by José Sert, who has added his distinctive signature to the Charles River skyline in several places. The pedestrian arcade under Holyoke will take you to Mass. Ave., near the Harvard Information center.

Summer **tours of Harvard** leave from the Information Center at 10 and 11:15 a.m.; at 2 and 3:15 p.m. Monday through Saturday; and at 1:30 and 3 p.m. on Sundays and holidays. During the school year, there are three tours daily from the Admissions Office on the ninth floor of Holyoke Center: at 10 and 11 a.m. and at 2:30 p.m. Monday through Friday. Except for large groups no special arrangements need be made.

BRATTLE STREET

If Socrates were here we could go and talk with him; but Longfellow, we cannot go and talk with; there is a palace, and servants, and a row of bottles of different coloured wine, and wine glasses, and fine coats.

Emerson in his *Journal*

In colonial days, Cambridge was a country town notable for its sedate college yard, modest houses, and few magnificent summer homes built along Brattle Street, "Tory Row", by wealthy and conservative Bostonians. After the rapid growth of the last 100 years, Brattle is still a lovely street, with an exciting juxtaposition of building styles and functions. This walk follows it past Harvard Square shops and college buildings to the area near Longfellow House, then returns by another route. Lovers of old houses should stay with Brattle further, especially on a Thursday afternoon, when the Lee Nichols House at number 159 is open.

L'IL ABNER LIVES ON BRATTLE STREET

63

(1) **William Brattle House**, built in 1727 for loyalist William Brattle, gives the street its name. It is now used by the Cambridge Center for Adult Education. The center's parent organization, the Cambridge Social Union, bought the property in 1889 and built the Brattle Theatre building next door.

(2) **Design Research**, 1969, is what it's meant to be—a showcase for the things inside, people as well as goods. Go in and join the design.

MERIMEKKO LIVES HERE.

(3) **Education Library and Research Center.** is under construction in the block between Farwell Place and Appian Way. Harvard is moving two neighborhood houses to this block, Read House (1772) and Nichols House (1827). Look for them off Farwell Place.

(4) **Window Shop Restaurant**, 1808. This house was once owned by Dexter Pratt, Longfellow's village smithy. Look for relatives of the spreading chestnut.

(5) **Loeb Drama Center** was built in 1959, with advanced stage rigging by George Izenour. The Loeb can have a conventional proscenium stage, an arena theatre, or a theatre-in-the round at the flick of a switch.

SCULPTURE IN THE "SERPENTINE-WALLED" GARDEN.

In this neighborhood are several buildings belonging to Radcliffe, the feminine side of Harvard. Although the administration of the two schools is separate, classes are coeducational. Greenleaf House (1859) at 76 Brattle, has been the Radcliffe President's house since 1913. We will return for a look at Radcliffe Yard.

(6) **Stoughton House**, the dark shingled building at 90 Brattle St., was built in 1883. Students of H. H. Richardson will recognize it as a national architectural momument, a prototype for hundreds of suburban houses all over the country. Imitation has given it such old-fashioned familiarity that most people walking by hardly give it a second look. Turn left on Ash St. for a look at another sort of architectural momument.

WE DEDICATE THESE TWO "MOMUMENTS" TO OUR PROOF-READERS.

(7) **9 Ash Street** is just what it looks like—a fenced lot roofed on one end to form a house. A glass wall separates the dwelling from the yard. Philip Johnson, whose influential

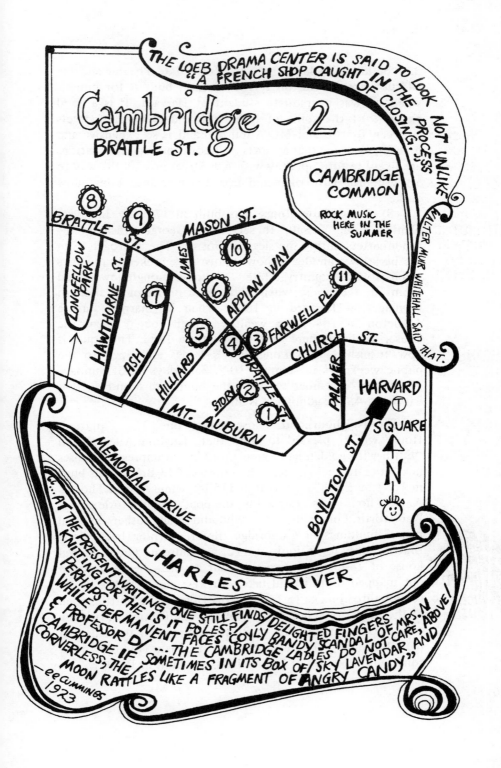

THE LOEB DRAMA CENTER IS SAID TO LOOK "A FRENCH SHOP CAUGHT IN THE PROCESS OF CLOSING." NOT UNLIKE WALTER MUIR WHITEHALL SAID THAT.

Cambridge — 2
BRATTLE ST.

CAMBRIDGE COMMON
ROCK MUSIC HERE IN THE SUMMER

BRATTLE ST.

LONGFELLOW PARK

HAWTHORNE ST.

MASON ST.

JAMES

ASH

HILLIARD

STORY

MT. AUBURN

APPIAN WAY

BRATTLE ST.

FARWELL PL.

CHURCH ST.

PALMER

BOYLSTON ST.

MEMORIAL DRIVE

CHARLES RIVER

HARVARD SQUARE Ⓣ

N

8 9 10 11 7 6 5 4 3 2 1

...AT THE PRESENT WRITING ONE STILL FINDS/ DELIGHTED FINGERS KNITTING FOR THE/ IS IT POLES?/ PERHAPS. PERMANENT FACES COYLY BANDY SCANDAL OF MRS. N/ WHILE ...THE CAMBRIDGE LADIES DO NOT CARE, ABOVE!/ & PROFESSOR D/ SOMETIMES IN ITS BOX OF/ SKY LAVENDAR AND CAMBRIDGE IF/ MOON RATTLES LIKE A FRAGMENT OF ANGRY CANDY"/ CORNERLESS, THE —ee cummings 1923

new buildings include the New York State Theater and the addition to the Boston Public Library, built it for himself when he was a graduate student at Harvard. It is a good example of the spirit of housing found along side streets between Brattle and Mt. Auburn. Land is so expensive and housing so scarce that all sorts of innovations and renovations are likely to turn up. Stay with Ash Street now all the way to Mt. Auburn. Turn right and take the gate into Longfellow Park.

ATTRIBUTED TO PETER HARRISON OF NEWPORT.

(8) **Longfellow House** was built in 1759 by Jamaican planter John Vassall. It served as George Washington's headquarters during the siege of Boston. The approach from the park gives an idea of how it must have looked in the days when it was a country estate. The young Longfellow rented rooms in the house when he became professor of modern languages at Harvard in 1837. When he married Fannie Appleton in 1843, her wealthy father bought them the house. He lived there until his death in 1882. The house is now furnished with Longfellow's things and open to the public weekdays in summer 10-5, Saturdays 12-5, Sundays 1-5. From November to April the hours are Mon-Fri 10-4, Sat-Sun 2-4. The admission is 30¢.

The Neighborhood. Those raised on "The Children's Hour" will be pleased to know that "laughing Allegra" and "Edith with golden hair" grew up to live in impressive houses next door to their father. The house at 113 Brattle was built in 1887 by Edith Dana, that at 115 by Annie Allegra Thorpe. Annie's house was designed by the poet's nephew, Alexander Wadsworth Longfellow, Jr., who did many other colonial revival buildings in Cambridge. Before turning back along Brattle, stop for a look at 112, a handsome Greek revival house of 1846. An interesting—but longish—digression from our mapped route would take you west along Brattle Street

LEE-NICHOLES HOUSE

two or three blocks to Lee-Nichols House, 159 Brattle, open to the public on Thursdays from 3-5, admission 25¢. It is the oldest house on this part of Brattle and one of the oldest in the city. Most of its neighbors are Victorian. Number 146, a conscious reflection of Lee-Nichols, was built in 1939.

(9) St. John's Chapel at the Episcopal Theological School was built in 1868, modeled after English parish churches of the 13th and 14th-centuries. Notice how the landscaping and paving have been used to integrate the old buildings of the ETS with the new Sherrill Building, 1965.

Now walk back along Brattle a short way until you come to a gate leading into **(10)** **Radcliffe Yard**. The three main buildings in the yard, turn-of-the-century buildings by different architects, are linked by colonnades. The multiple chimneys on Byerly Hall, 1931, vent the laboratories inside. White-pillared Agassiz House (1904), one of Alexander Wadsworth Longfellow's buildings, contains a small theatre used for student productions. That brick tower looking down on the Yard from Appian Way is **Larsen Hall** of Harvard's School of Education. Quite ordinary on the inside, it is best appreciated from the Yard. Can you see how it emulates Radcliffe's chimneys? The closed façade on this side respects the privacy of **Radcliffe Garden** a left-over corner of the Yard between Cambridge Common and Appian Way, transformed into a quiet and secluded urban space. Look for the path between Byerly and Longfellow Hall.

DON'T MISS THE YURT IN RADCLIFFE GARDEN.

(11) **Christ Church**, built in 1760, is one of Cambridge's most interesting buildings. Designed by Peter Harrison for a Tory congregation, it has a more cosmopolitan air than the Puritan churches built around the same time. Still, it is modest beside Harrison's more famous King's Chapel (on the Freedom Trail) and tells something about Cambridge's rural character at the time. The Redcoats retreated this way after the first battle at Lexington and Concord; a plaque in the foyer marks a hole made by a stray bullet. Some of the Revolutionary soldiers ended in the adjoining burying ground. The graves there include those of Harvard's first presidents. At the southern boundary of the graveyard is First Church, Unitarian, built in 1833, an early example of "medievalism." Wooden finials along the roofline once gave it even more a storybook look.

MASSACHUSETTS INSTITUTE OF TECHNOLOGY

In contrast to Harvard's cloistered yard, MIT's central court is open to the river. The best introduction to the school is a drive along Memorial or Storrow Drive. The classical domed Maclaurin buildings may call forth images of gladiators and Roman baths, but the inscriptions carved in stone dedicate them unmistakably to the gods of science and industry. As any child can tell you on his first visit, MIT has a hum. If you are vitally interested in the inner workings, you might want to take a **guided tour.** (Mon.-Fri. at 10 and 2 year round. Go in the Mass. Ave. entrance and ask the guard for directions to the Admissions Office, building 3, Room 108).

For a casual walking tour, start with the courtyard west of Massachusetts Ave. The dome-theme is picked up here by **Kresge Auditorium,** designed by Eero Saarinen in 1953. The concrete roof is supported at only three points and is only a few inches thick at the top. The auditorium is occassionally used by Boston opera and theatre companies as well as for MIT functions. All 1200 seats are said to have a front view. The neighboring **Chapel,** a cylinder set in a moat, is also by Saarinen, the sculptural bell-tower by Theodore Roszak. Inside, the world is obliterated. Light reflected from the water casts a changing pattern on the brick walls and the delicate bronze altar screen.

From the Chapel walk across the plaza, past the **Julius Stratton Building,** MIT's new student center, and cross Mass. Ave. Giant anchors flank the entrance to the School of Naval Architecture. If you like ship models, go inside to see the **Nautical Museum** (see page 142). Otherwise, go through the main entrance into the **Rogers Building.** Since all buildings on this side of the Institute are connected, you can cover a block without getting out in the rain. Follow the corridor straight east. You might stop when you come to the foyer opening onto the **Great Court,** the face of MIT seen from the river. Its austerity is relieved in June with the blossoming of rhododendrons as monumental as the buildings, which

68

were built in 1913 when MIT left Back Bay for Cambridge. The inscriptions will test your knowledge of science history.

Back inside, continue along the main corridor as far east as it goes, then go right until you see the glassed-in passageway leading to **Hayden Library**. MIT's first library on this campus was housed under the dome; Hayden was built in 1949. Changing art exhibits, open to the public, sometimes have a technological twist.

McDermott Court outside Hayden is noted for the giant stabile by Alexander Calder, commissioned for the spot. It is directly in front of the new **Green Building** (the color is concrete), designed by I. M. Pei in 1964. It is identified by the bubble on top. Beyond the laboratories north of McDermott Court look for the secluded garden facing the window wall of **Alumni Swimming Pool** (1939), the first "International Style" building at MIT.

Sometime as you drive past the Institute west along Memorial Drive, notice the curving brick walls of **Baker House**, 1947, one of Cambridge's best-known modern buildings. The pace-setting design by Alvar Aalto gives most of the dormitory rooms a view of the Charles.

Food

MY DICTIONARY
SAYS: "SCROD,
A YOUNG COD-
FISH" IN CASE
YOU WONDERED.

Every noon a businessman we know goes to a cafeteria near Post Office Square for a ham-and-banana sandwich. Academic types with the proper credentials can lunch on horse steak at the Harvard Faculty Club. What you eat is up to you. If you don't like Yankee Pot Roast, try Schrod. Or eat Fleefly at one of the Syrian restaurants in town.

Prices change, but to give you a rough idea of what you're up against we have marked each restaurant according to what an average meal might cost at this writing. E—expensive, $6 and up. M—moderate, $4-6. I—inexpensive, under $4.

DOWNTOWN BUSINESS DISTRICT

Durgin-Park, 30 North Market St., Boston 227-2038
Luncheon 10:30-4, Dinner 4-9. Closed Sundays and Holidays.

An old Boston favorite, now somewhat blighted by fame. Located in the middle of the market area over a warehouse, it is known for its roast beef, strawberry short cake, long crowded tables, and sassy waitresses. Prices are lower at noon. At the dinner hour or during tourist season, be prepared to wait 45 minutes, unless you know about the backstairs from the bar. I to M.

Locke-Ober, 3 Winter Place, 542-1340
Lunch 11-3, Dinner 3-10. Closed Sundays and Holidays.

Down a narrow alley between Winter St. and Temple Place, famous for fine cuisine and unbending tradition. Women are excluded from the downstairs dining room except of New Year's Eve and the day Harvard plays Yale. If the dinner prices are beyond you, splurge on an unforgettable bowl of Lobster Bisque for lunch. Reservations are necessary for dinner and will not be held more than 15 minutes. E.

Marliave, 11 Bosworth St. 542-2680
Lunch 11-4, Dinner 4-11. Closed Sundays.

Convenient to "Ye Old Province Steps." Good Italian food, charmingly dated decor, circa 1930. In summer try the roof garden. M.

Union Oyster House, 41 Union St., Boston, 227-2750
Lunch 10-3, Dinner 10-9 (9:30 on Friday, 10 on Sat.)

Once the home of exiled King Louis Philippe—an oyster house since 1826. More atmosphere downstairs. Other Union Oyster Houses are at 122 Canal St. and 143 Stuart St. M.

Warmuth's, 280 Devonshire St., Boston, 542-4772
Lunch 11-4, Dinner 4-10:15. Closed Sundays and Holidays.

A good place to go while downtown shopping. A large variety of items with an emphasis on sea food. I to M.

BEACON HILL

Au Beauchamp, 99 Mt. Vernon St., Boston, 523-9299
Lunch 11:30-2:30, Dinner 6-9, daily except Sunday.

A reasonably good French restaurant, located in a pleasantly respectable cellar. M.

The Charles, 75a Chestnut St., Boston 523-4477
Dinner 5-11, closed Sunday.

A relatively new but popular Italian restaurant. E.

Maître Jacques, 10 Emerson Place (Charles River Park), 742-5480
Lunch 12-2:30, Dinner 6-10.

French. Elegant food and good service. On the "other side of the hill" in a new tower overlooking the river. E.

·MENU·

ARTICHOKE BOTTOMS WITH FOIS GRAS · CHICKEN KIEVSKI · SEMOLINA GNOCCHI · PETITS POIS · ENDIVE BRAISSÉES · FRAISES MOUSSE · VIN

71

··VERS POUR UN GOURMET··

SI QUAND TU VAS A L'ETRANGER
TU VEUX COMME EN FRANCE MANGER,
JE NE VOIS PAS POUR QUOI LE CANNIBAL EN SOMME
SERAIT PLUS FOL, CHEZ NOUS, A DEMANDER DE "L'HOMME".
RAOUL PONCHON (1848-1937)

BACK BAY–SOUTH END

Cafe Budapest, 47 Huntington Ave., Boston, 734-3388
Lunch 12-3:30, Dinner 4-10.
A very fine restaurant located in the Copley Square Hotel. A strolling violinist adds romance to the goulash. Try to avoid weekends. M.

English Room, 29 Newbury St., Boston 262-8631
Daily 11-9
Anti-atmosphere but one of the best food buys in Boston. Home-cooked meals with hot rolls, dessert, and a bottomless salad bowl. Quick service. I.

Joseph's, 279 Dartmouth St., 266-1502
11:45-11
Under Locke-Ober management. Continental cuisine, disappointing atmosphere. E.

Kon Tiki, 39 Dalton St., Sheraton Boston Hotel, Boston, 262-3063.
Lunch 12-3, Dinner 5:30-12
For polynesia-collectors, a good risk. M.

Le Languedoc, 914 Beacon St., Boston 262-9652
Dinner, 5:30-9:30, closed Sunday and Monday
Excellent French-cooking in an intimate, family-run restaurant. M.

The Ritz-Carlton Hotel, 15 Arlington St., Boston, 536-5700
Breakfast 7-12, Lunch 12-3:30, Dinner 6-9:30.
The dining room lives up to the reputation of the hotel. The food is wonderful, the service excellent, the décor elegant. But, watch your skirt, ladies. The Maître will, and if by his conservative estimate it is too short, you will not be seated. Ties of course. E.

Top of the Hub, Prudential Center, Boston, 536-1775.
Lunch 11-2, Dinner 5-9:30, Sunday Brunch 11:2:30, Sunday dinner 4-9.

A Stouffer restaurant located at the top of the Prudential Tower. Enjoy the panorama—and sometimes the food. E.

Trader Vic's, Park Square, Boston (in the Statler Hilton), 426-2000.
Lunch 11:30-2:30, Dinner 5-11:30, Saturday and Sunday dinner only is served.

Out-rigger canoes, giant sea shells, and other South Sea artifacts cover the walls and ceiling. The food and service are good. Ordering à la carte is dangerous. We recommend ordering one of the dinners, as you get a good sampling of dishes, all delicious. E.

Sahara, Corner of Waltham St. and Shawmut Ave. No phone listing.
Open 6 p.m. to the wee hours.

Authentic Syrian restaurant in one of the South End's oldest neighborhoods. One "Combination Special," at $5.50, is ample for three. An herbed green salad is a nice extra, but skip the baklava. The crowd gets more interesting after 11. I.

Kyoto, 337 Massachusetts Ave., Boston, 536-9295.
Lunch 12-2:30, Dinner 5-11, Closed Mondays.

A fine experience in authentic Japanese cuisine. The atmosphere in the main room is plain; but there is a separate section for Japanese style eating. I-M.

73

THEATRE DISTRICT—CHINATOWN

Athens-Olympia Cafe, 51 Stuart St., 426-6236
Open 11-midnight.
 Famous old restaurant highly recommended by Walter Muir Whitehill and a Greek repairman we know. I to M.

Jacob Wirth's, 31-37 Stuart St., Boston, 338-7194, 338-8586
Hours 11-11, closed Sundays.
 German food, sawdust on the floor. Famous and fun. M.

Nine Knox, 9 Knox St., Boston, 482-3494.
Dinner 8:30. Be prompt.
 Run by two men who do all the cooking and serving, it is located in an unusually decorated town house in the gas lamp section of Boston between the theater district and the Mass. Pike. The set menu changes monthly. The dining room holds about 25 to 30 people and reservations must be made weeks in advance. The price is $10 a person. After dinner you may be invited to tour the house; don't miss the Ladies Room. E.

The Nile, 227 Harrison Ave., Boston, 426-7855.
Dinner 4:30 to 12:30, Saturday and Sunday noon-12:30 a.m.
 Exceptionally good Near Eastern food. The place is new and pleasantly Byzantine in atmosphere. I-M.

Yee Hong Guey, 34 Oxford St., Boston, 426-6738, 338-7337
Daily 11-10
 A Chinatown favorite. Particularly recommended is the fried shrimp and beef in oyster sauce. I-M.

Fung Won, 8 Tyler St., Boston, 542-1175 Daily 11-10
 Highly recommended by Chinese graduate students at Harvard, who gather at Fung Won to feast on a budget. I-M.

叉 燒 炒 飯
MEANS: "FRIED RICE WITH PORK"

NORTH END

Mother Anna's, 211 Hanover St., 523-8496.
Lunch 12-3, Dinner 5-11:30.

Your explorations of the North End need go no further than Mother Anna's, situated beside Callahan Tunnel in the shadow of the expressway. An order of Shrimp Scampi makes a spectacular beginning for four. Sop up the juices with your bread as the Italians do. For an entree, try Scallopine a la Marsala and spaghetti or ravioli. The pastries, when they have them, are great, but tortoni lovers will need a pick and a shovel. M.

Joe Tecce's, 53 No. Washington St., 523-8975.
Dinner 5-11, closed Sundays.

Artistic antipasto. One platter is a meal for two or a starter for eight. The word has gotten around and there's not much room inside so after 6:30 you risk waiting in line on the street even on a weeknight. I-M.

Jennie's, 10 Bartlett Place, Boston, 523-9521.
Daily 4-12.

Italian home cooking. Make this your last stop on the Freedom Trail. Asking directions to Bartlett Place is half the fun. M.

WATERFRONT

Anthony's Pier 4, Pier 4, Northern Ave., Boston 482-6363.
Lunch 11:30-3, Dinner 5-10:30. Sunday 12:30-9:30.

Good fish and popovers in an impressively nautical setting. Lunchtime is less busy and the daylight allows you to enjoy the activities of the harbor. E.

Boston 1800, 25 Lewis St. East Boston, 569-1800.
Lunch 12-4, Dinner 5-11.

In the new East Boston waterfront development. Food and service are of good quality, although on some weekends the crush is overwhelming. E.

Jimmy's Harborside, 248 Northern Ave., Boston, 426-5343.
Open 11:30-9:30, Closed Sunday.

The other famous one. When in doubt order the Finnan Haddie Jimmy-style. Try to reserve a table with a harbor view. M-E.

"No-Name" Restaurant," 15½ Fish Pier, Boston, 338-7539.
Mon-Tues-Thurs 'til 4:30, Wed and Fri 'til 9.

Fish right off the boat into the pan, homemade bread and pies, all the charm of a fisherman's diner, and nothing costs over $2. Durgin-Park must once have been like this. Mobbed on Friday nights, naturally. I.

HARVARD SQUARE AREA

Acropolis, 1680 Mass. Ave., Cambridge, 354-8335.
Weekdays 4-11:30, Weekends 11:30-11:30.

Greek. Quick, friendly service. Reliable lemon soup and fried squid. Though popular with Harvard-Radcliffe students, it is rarely overcrowded. I.

Casa Mexico, 75 Winthrop St., Cambridge, 491-4552.
Dinner Sun-Thurs 6-10, Fri and Sat 6-11.

Mexican. Though the prices are a trifle disconcerting ($3 for two tacos, rice and beans), the food is reasonably authentic if you're not expecting the Great Southwest.

Chez Jean, 1 Shepard St., Cambridge, 354-8980.
Dinner Mon-Sat 5:30-10.

Fine French food with good service and a pleasant atmosphere. M.

Iruña, 56 Boylston St., Cambridge, 868-5633.
Lunch 12-2, Dinner 6-9, Sat. 6-10, closed Sunday.

Spanish. Nicest in summer when you can eat on the patio behind the house. I-M.

Taj Mahal, 14a Eliot St., Cambridge, 354-4764.
Dinner weekdays 5:30-10, Weekends 5:30-11.

The fanciest of the Indian restaurants which have opened in Cambridge recently. The food is consistently good—but novices should be warned that even the mild curry can have you reaching for your water glass. I.-M.

Window Shop, 56 Brattle St., Cambridge, 354-7874.
Lunch 11:30-3, Tea 3-5, Dinner 5:30-8:15. Closed Sunday.

Continental specialties in the house of Longfellow's "smithy." In summer eat on the terrace under the spreading chestnuts and watch the world walk by. M.

OTHER CAMBRIDGE LOCATIONS

Five Chateaux, 5 Cambridge Parkway, Cambridge (Sonesta Motel), 491-3600.
Lunch 11:30-2:30, Dinner 5-10.

French cuisine. Elegant décor and prices. E.

Joyce Chen, 500 Memorial Drive, Cambridge, 494-7373, 617 Concord Ave., Cambridge, 868-7474. Open 12-9:30, closed Monday.

Superb Chinese food including hard to find Mandarin specialties. The owner, author of the well-known Joyce Chen Cookbook, has a show on Channel 2. The Tuesday night buffet is $3 a person. Other times the bill depends on what you order from the huge menu. I-E.

Fantasia, 617 Concord Ave., Cambridge, 354-0285.
Daily 12-10:30.

Prize-winning American restaurant known for good meat and excellent service. Reservations are a good idea even at noon. M.

ICE CREAM

Bailey's, 45 West St., Boston (branches in other areas) 354-2772. 9:30-11 daily, Sunday 12-12.

You haven't seen Boston 'til you've eaten a sloppy Bailey's sundae and watched little old ladies in flowered hats eating them too at the tables all around you. Bailey's has lost some of its antiquated charm since it expanded and added sandwiches and that St. Louis invention, the ice cream cone. (Even Bailey's ice cream cones are sloppy. Unless you have tremendous faith in your child, ask for a dish). The hot fudge sundaes are still worth skipping a meal for. Hand-dipped quart of ice cream, $1.50, sundae, 75¢ (with whipped cream, 80¢).

Brigham's, All over the Boston area.

The service varies from store to store, but the hand-packed ice cream is uniformly excellent. Plain old vanilla tastes like you turned the crank. Jimmies on cones are free. Hand-dipped quart $1.30, sundaes, 50¢.

Friendly Ice Cream, Suburban locations.

Respectable ice cream, juicy beefburgers on toast, and lots of smiles. Good place to take the kids when you're not up to McDonald's. Highchairs and bibs provided. Sundaes 50¢ hand-packed quart, $1.05, half-gallon pre-pack, $1.15.

Baskin-Robbins, Needham, Belmont, Newton Centre and elsewhere.

New to New England, but famous in California. Flavors run to Red-White-and-Blueberry, Grasshopper, and Cherry Cheesecake. Good fruit sherbet. Sundaes 57¢, hand-packed quarts $1.45 to $1.92 depending on flavor.

FURTHER AFIELD

Chardas, 1306 Beacon St., Brookline (Coolidge Corner), 232-2596. Dinner 5-10:30.

This is considered one of the best Hungarian restaurants in town. The décor is plain, the service friendly, and the cherry soup delicious. M.

Jack and Marion's, 299 Harvard St., Brookline (Coolidge Corner), 277-4455. Open 8 a.m.-3 a.m.
Crowded, noisy delicatessen-restaurant with an over-sized menu and sandwiches for *fressers* and other people with over-sized appetites. I-E.

Peking on the Mystic, 66 High St., Medford, 396-0850. Weekdays 11-10, Friday and Saturday 11-12.
The romance is in the name only, but the cooking is tops. I-M.

Rita's Place, 88 Winnisimmet St., Chelsea, 884-9838. Open daily for lunch, Dinner Friday and Saturday only.
A very small family-run Italian restaurant located in the back room of a submarine sandwich parlor. It is necessary to make reservations and advisable to arrive before 8 p.m. since the choices become fewer. There is no written menu so unless you know your dishes you will have to rely on the waiter's recommendations. Delicious antipasto. M.

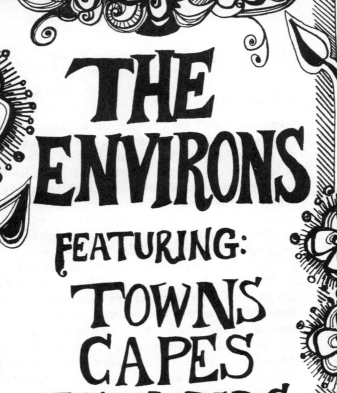

THE ENVIRONS

FEATURING:

TOWNS
CAPES
ISLANDS

AND: HOW TO GET LOST ON A COUNTRY ROAD

CWD

Famous Towns

PLYMOUTH

Plymouth wasn't the first English settlement in America, nor the biggest. In New England she was soon overshadowed by the larger migrations to neighboring Massachusetts Bay Colony. Yet to most Americans, that little Pilgrim band fathered a nation—literally as well as spiritually, if we can believe all the people who claim to be their descendants. To most of us, a visit to Plymouth is a favorite old story. The Mayflower Compact, Massasoit, "a herring to a hill of corn," the First Thanksgiving, Myles Standish—all are represented. Plymouth Rock is there too, surprisingly tamed.

Most visits begin on the waterfront, where you can climb aboard **Mayflower II**, listen to a costumed guide at the Rock, then for a dime visit two houses similar to those at **Plimoth Plantation**, a re-creation two and a half miles south on Route 3A. The local people argue over the relative merits of the Plantation and the three original 17th-century houses still standing in town. Certainly a visit to the Plantation gives you a unified picture of how it was those first years. You see a carefully documented color film at the orientation center, then visit the old fort and 12 reconstructed houses in their beautiful hilltop setting. Costumed guides demonstrate Pilgrim crafts; an adjacent camp portrays Indian life.

On the other hand, no replica can claim as can the **Howland House**, (1666) that "its floors have been trodden by two passengers of the Mayflower." **Harlow Old Fort House**, though built in 1677 after all the settlers had died, has the hand-hewn beams of the first Pilgrim fort, torn down after King Phillip's war and used in the construction. Here costumed hostesses dip bayberry candles and demonstrate spinning and weaving from flax and wool. **Sparrow House,** possibly Plymouth's oldest, has been remodeled over the years, but parts of it have been restored. The owner—and sometime guide—is an Alden.

If you have the energy—and money—the town makes it easy for you to do everything. Starting in mid-May **Combination Tickets** are sold: Adults $3.75, children $1.75. They are transferable and admit you to the Plantation, Mayflower II, the three 17th-century houses, as well as **Spooner House,** since 1754 occupied by one family; the **Antiquarian House,** interesting octagonal rooms and nineteenth-century furnishings; **Pilgrim Hall,** museum of Pilgrim possessions; and the **Mayflower Society House,** twelve period rooms.

A separate attraction is the **Wax Museum,** not far from the Rock, which reconstructs the Pilgrim story in a series of scenes using sound and animation.

As you might imagine, **Thanksgiving Day** is special. Most of the houses are open without charge; cranberry juice, cider and donuts are served. Plymouth residents, costumed to represent the Pilgrims who survived the rigors of the first winter, assemble at the beat of the drum and march up Leyden Street to the site of the Fort on Burial Hill, where they sing from the Book of Psalms. (This same pageant, called **Pilgrim's Progress,** is enacted every Friday in August at 5 p.m.)

OVER ONE-HALF OF THE PILGRIMS DIED THE FIRST WINTER. ONLY 12 HEADS OF FAMILIES SURVIVED.

To Read: William Bradford's own story *Of Plymouth Plantation* 1620-1647 is now available in a Capricorn paperback edited by Harvey Wish. Your library probably has a hardback edition with an introduction and notes by Samuel Eliot Morison. *The Coming of The Pilgrims,* by E. Brooks Smith and Robert Meredith, is a story for children told from Governor Bradford's account.

Food: The Plantation has a snack bar and limited picnic facilities. Not far beyond it, along Rt. 3A towards the Cape, try Bert's for moderately-priced shore dinners and excellent scallops. The waterfront area is distractingly well-supplied with souvenir and snack shops. A good bet in this area is the Mayflower Restaurant, which has excellent fish plates in an informal atmosphere. No tipping; you serve yourself. On Fridays fish markets nearby sell delicious fish cakes for a pittance. Lovely Brewster Gardens on Leyden Street has no tables, but you can still drink from the spring the Pilgrims used.

WHEN THEIR ENGLISH SEEDS FAILED, THE INDIANS SHOWED THEM HOW TO PLANT CORN.

(1) **Mayflower II.** April 'til November open 9-5, weekends 9-7; July and August 9-9. Adults $1.00, children 50¢

(2) **Replicas of First Houses,** 10¢

(3) **Plymouth Rock**

(4) **Cole's Hill Burying Ground**

(5) **Spooner House,** 27 North St., near Plymouth Rock. Open mid-May to mid-Sept 10-5 daily, Sun. 1-5. Adults 50¢, Children 25¢

(6) **Wax Museum,** 16 Carver St. Open summer 9-9:30, spring and fall 9-5. Adults $1.00, children 5-12 50¢

(7) **Mayflower Society House,** 4 Winslow St. Open June-Sept daily 10-5. Adults 50¢ children 25¢

(8) **Antiquarian House,** 126 Water St. Open mid-May to mid-Sept. daily 10-5. Adults 50¢, children 25¢

(9) **Pilgrim Museum,** 75 Court St. Open year round 10-5, winter 10-4:30, Sun. 1-4:30. Adults 75¢, children 25¢

(10) **Sparrow House,** Summer St. Open Mon-Sat 10-5, closed Sun. Adults 50¢, children 25¢

(11) **Howland House,** Sandwich St. Open May 15-Oct. 15, Mon-Sat 9:30-5, Sun 10-5. Adults 50¢, children 25¢

(12) **Harlow Old Fort House,** 119 Sandwich St. Open May 15-Sept. 30 10-5 daily. Adults 50¢, children 25¢. Craft classes are conducted here during July and August, Mon-Fri 2-4.

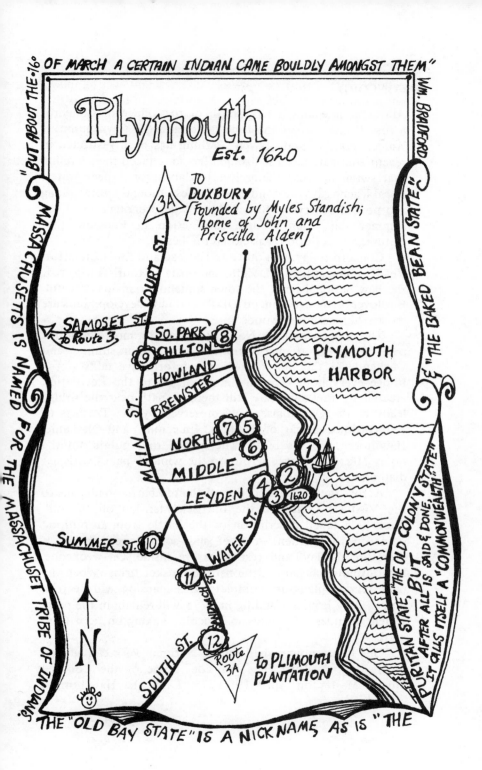

"BUT ABOUT THE .16.

WM BRADFORD

Plymouth
Est. 1620

TO
DUXBURY
[Founded by Myles Standish;
home of John and
Priscilla Alden]

3A

COURT ST.

SAMOSET ST.
to Route 3

SO. PARK
CHILTON
8
9

HOWLAND

BREWSTER

MAIN ST.

NORTH
7 5
6

MIDDLE

LEYDEN
4 2
3 1620
1

PLYMOUTH
HARBOR

SUMMER ST. 10

WATER ST.

11

SANDWICH ST.

N

SOUTH ST.

12
Route
3A

to PLIMOUTH
PLANTATION

"MASSACHUSETTS IS NAMED FOR THE MASSACHUSET TRIBE OF INDIANS"

E "THE BAKED BEAN STATE"

"PURITAN STATE," "THE OLD COLONY STATE," BUT, AFTER ALL IS SAID & DONE, IT CALLS ITSELF A "COMMONWEALTH"

THE "OLD BAY STATE" IS A NICKNAME, AS IS "THE

CONCORD

About a mile and a half south of the village of Concord, across Route 2, past the trailer park and the town dump, is Walden Pond, a state beach. Bathing has been restricted in recent summers because drought has so reduced the shoreline that swimmers find themselves too abruptly in deep water. Local legend says the pond is bottomless, though Thoreau long ago proved otherwise. Still Walden is deep enough. On a hot summer day there's some satisfaction in knowing that Nature, not pollution, has closed the beach.

Concord today isn't quite as Thoreau and Emerson left it. Yet its name still fits. Despite the hosts of tourists who visit the new national park, the town somehow remains peaceful. Birdlovers long ago banned DDT. The new developments are mostly hidden in the woods.

The area around the North Bridge is the most developed part of the **Minuteman National Park.** Daily in summer and weekends in the fall, rangers give informative talks at the bridge every hour. The first monuments to the Revolution erected by the village are still there. A path near the Bridge leads to the **Old Manse,** now preserved by the Trustees of Reservations, home of Ripleys, Emersons, and Nathaniel Hawthorne and his bride. The guided tour points out the notes Mrs. Hawthorne wrote on the window panes with her diamond.

Across the bridge a portion of the old battle road leads to the **Visitor's Center** in the Buttrick Mansion on the hill. There is a taped description of the battle from an outlook point in the garden. A brief slide-sound presentation, a literature display, and restrooms are inside. On weekends, local Minuteman units demonstrate musket firing. When the park service plans are complete, this mansion will be torn down. Only houses standing in 1775 will remain in the park, which includes 750 acres in Lincoln, Lexington, and Concord.

One house now owned by the National Park can be seen on Lexington Road, **The Wayside,** home of the Concord Muster Master on April 19, 1775. Later the Hawthornes,

86

Alcott, and Margaret Sidney lived there. There are other houses of literary note nearby. **Orchard House** has echoes of *Little Women*. The weathered building of Bronson Alcott's Concord School of Philosophy is out back. Visitors may see four rooms of **Emerson House**, furnished as they were when Ralph Waldo Emerson lived there between 1832 and 1882. The fourteen rooms of the **Antiquarian House** preserve such things as Paul Revere's lantern and Thoreau's flute. In another part of town the Thoreau Society maintains a museum, library, and shop at **The Thoreau Lyceum**, past the town center near the railroad station. **Wright Tavern**, near Monument Square, is now a gift shop run by the ladies of the Congregational Church.

"MR. ALCOTT, A LADY NEAR ME DESIRES TO INQUIRE WHETHER OMNIPOTENCE ABNEGATES ATTRIBUTE?"

PAUL REVERE'S LANTERN

The National Park is excavating the old battle road, parts of which can be seen along Rt. 2A between Lexington and Concord. A one-mile self-guided historical trail across woods and fields begins at the **Fiske Hill Information Station**, near Rt. 128.

April 19, **Patriot's Day**, is an important holiday to Concordians. The celebration begins with a Military Ball the night before. Just after midnight "Dr. Samuel Prescott" rides into town and is greeted at Wright Tavern. (Longfellow notwithstanding, Paul Revere was captured in Lincoln and never made it.) At dawn the Concord Independent Battery fires a 21-gun cannonade on the Buttrick Hillside overlooking the Bridge. Most years the Parade steps off at 9 a.m., with 100 marching units, most in colonial garb.

Food: There are picnic areas at Fiske Hill and North Bridge in the National Park and at Walden Pond. The Colonial Inn is noted, but on the expensive side. Less venerable, but with a following all its own, is the Willow Pond Kitchen on Rt. 2A, affectionately known as "the hanging junkyard." Buttrick's Ice Cream is on Rt. 2A.

To Read: *Walden* is restorative. Hawthorne's Preface to *Mosses from an Old Manse* has an interesting description of the house and the battleground.

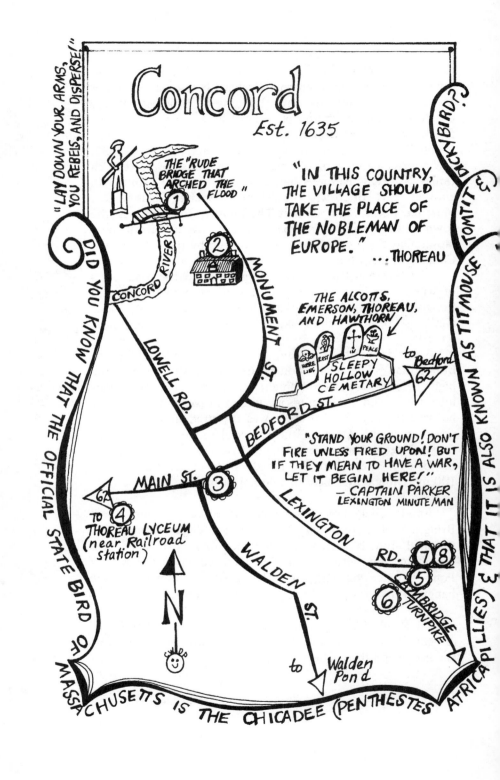

(1) North Bridge. Visitors' center is open year round free.

(2) Old Manse. Open June 1-October 15, Tues-Sat 10-4:30, Sun 1-4:30. Adults 50¢, children 25¢.

(3) Wright Tavern. Gift shop.

(4) Thoreau Lyceum, 48 Belknap St. Open Tues-Sun year round. Summer 10-5, winter 1-5, Sundays 2-5. Free.

(5) Antiquarian House. Open Feb-Nov weekdays and holidays 10-5, Sundays 2-5. Adults 75¢, children 35¢.

(6) Emerson House. Open April 19-Dec. 1. Tues-Sat 10-11:30, 1:30-5:30, Sundays 2:30-5:30. Open on Monday holidays. Adults 50¢, children 35¢.

(7) Orchard House. Open April 19-Nov. 11. Mon-Sat 10-5, Sun 2-6. Adults 60¢, children 25¢.

(8) The Wayside will open eventually as part of the Minute Man Park.

LEXINGTON

In the midst of a busy and affluent suburb is the quiet oasis of Lexington Green, "birthplace of American Liberty." Monuments and markers relate the story of the first battle of the Revolution. Not far away are three houses open to the public which commemorate the events of April 19, 1775. **Buckman Tavern,** 1 Bedford Street, was the rendezvous of the Minute Men on the morning of the Battle. In **Hancock-Clarke House,** now at 35 Hancock St., Samuel Adams and John Hancock were sleeping when aroused by Paul Revere and told the Redcoats were coming. **Munroe Tavern,** at 1332 Massachusetts Avenue, was headquarters of Earl Percy for awhile that day. A new **Chamber of Commerce Visitors Center,** at Massachusetts Avenue and Meriam Street, to the right of Buckman Tavern has a diorama of the Battle of Lexington, and helpful literature and displays.

There is a big parade in Lexington on **Patriot's Day.** "Paul Revere" arrives at Lexington Green around 1, and "William Dawes" a few minutes later. The parade begins at 2, but it can take at least an hour to reach the Green from the starting point. Out-of-towners had best arrive early as all roads leading into Lexington Center are closed at approximately 1 p.m.

Lexington Visitor's Center, open daily April 1-Oct. 31, 9-5; Nov. 1-March 31, 10-4.

Historic Houses, open April 19-Oct. 31, Mon-Sat 10-5, Sun 1-5. Adults 50¢ for each house, children 15¢. Combination tickets $1.25.

SALEM

It can be said in Salem's defense that the whole thing started in Danvers. Furthermore it never reached the proportions it did in Europe and England during the late Middle Ages. Still, in one hysterical year, 1692, Salem executed 20 witches and two dogs possessed of the devil, an outstanding record when we consider that in the whole of the 17th-century there are only 34 executions for witchcraft on record in all the New England colonies. "Let us thank God for having given us such ancestors," wrote the famous descendant of Judge John Hathorne of the Witchcraft Court, "and let each successive generation thank Him, not less fervently, for being one step further from them in the march of ages."

Tourists will be pleased to know that Salem hasn't forgotten Nathaniel Hawthorne or his witchhunting ancestors. Witches on broomsticks mark the Historic Trail signs. Gallows Hill is now a park, but the restored home of Judge Jonathan Corwin, where preliminary examinations were held, is open to the public as the **Witch House**.

Hawthorne is memorialized in the restored **House of Seven Gables**, complete with secret staircase. In summer the guided tour includes three smaller houses grouped in the garden, including Hawthorne's birthplace, built in 1750. If the admission fee seems steep, proceeds go to settlement work. Within walking distance of the Seven Gables is the old Salem **Custom House**, where Hawthorne worked as Surveyor of the Port. The exhibits include his office with a taped description taken from the preface to the *Scarlet Letter*.

The Custom House is part of the **Salem Maritime National Historic Site,** which includes several other buildings from the heyday of shipping. **Derby House** was built in 1761 by a clipper-ship captain who later became America's first millionaire. Notice the unusually ornate staircase and the painted paneling.

DERBY HOUSE HAS UNUSUAL EXAMPLES OF EARLY BRASSWORK (BUILT FOR ELIAS HASKET DERBY).

The **Peabody Museum,** a few blocks away on Essex Street, is a fascinating mariner museum dating from the days when Salem captains circled the globe, (see page 143). Nearby is another free museum, the **Essex Institute,** which has naval and medical items, early American decorative arts, and a major collection of 18th and early 19th century portraits. A shoe shop, a Quaker meeting house, and the **John Ward House,** (1684), are grouped on the museum property. Essex Institute maintains other houses in Salem. Two—the **Crowninshield-Bentley House** (1727) and Samuel McIntire's **Pingree House** (1804)—are next door.

A well-marked "Historic Trail" makes it easy to find the major attractions in Salem. Students of American architecture may enjoy strolling along Chestnut Street or exploring other mansions by Samuel McIntire. Children who have not been to Plimoth Plantation might like the **Pioneer Village,** a replica of the wilderness settlement of 1630. For newcomers, we suggest concentrating on one area and walking. Salem's narrow old streets, many marked one-way, are charming on foot but frustrating in a car.

Food: Salem Willows, a town beach and amusement park has hot dog stands and a picnic area. Ye Olde Pepper Companie, 37 Turner St., near the House of Seven Gables, has marvelous homemade "Gibraltars," "Black Jacks," toffees, caramels, and creams. You won't go hungry on Route 1A.

To Read: Indispensable on witches is Marion Starkey's, *The Devil in Massachusetts,* a Dolphin paperback. Impressively documented, it reads like a suspense story. Hawthorne's *House of Seven Gables* and the "Custom House" preface to the *Scarlet Letter* are o.k. too.

ALSO READ: CHADWICK HANSEN'S WITCHCRAFT IN SALEM.

91

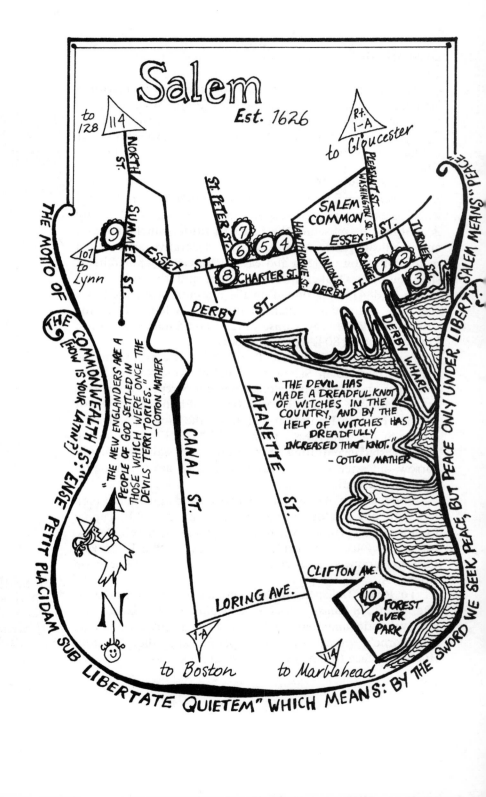

(1) Custom House. Open daily 8:30-5. Free.

(2) Derby House. Open year round 8:30-4:30. Adults 50¢, children free.

(3) House of Seven Gables. Open year round 10-5 daily except 9:30-7:30 in July and August. The daytime tour in summer includes two other buildings. Adults $1.50 in summer, $1.25 winter. Students 75¢, children 35¢.

(4) Crowninshield-Bentley House. Open June-September Tues-Sat 10-12:30 and 2-4:30, Sundays 2-4:30. Adults 50¢, children 25¢.

(5) Pingree House. Same hours as Crowninshield-Bentley. Adults $1, children 50¢.

(6) and (7) Essex Institute. Open Tues-Sat 9-4:30, Sundays and holidays 2-5. Free. Garden buildings, 25¢.

(8) Peabody Museum. Open year round, March 1-October 31 from 9-5, November 1-February 28 from 9-4. Sundays and holidays 2-5. Free.

(9) Witch House. Open May 1-October 31 daily 10-6. Adults 50¢, children 25¢.

(10) Pioneer Village, Clifton Avenue. Open June 1-October 12 from 9:30-6:30. After Labor Day 10-5. Adults 50¢, children 25¢.

OLD STURBRIDGE VILLAGE

Sturbridge Village is a re-creation of a typical New England rural village of the early 1800's. The buildings are not reproductions, however, as they are at Plimoth Plantation or Colonial Williamsburg, but are original structures moved from many New England locations. Costumed adults and children demonstrate typical farm, trade, and household crafts. See the broommaker, the blacksmith, the printer, the potter, the herbalist at work. Taste gingerbread fresh out of the oven at the farm house or buy "Pine Schillings" or other old-fashioned cookies at the village bakery. Take pictures of your family in the pillory. Watch a Punch and Judy Show or listen to a folksinger on the village green. Activities vary according to the season; the village is delightful year-round.

Plan to arrive early in the morning as there is more than a day's activity. You will be outdoors much of the time, so dress accordingly. Bring a carriage or stroller for little ones.

Sturbridge is 60 miles west of Boston, an hour and a half drive on the Mass. Turnpike. The exit is well marked. It is Open 9:30 to 5:30 everyday from mid-March until December. In winter the hours are 10-4. **Admission** is $2.50 for adults, $1.00 for children six through 14. If you visit the village twice in one year, it is well worth exploring the advantages of **membership**. Members may visit the Village free and bring a guest (or more according to classification) for half price. They also receive a 10% discount at the gift shop, and a subscription to two publications.

Special days at Sturbridge include **Militia Day,** the third Sunday in May, when you can see uniformed and marching Ancient and Honorable military units from throughout New England. Events include the raising of a Liberty Pole and the capping of it with a Liberty Cap. Ceremonies begin at noon. On **Thanksgiving** a traditional New England dinner is prepared and cooked at the Village. Reservations must be made with the Secretary for Special Events, Old Sturbridge Village, and are often filled by July. In October, the village sponsors an **Antique Collector's Weekend,** three days of lectures, discussions, and sociability.

Food: A Buffet is served in the Village Tavern—but there is apt to be a long wait for tables. The Cafeteria downstairs is inexpensive and you can eat on the patio in good weather. In the summer, light lunches are served at the Farmer's Nooning. Better yet, bring a picnic; there are tables under the trees.

Capes & Islands

CAPE COD

There are many Cape Cods—the winter Cape where 55,000 permanent residents settle down to cranberry production or fishing or chicken farming or recuperating; a springtime Cape of uncertain weather, when the herring fight their way from the ocean to Herring Pond to spawn, or when the rhododendron bloom at Shawne Forest; the summer Cape, July and August, when summer homes, motels, and beachside cottages are full, when Cape Cod stores from Peck & Peck to the local sandal maker extend their hours, when roads jam on Friday nights and Sunday evenings, and the beaches are warm, spirits are high, and there is no summer pleasure not close at hand. Then there is the Cape of Indian Summer. From Labor Day to Columbus Day is considered by many the ideal time to visit the Cape. Many of the shops are still open, the air is clear and the weather as consistently beautiful as at any other time of the year. Rates go down, but the water is still pleasant.

Some facts to remember about the Cape no matter what time of year you visit it:

. . . it is 70 miles from the canal, which divides it from the mainland, to Provincetown at the tip. Check mileages before you head for any particular point.

. . . once you cross the bridge you might well be entering the 51st state of the union—Cape Codders seem not to consider themselves part of Massachusetts. Be sure to bring enough cash or be prepared with traveler's checks as local banks will not cash anything else.

95

. . . it is an area of great diversity. The Pilgrims landed here, of course, and Cape Codders have not forgotten it. Most people visit the Cape mainly to "beach it." There are numerous other attractions for those willing to explore. At the end of August you can find wild beach plums, blackberries, raspberries and rose hips—delicious for making into jams and jellies. Cranberry bogs are located near swamps or meadows.

Cape Cod beaches are famous. In choosing one it helps to know that the three sides of the Cape are very different. The Atlantic (south) side gets the warm Gulf stream producing comfortable water temperatures, and, as you would expect, is the most crowded. The Atlantic outer (east) side gets the big breakers and it is here you find the spectacular unspoiled dunes, cliffs, the great outer beach—and cold water. The waters of Cape Cod Bay on the north and west side are shallow, calm and warm. You can walk out for a mile from the shoreline at low tide and see all sorts of sea life from tiny fish to hermit crabs. Children and adults love to go through  the wrack left by the tide and discover shells, skate egg cases, and horseshoe crab shells. Each town operates the public beaches (except for those in the National Seashore) and requires a permit, available from the town hall. Shellfishing permits are also obtained at the town halls. Clam digging is best at low tide. Swimming is best on the bay beaches at high tide, on ocean beaches at low tide.

A visit to the **Cape Cod National Seashore**, a beautiful strip of the Cape from Chatham to Provincetown, is the best way to learn about and enjoy Cape Cod. The Pilgrim Spring, the Marconi Wireless Station site, the Provincetown sand dunes, the Cape Cod Lighthouse, and famous Nauset Beach are all in the National Seashore. The Seashore includes walking trails, guided tours, children's field trips, a dune caravan, demonstrations of shellfishing and surfing and bicycle trails. An entrance fee of $1 is required at beaches and bath houses. Surfing areas are set aside at Nauset and Coast Guard beaches.

The National Seashore Visitor's Centers, Route 6, Eastham and at Provincetown, are open daily during the summer

8-8. After Labor Day to April 1 they are open 9-4:45 Wed-Sat. Both centers have exhibits, national seashore information, and a free movie about the Cape every hour. Every evening at 8 during the summer there are excellent free illustrated lectures on Cape history, wild life and geology.

Bicycles and surfboards may be rented from gas stations, motels and shops along Rt. 6 in Eastham or in Provincetown. Bicycles are $1 for two hours or they may be rented by the day or week. Surfboards rent for $5 a day including a car rack. Low tide is the best time to surf so consult your tide schedule before you begin.

To see the Cape you have to get lost on the back roads; leave either Rt. 6 or 6A and wander. The Cape is famous for seascapes; people who have taken the trouble to meander in the interior claim that the freshwater scenes deserve fame as well. The fresh water lakes or kettle ponds are filled with fish and have shallow sandy beaches ideal for children to swim, sail and fish.

Each of the small towns on the Cape cherishes its individuality. At the canal is the town of **Bourne**. Don't rush by every time. Stop to see the railroad bridge over the canal raised and lowered to let ships pass. In late April you can watch the Herring run. For about two weeks hordes of fish swim upstream from the ocean to spawn. The best outlook is in Bournedale, on Rt. 6 halfway between the Sagamore and Bourne traffic rotaries. As the natives say, if the run is on you can't possibly miss the spot.

Chatham is known for yacht races every Sunday at three. In **Dennis** summer stock is an important enterprise. The Dennis Playhouse is the oldest of the theatres and gave a first start to such stars as Robert Montgomery and Bette Davis. It is only one of many playhouses whose productions range from serious drama to musical comedy.

The Old Windmill in the center of **Eastham** is worth a visit, especially to hear the stories told by the guides. It is one of the few things left on the Cape that is free.

The streets of **Hyannis** in July and August are as crowded as a big city. Major department stores have branches there and at the south end of the central street exclusive shops

97

reign. Best shopping on the Cape includes the Colonial Candle Company. They have seconds of candles at a discount and will let you walk through the factory and see how the candles are made. Major supermarkets are here and in **Orleans**, where the Peter Hunt Studio on Rt. 6 is great for browsing.

Provincetown used to be a major art colony but now is noted for its shops which abound in imports and unusual gifts. The Pilgrim Monument and Museum are worth a visit. Let your children climb to the top of the 252 foot high monument—they'll be too tired to fight in the car on the way home. It is open daily year round 9-5 except mid-June-Sept. 9-9. Adults 75¢. The Dolphin II, a deep sea fishing boat, sails out of MacMillan Wharf every morning at 8 and afternoon at 2. The fare is $5 for adults and $3 for children under 12. Rod, reel, bait, and parking are free. Telephone 487-1900 for reservations.

Quaint and salty **Wellfleet** replaced Provincetown as the major art colony. It's fun to watch the fishing fleet return and see the catch taken from the boats.

Sandwich is a very lovely bayside town. Stop in at the Glass Museum to see exhibits of authentic Sandwich blown and pressed glass. It's at Town Hall Square, Rt. 130, open May 1-Nov 1 daily and Sun 10-5. Adults 50¢, children 25¢.

The marvelous collection of dolls at the Yesteryears Museum is another favorite attraction in Sandwich. It's open May 30-Oct 15 daily 10-5, Sunday 1-5. Adults 75¢, children 25¢.

In **Woods Hole**, a renowned center for oceanographic research and exploration, an important spot is the Aquarium, Albatross St., open in summer 10-5 daily. Free. Fifteen tanks exhibit live ocean creatures. Other displays describe marine life and oceanographic equipment.

A Weekly Guide to Cape Cod available everywhere on the Cape, gives details on the theatre, races, and other current happenings. *The Cape Cod Vacationer,* published by the Chamber of Commerce, is an excellent guide. It has listings of all museums, beaches, boats and about anything else you might want to know. Additional information can be had at the Chamber of Commerce Information Center at the rotary before the Sagamore Bridge. Each town has its own information center and these are very helpful in finding accommodations. During the height of the tourist season, write well ahead for reservations.

A good book to put you in the spirit of Cape Cod is Henry Beston's *The Outermost House.*

CAPE ANN

Champlain called it the Cape aux Isles for the three wooded islands just offshore. Captain John Smith named it Tragabigzanda for a Turkish lady he knew. Prince Charles, in honor of his mother, made it plain Cape Ann. A fishing port since 1623, it's a haven for artists, birders, hikers, beachcombers, and browsers. Route 127, with diversions along the way, is as beautiful a drive as you'll find in New England.

Gloucester is the biggest and best known of the Cape Ann towns. The sea-green granite statue overlooking the Harbor is a memorial to the more than 10,000 Gloucester fishermen who have lost their lives at sea. If that rugged face looks familiar, you may have seen it on a package of frozen fillets. Gloucester is still a major fishing port. In summer, Gorton's seafood center has tours of the works twice a day.

Rockport, at the tip of Cape Ann, is a famous artists' colony. A tourist favorite in summer, it's an unbeatable winter hideaway. Lots of local artists exhibit at the Rockport Art Association on Main Street, open year round, afternoons only in winter. Next door is the Christmas Dove, a tinselly enticement from May through December. Most of the shops and craftsmen's studios on **Bearskin Neck** are open year round. Look for the marker that tells the story of the bearskins. At Christmas time, tiny lighted trees above doorways lure sightseers from the windy ocean view at the end of the street.

For the nature lover, the choicest spots on Cape Ann can't be reached by car. One of these is **Dogtown Commons,** the center of settlement in the 1600's. The jutting boulders made a natural defense against Indians and pirates in the early days. When those dangers passed and fishing became more lucrative than farming, the commons was deserted for the coast—left to the dogs. For a hundred years this northeast ghosttown has been woods; the last house was torn down in 1845. Wild roses, blue asters, and wild berries reward the hiker. History hunters like to search for the foundations of old houses and streets, some still discernible if you know where to look.

ASTERS

Eastern Point in Gloucester is an unspoiled rocky headland with tidal pools for studying marine life. Patches of seaside goldenrod welcome migrating Monarch butterflies. The Audubon Society maintains a sanctuary here. Another beautiful seaside trail is at **Halibut Point,** north of Rockport, a property of the Trustees of Reservations. Halibut and Andrews Points are the nearest points of land to Britain in the United States.

True to its heritage, Cape Ann has a number of 17th-century houses, historical exhibits, and local relics—and one surprise. Along the rock-bound coast south of Glouces-ter, with a splendid view of the reef of Norman's Woe (made famous by Longfellow in "The Wreck of the Hesperus"), is a medieval castle. **The Hammond Museum,** designed by Allen and Collens, who later did the Cloisters in New York, was once the home of millionaire-inventor John Hays Hammond. June 15 to September 15 it is open to the public for guided tours at 10, 11, 12, 2 and 3. Admission for adults is $1.25, for children 75¢. Not far from the museum is **Ravenswood Park,** a wooded height with a magnificent view of Gloucester Harbor and the site of a hermit's hut.

A bonus for Cape Ann sightseers is the annual **blessing of the fleet** in Gloucester. The festival is held on the weekend closest to the Feast Day of St. Peter, June 29. It lasts four days, beginning with a Block Dance on Thursday night. Sports events take place both Saturday and Sunday at 4:30. They include seine boat races, dory races, and the "greased pole" contest in which teen age boys slither up a fifty-foot greased spar extending over the water and attempt to capture a flag at the end. Failure means a good dunk in the cold Atlantic.

All during the festival, street booths sell Italian ices and bands play. Fifty archways hung with colored lights are erected over the streets in the Italian section and an enormous altar supports a lifesize statue of St. Peter which is decorated with hundreds of flowers.

The religious part of the celebration begins with a Solemn Pontifical Mass at 10:45 on Sunday. Immediately following, a procession of clergy, floats, and bands escorts the Statue of St. Peter to the waterfront for the Blessing. All the fishing boats are decorated with signal flags and massed in the harbor. At the conclusion of the Blessing they blow their fog horns in a blast of gaiety heard through Cape Ann.

The Blessing may be viewed from Pavillion Beach and Stacey Boulevard in Gloucester. The events follow the same schedule from year to year, but the dates vary. Write the Chamber of Commerce, Gloucester, and ask for an advance program, or watch the Boston papers for information.

THEY THAT GO
DOWN TO THE SEA
IN SHIPS

THE ISLANDS

Martha's Vineyard and Nantucket: even the names are resonant of the sea, of quaint villages and half-deserted beaches, weathered fishing shacks and rose-covered cottages. Tales of whalers and Indians and persecuted Quakers seem closer in time than the mainland hubbub a few miles away.

The two islands are quite different. Martha's Vineyard is only six miles from Cape Cod, is larger and more varied than Nantucket. A car is an advantage. A bicycle is more in scale with romantic Nantucket, thirty miles out to sea. Neither island is crowded, even on holiday weekends. Both are especially lovely in late June or early July when the wild and cultivated roses are in full bloom.

On Martha's Vineyard you'll probably spend most of your time relaxing on the beautiful beaches. Plan some time, too, for exploring the diverse communities around the island. **Edgartown** is a good place to stay overnight. Many of the houses date from whaling days. There are lovely gardens all along the tree-lined streets. Although many houses are tourist homes, they are hard to distinguish from residences and the feeling is never commercial. **Gay Head** is the site of the spectacular red-clay cliffs which attracted early explorers. Once an Indian reservation, it is now a quiet village. Indian islanders run a small museum and shop. Small craft line the harbor gut at **Menemsha**, a small fishing village and art colony, one of the most picturesque spots in New England. **Vineyard Haven** and **Oak Bluffs**, the landing points for the steamships, are less appealing to most people, although they do have good beaches and shopping. Oak Bluffs has a storybook cluster of "gingerbread houses," little one-room cottages frilled with wooden trim. Originally built as part of the Methodist Camp Meeting complex, they are hung with lanterns the third Wednesday in August for "Illumination Night."

Nantucket has a low-keyed, somewhat self-conscious charm, with miles of sand and shells and good swimming. It has a golf course, tennis club, boats to rent, and good surf

MENEMSHA IS NEAR GAY HEAD

fishing. Night entertainment is limited to a summer play-house, a movie theatre, some good restaurants, and strolling.

The restorations and improvements on the **harbor front** have been much in the news. The S & H Green Stamp inheritance provided the money, but not the flavor. The cobbled plaza has tastefully restored shops where candles are dipped from sperm oil wax and a pewtersmith fashions creamers and sugars. Modern comforts include a multitude of docking facilities, even a sink with garbage disposal for cleaning newly caught fish. Toward the center of town, handcraft stores carry material woven on the Island, as well as the famous lightship baskets with carved ivory tops.

Main Street is known for beautiful houses of the 1820's and 30's with silver name-plates on the doors. All are in the hands of private families except for number 96, the Haden House-Satler Memorial. Most of the houses on Nantucket are more modest, small weathered shake cottages. The Jethro Coffin House, built in 1686, is easily reached from the center of town. The old mill, built in 1746 by Nathan Wilbur, has the original grinding stones and wooden machinery. **The Whaling Museum**, in an old brick candlehouse, has relics of Nantucket's adventuring past. An Old Quaker meetinghouse recalls the first migrations.

If you feel inclined to leave the center of town there are taxis available or several rental bicycle shops. Well laid out bicycle paths lead to other parts of the island. **Siasconset** is one of the most picturesque areas of the island with tiny row-houses lining the streets.

The most popular way to reach the islands is by **steamer** from Woods Hole, 45 minutes to the Vineyard, three hours to Nantucket. The fastest approach is by Northeast Airlines from New York or Boston. The Woods Hole, Martha's Vineyard & Nantucket Steamship Authority has a phone in Boston 426-1855. The schedule can be obtained by writing to P.O. Box 284, Woods Hole, Mass. 02543. The fares change four times a year. Passengers don't need reservations, cars do. In high season, a round-trip fare for an adult is about $4 to the Vineyard, $7 to Nantucket. Children 5-15 pay half fare.

Information on Summer Seminars on art, literature, history, film, drama, etc. can be obtained by writing Nantucket Summer Seminars, Chamber of Commerce, Nantucket, Massachusetts 02554 (617-228-1700). Places to stay, things to see and general information can also be had from the Chambers of Commerce of either island.

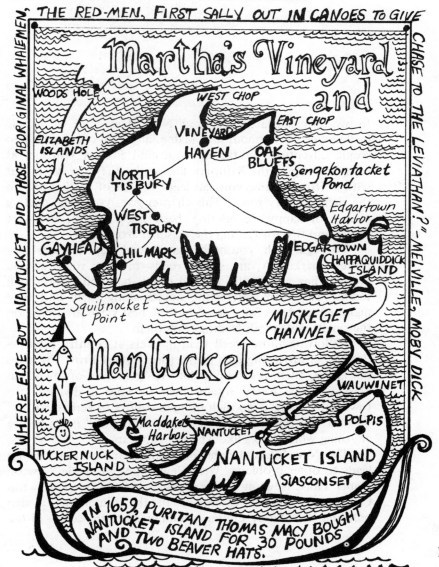

105

How To Get Lost
On A Country Road

In western Massachusetts and New Hampshire or in the backwoods of Vermont and Maine, any turn-off can lead to scenic adventure. In the areas around Boston you can as easily end up in the Saturday line at the Jiffy Car Wash. But with a little practice you can learn the art of getting lost on the right country roads. This chapter gives you some starting places for happy meandering—basic north, south, and west routes and tips for finding the seasonal attractions.

To begin with, you need a good road map. The alternate routes, marked A, are scenic roads—or slow roads as you prefer. They are usually the old routes between and through towns. There are interesting points along them and they make a good basis for a drive, but the best views are found on the smaller side roads leading from them.

Following those small road markers at country intersections is an intriguing dice game. (See Robert Frost.) It helps to know that it's impossible to get "out-of-town" in Massachusetts. Every square inch of land is divided into townships; there is no such thing as county or state territory. So you will find yourself "Entering Abington" miles before anything which looks like Abington appears.

The New England habit of economizing on town names leads to other problems. West Newton, Newtonville, Newton Upper Falls, Newton Lower Falls, Newton Corner, Newton Centre are familiar examples. In the hinterland, a sign pointing to "Shirley Center" could mean to the center of the town where you might find a grocery store; it more probably means a gas-pump and a post office in a separate village six or seven miles away.

Asking directions can be tricky, too. The proverbial New Englander who speaks only when spoken to and answers questions without elaboration does exist. More dangerous is the helpful soul with a vague sense of geography who's sure he knows the place you mean. When tired of such local color, get out your map and take the nearest expressway home.

NORTH SHORE

When you're feeling land-locked head for Marblehead. Once a fishing village, now a yachting center, it is famous for blue water, quaint houses, and rocky beach. Combine it with a visit to Salem; from the suburbs take Rt. 128 to Rt. 114. Or meander up the coast along Rt. 1A. The traffic can be snarled at least as far as Lynn, but at **Revere Beach** you'll get your first view of open water. Because Revere can be reached by MBTA, the beach gets pretty crowded in summer, but off-season it's a favorite look-out point. Bundle up and walk along the shore on a sunny December day.

Nahant is a nice diversion if you like to see water all around you. Further up the coast at Swampscott, take Rt. 129, then watch for the right turn to **Marblehead Neck**, where you'll find a small park, a lighthouse, and a jumble of rocks to explore at low tide. During yacht race week the end of July, the Neck has "front seat" views, but any summer weekend you might see boats warming up for the competition.

From the Neck, follow Rt. 129 into **Marblehead** proper. If you're seaworthy you can take a harbor cruise or rent a sailboat for the day. For landlubbers just walking the narrow streets is fun. There are free historic trail maps at the tourist information center, but you don't need a map to enjoy the nautical views from Front Street or old Ft. Sewell on the hill. The local historical association maintains the Jeremiah Lee Mansion, a Georgian town-house of 1768. It's at 161

Washington St., open Mon-Sat 9:30-4. Adults 50¢, 75¢ on holidays.

The Marblehead Arts Association owns the King Hooper Mansion, using the third-floor ballroom for exhibitions. It's at 8 Hooper St., open Tues-Sun 1:30-5. Adults 50¢.

Willard's "Spirit of '76" is in Abbot Hall, the spired Victorian town hall. A small bakery on Washington St. preserves another Marblehead tradition—Joe Froggers, saucer-sized molasses cookies like those the sailors once took to sea. The Garden Spot nearby is another shop worth looking into. Besides the usual garden supplies there are imaginative gifts and seasonal decorations for purchase or inspiration.

From Marblehead some people like to continue on up the coast as far as Cape Ann. It's a matter of energy. Actually the coast road below Cape Ann has rather skimpy water views. Cape Ann itself was described in the last chapter.

An interesting alternative to Rt. 1A is the land route via the **Saugus Ironworks Restoration**. From the northwest suburbs the Lynn Fells Parkway, a pretty drive past Breakhart and the Lynn Woods, will put you in the right neighborhood. Or from Rt. 1, take Main Street to Central Street and follow the signs. The Saugus Ironworks brings to life the birthplace of America's iron and steel industry. The blast furnace, forge and slitting mill are as they were in 1650. Massive wheels power the huge bellows used to melt the ore and a deafening hammer which beats the iron into bars. The restored ironmaster's house is younger than the works, but it's still old enough to merit attention and is a nice addition to the tour. The restoration was first opened to the public by an industrial foundation. It's now administered by the Minute Man National Park. Nature trails, additional displays and an expanded schedule are all future possibilities.

The Saugus Ironworks is open from April 19 to mid-October, Tues-Sun 9-4. Be sure to time your visit so you can see a demonstration. They are given Tues-Fri at 10 and 3 and on Saturdays, Sundays, and holidays at 11, 1:30, 2:30 and 4. Adults 50¢, children free. Phone 1-233-0050 for further information.

108

Food: The Clambox on Rt. 1A in Revere is handily located across the street from McDonald's; finicky eaters can have a choice. Lobster rolls and chowder are easy to come by on Front St. in Marblehead. Serious picnicking is possible at Fort Sewell, Chandler Hovey Park on the Neck, or at Breakhart Reservation in Lynn. Don't forget Stowaway Sweets, 154 Atlantic, Marblehead, a cozy shop featuring original candies in a gracious antique-filled house.

SOUTH SHORE

You can zip down the expressway to Plymouth in no time, but you miss a lot of fun on the way. Next time leave the expressway at Neponset Circle and join Rt. 3A. You'll go through some traffic for a few miles, but there are advantages. For Irving Stone fans or history lovers, a right on Hancock Street in Quincy leads to the **Adams Historical Sites**. The 17th-century cottages where two presidents were born are side by side on Franklin St. in the center of town. (Open April 19-Sept. 30, Tues-Sun 10-5. Adults 50¢, children 10¢.) A short drive away on Adams Street (follow the historical trail markers) is the lovely country estate bought by John and Abigail while he was vice-president. Four famous generations of Adamses lived here—John Quincy, Charles, Francis, and Henry among them. The house is now a National Historic Site. (135 Adams St. Open April 19-Nov. 10 daily 9-5. Adults 50¢, children under 16 free.)

Back on Rt. 3A, wives like to stop at the Quincy Bargain Center on the Weymouth line. Husbands and little boys like the **Naval Shipyard**. Park your car just off to the side of the rotary and walk up onto the bridge to watch the men and machinery building and repairing ships.

If none of these things interests you, stick with the expressway as far as the Hingham exit to Rt. 3A. From here you can make your own trip as interesting and as lengthy as you want. A right off Rt. 3A at the police station will take you into Hingham Center, where you can see the **Old Ship**

"THE CONSTANT ROAR OF THE CANNON IS SO DISTRESSING THAT WE CANNOT EAT OR SLEEP."

ABIGAIL ADAMS

109

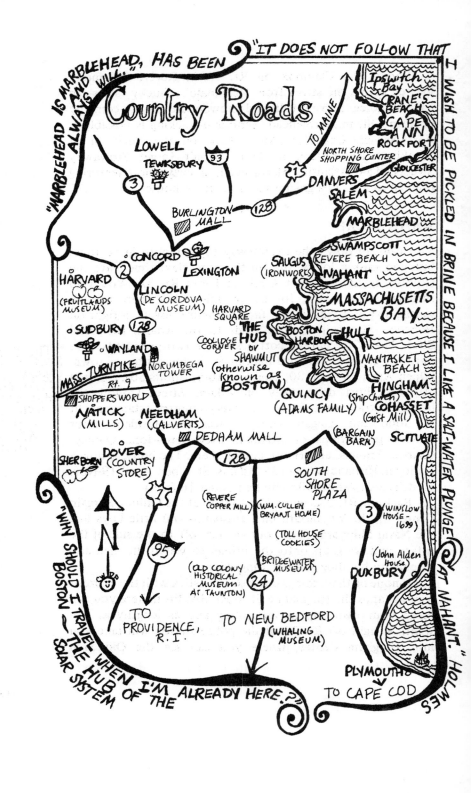

Church, so-called because the curved struts in the roof resemble the inverted hull of a ship. Built in 1681, it is the oldest surviving church in the original thirteen colonies and the only 17th-century church in New England. It has been remodeled, however—in 1731 and 1755. (Open July and August, Tues-Sat 12-5. Free.)

Back on Rt. 3A, look in at the Hingham Lobster Pound, then follow the signs to **Nantasket** and **Hull.** The road to **World's End** (page 165) lies in this direction, but in winter it's fun to take the Hull road to the end, past boarded-up summer houses and deserted beach, for a good view of Boston Harbor. In summer the beachgoing traffic here is likely to crawl.

From Nantasket take any road that seems to keep you within view of the ocean. If you run into a dead-end, go back and get on something more promising. As long as you keep the ocean on your left you'll know you're moving in the right direction. If you see an unusual looking tower on the horizon around Scituate, track it down. It may turn out to be **Lawson's Tower,** said to be the most expensive and most beautiful watertower in America. A public-spirited Mr. Lawson spent $60,000 to turn an ungainly sight into a replica of a 15th-century roman tower complete with a clock that strikes the hour and bells that play at 7 a.m. and 6 p.m.

"THERE ARE 3 CLASSES IN AMERICA; THE BUSY, THE TIPSY, & DANIEL WEBSTER."
HENRY JAMES

There are a handful of historic houses between Marshfield and Duxbury. **Winslow House** has Daniel Webster's law office on the grounds. It is on Webster and Carswell St. in Marshfield. (Open July 1-Labor Day every day but Tues. 10-5, Adults 50¢, children 15¢.) But most people prefer the ocean views. Follow the winding road off Rt. 139 as far as you can onto **Duxbury Peninsula.** When you're tired of dunes, drive to the wooded outlook at Standish Monument Reservation. Plymouth and the Cape are tantalizingly close across water and not too far by land. But if you've had enough, Rt. 3 will take you to Boston in less than an hour.

Food: South Shore suburbanites are flocking to the Cocke 'N Kettle, 78 Border St., off Gannett Road, Scituate. Kilted waitresses surprise you with extra nibbles and relishes

111

throughout the meal. Generous slabs of prime beef are a specialty. (Open Tues-Sat at 5 p.m., Sunday at 1, closed Monday. Moderately expensive.) Picnic at Nantasket or Standish Monument, or try one of the clam shacks along the road.

INLAND

Rt. 2A west of Lexington is a famous road between famous towns with cider mills and fruit stands to lure you on to Concord. Next time you go, take the long way home. From Concord follow Rt. 126 past Walden Pond via farmland and woods to Wayland. At Wayland turn right onto Rt. 20, the Old Boston Post Road, and head for the **Wayside Inn** in South Sudbury. (More adventurous souls might try less traveled roads from Concord to South Sudbury. As long as you keep bearing south you are bound to hit Rt. 20 sooner or later.) The Inn made famous by Longfellow is still a hostelry. Patrons are free to look through the restored public rooms; sightseers are charged fifty cents. A short walk from the Inn is the Little Red Schoolhouse which Mary's lamb once attended. In summer the old Grist Mill down the road is in operation. It is open April-November, Wed-Sun 10-5 for 10¢.

The **Sudbury Country Store** restored by Henry Ford is on Rt. 20 west of the Inn turn-off. Republicans and Democrats are invited to eat on separate benches outside. Inside there are antiques for sale and for browsing, barrels of pickles, and antique gum machines that still work. A mechanical circus, snack shop, and penny candy store are in adjacent buildings.

From Sudbury, blaze your own trail south. Rt. 27 makes pleasant wandering as far as you want to go, past woods, red-barns, rock walls, old burying-grounds, and not too many New Country Estates For Sale. The congestion around Natick is somewhat compensated for by Natick Mills (good fabric buys) and a Dairy Queen—(rare around Boston). Near Sherborn watch for the cider mill at Dowse and Son Apples. For a windingly beautiful drive, take the left-hand turn here to Dover.

In **Dover**, bargain hunters will head straight for the Country Store. If the furniture truck isn't in, spend a few minutes looking at the pretty white meeting house and the restored animal pound on the slope behind. On the other side of the store, across the railroad tracks, go inside the new public library to prove for yourself all those chimneys lead nowhere. Or look at the local history exhibits at the Sawin Building, open on Saturday afternoons free (closed during July and August).

Now head for Dedham. Pet-lovers will be pleased to know that Dedham Street out of Dover center takes you past the **Pine Ridge Cemetery for Small Animals,** maintained by the Animal Rescue League. Visiting hours for friends and relatives are from 10 to 5. In Dedham, look for the **Fairbanks House,** oldest frame dwelling in the United States. It's east of Rt. 1 a stone's throw from the shopping centers on Eastern Avenue. (Open May 1-Nov 1; Tues-Sun 9-12, 1-5. Adults $1, children 35¢.) A chatty 45 minute tour through the house points out changes and additions made by the eight generations of Fairbanks who lived there between 1636 and 1903.

Rt. 1 is drearily commercial, but it will take you back to Boston. You are near the source of the Charles River. Spring wildflowers give a hint of what these waterlands must once have been. At the Baker Street crossing, watch for the sign marking the site of the Brook Farm social experiment of the 1840's.

Food: The Wayside Inn is renowned and not terribly expensive, although on weekends you will have a wait. Women in slacks will not be admitted to the dining room. If you feel snubbed, try Friendly's up the road. Meat-lovers prefer J.T.'s Steak House, also on Rt. 20 in Sudbury. The steak dinners are $3.95 and you can concoct your own salad. There are drive-ins on Rt. 27 through Natick.

113

SEASON SPECIALS

When the days start to get warm and the nights stay cold, when you can smell spring but still need your winter coat, it's **sugaring-off** time in New England. New Hampshire sugaring is closest to Boston. You will probably see syrup buckets and steaming sheds on side roads near Derry or around Milford and Wilton. Call the New Hampshire Vacation Center in Boston (426-9818) to see if the season has begun. They'll send you a list of syrup producers most of whom welcome sightseers with a sample of the new, still-warm syrup. Some sponsor "sugaring-off" parties with advance notice. These cost around $1.25 per person and include fresh donuts, all the syrup on snow you can eat, and sour dill pickles so you can eat more syrup. If you are lucky you might spot a poster advertising a local church supper where a ham and bean dinner is included for the same price.

When the last of the snow melts and May arrives, plan a trip to see **blossoming fruit trees**. The AAA publishes exact routes each spring, but the more adventurous might start on Rt. 117 and drive toward the Harvard-Boxboro area. With this road as a guide some happy wandering can be done on the many side roads that branch off it. If you want to go a little farther afield, the Monadnock Region Association in Peterborough, New Hampshire, posts information on marked tours May 15 of each year.

At harvest time follow the same roads and come home laden with apples. On the way stop at **Fruitlands**, an informal group of museums on a beautiful hilltop in Harvard, Mass. (Open May 30-Sept. 30, Tues-Sun 1-5, Adults $1, children 25¢.) The farmhouse was the setting for Bronson Alcott's short-lived experiment in communal living, described by his daughter Louisa May in "Transcendental Wild Oats." A Shaker house, an American Indian museum, and a picture gallery complete the Fruitlands group.

In mid-June the **mountain laurel** begins to fill the woods with its delicate pink and white flowers. This plant needs high altitudes and a cool climate. A favorite location is in the Berkshires. Plan on spending a full day whether you go by the turnpike or the more leisurely 20-23 Rt. to Great Barrington. From Barrington head for South Egremont and follow the signs up Mount Washington on the dirt road to the Mount Everett State Reservation. Picnic facilities are available here and a ranger is on duty to give you information. Campers will find excellent facilities at the bottom of the mountain on the west side, and hikers will be interested to know that the Appalachian Trail runs through the reservation.

Two of the properties of the Trustees of Reservations also have excellent laurel displays. One of these is the Elliott Laurel Reservation in Phillipston on the Petersham-Templeton Road. The other is Tantisques near Sturbridge, which can be reached by taking exit 9 from the Mass. Pike, following Rt. 15 south for 6.7 miles and bearing right on Leadmine Road for one mile.

New Englanders take the **fall foliage** season seriously. Newspapers publish time charts and route guides and governors issue proclamations. Unfortunately all the excitement can put you in bumper to bumper traffic. Your best bet is to use the published routes as a starting point for getting lost on the back roads. The Mohawk Trail, a spectacular—and popular—drive is a 63 mile strip of Rt. 2 in the western part of the state. Even plain old Rt. 2 between home and Walden Pond isn't bad. A drive to Dover Country Store or along the Charles River in Newton and Weston is a handy substitute for a weekend in Vermont. Or repeat your spring sugar tour of New Hampshire. Where there are sugar maples, there's sure to be color.

IF THE TREES LOOK LIKE THIS, YOU ARE TOO LATE.

115

For more information on scenic drives write any of the following:

New Hampshire Vacation Center, 19 The Arcade, Statler Building, Boston, 426-9818. Seasonal tours, lists of sugar producers.

Berkshire Hill Conference, 100 North St., Pittsfield, Mass. 01201. Free detailed map of six circular drives in the Berkshires.

Mohawk Trail Association, Charlemont, Mass. 01339. Map and color brochure.

Vermont Development Department, Montpelier, Vt., 05602. Free brochures.

MORE

Once you get the hang of it, there are lesser known sights to be pursued on country roads. When you're sick of history, try **pre-history.** In the Connecticut Valley, dinosaur tracks are commonplace. A footprint quarry on Route 116 north of South Hadley has thousands. Charles Boland says you can see Phoenician sacrificial stones near Salem, New Hampshire, an Icelandic tower at Newport, Rhode Island, and viking inscriptions at the Aptuxcet Trading Post at Bourne on the Cape. He tells all about it in his fascinating popular history of pre-Columbian explorations, *They All Discovered America.*

If this doesn't suit you, spend a day tracking down mementos of **non-favorite sons.** Thomas Morton, the Plymouth pilgrims' rowdy neighbor, didn't last long enough to found a city, but Merrymount is still on the map. For an opposition view of our Founding Fathers, see his *New English Canaan.* In a rocky field outside of Whitingham, Vermont, a granite marker honors another famous maverick: "Brigham Young, born on this spot 1801, a man of much courage and superb equipment."

Rebecca Nurse, the first witch hung in 1692, was once considered a threat to the godly commonwealth. Her house in Danvers is now maintained by the Society For the

Preservation of New England Antiquities. You might enjoy looking up other houses of famous ladies. Clara Barton's birthplace is on Clara Barton Road in North Oxford. Mary Baker Eddy's house is on Paradise Road in Swampscott. Both are open to visitors. Emily Dickinson's house in Amherst never was.

MARY BAKER EDDY ALSO LIVED IN LYNN WHERE SHE WROTE SCIENCE & HEALTH, AND ALSO IN CHESTNUT HILL AT 400 BEACON ST. THE LONGYEAR FOUNDATION AT 120 SEAVER ST. IN BROOKLINE IS A MUSEUM TO HER MEMORY.

If you are so inclined, you can go in search of **anti-scenery.** Like the bumper crop of junk autos in the field near Robert Frost's old farm in Derry, New Hampshire. Or the antique covered-bridge near Greenfield, Mass. burned by Halloween pranksters in 1969. If this sort of thing gets you down, you might like to know that public spirited citizens are raising money to restore the bridge. In the meantime, there are seven others in western Massachusetts just waiting to be discovered. Who knows where the next road may lead?

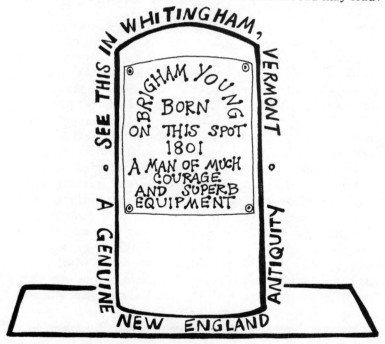

SEE THIS IN WHITINGHAM, VERMONT · A GENUINE NEW ENGLAND ANTIQUITY

BRIGHAM YOUNG BORN ON THIS SPOT 1801 A MAN OF MUCH COURAGE AND SUPERB EQUIPMENT

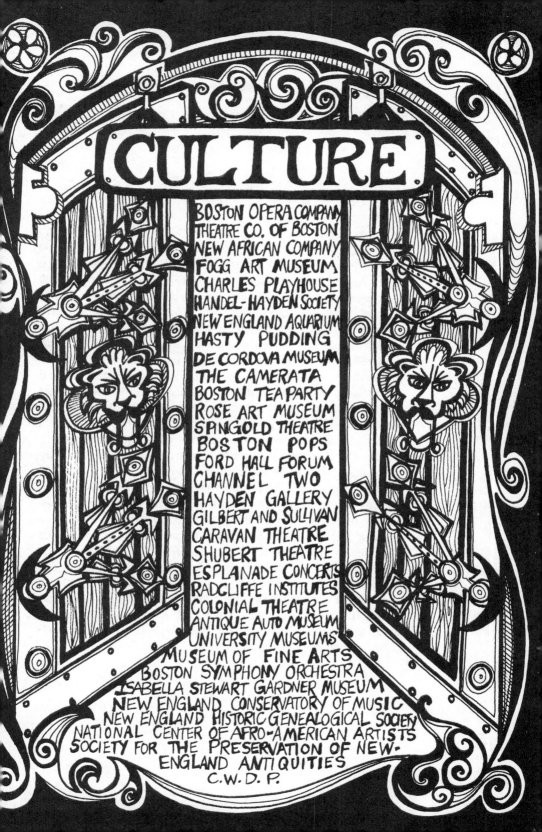

CULTURE

BOSTON OPERA COMPANY
THEATRE CO. OF BOSTON
NEW AFRICAN COMPANY
FOGG ART MUSEUM
CHARLES PLAYHOUSE
HANDEL-HAYDEN SOCIETY
NEW ENGLAND AQUARIUM
HASTY PUDDING
DE CORDOVA MUSEUM
THE CAMERATA
BOSTON TEA PARTY
ROSE ART MUSEUM
SPINGOLD THEATRE
BOSTON POPS
FORD HALL FORUM
CHANNEL TWO
HAYDEN GALLERY
GILBERT AND SULLIVAN
CARAVAN THEATRE
SHUBERT THEATRE
ESPLANADE CONCERTS
RADCLIFFE INSTITUTES
COLONIAL THEATRE
ANTIQUE AUTO MUSEUM
UNIVERSITY MUSEUMS
MUSEUM OF FINE ARTS
BOSTON SYMPHONY ORCHESTRA
ISABELLA STEWART GARDNER MUSEUM
NEW ENGLAND CONSERVATORY OF MUSIC
NEW ENGLAND HISTORIC GENEALOGICAL SOCIETY
NATIONAL CENTER OF AFRO-AMERICAN ARTISTS
SOCIETY FOR THE PRESERVATION OF NEW-
ENGLAND ANTIQUITIES
C.W.D.P.

Theatre

Boston has no Lincoln Center. The critics lament her shabby stages and her status as a Tryout Town. Yet theatrical enthusiasm is high. A British critic in a recent year found the best play of his U.S. tour off off-Broadway at Theatre Company of Boston. Much of the excitement on stage has come from Boston's two grand women of the theatre—Sarah Caldwell, whose Boston opera company has attracted national raves, and Elma Lewis, whose Afro-American cultural center is becoming a reality. On the area's most modern, best equipped stages—those in the universities, the new resident dance and opera companies occasionally perform as well as a variety of student groups, some of which are well worth seeing. On the fringes, the experimental groups are flourishing in make-shift halls and church basements.

To keep up on the happenings, you will need a source of current information. The event guides in the Sunday newspapers help. We have listed program guides available from specific institutions. For comprehensive coverage, look for the weekly newspaper, *Boston After Dark,* 25¢ on the newsstands or by subscription (write 1108 Boylston St., Boston 02215, $3.50 for 6 months, $6.50 a year). In addition to events listings and reviews, BAD has an FM music guide. It also offers a priority ticket service for its readers, advance tickets to many of the best plays, films and concerts at box office prices or lower.

BROADWAY RUNS

If you choose your play carefully and get tickets early you can say you saw the big hit first in Boston. That is, if you can recognize it. In a "try-out town" new productions often undergo nightly revisions. The three major theatres also feature road companies in established shows. Tickets are usually sold in advance, although occasionally a run is extended on an especially popular play. The pre-Broadway theatres are:

The Shubert, 265 Tremont St., Boston, 426-4520, tickets at the box office only.

The Colonial, 106 Boylston St., Boston, box office 426-9366, offices, 426-5827.
Ornately decorated in rococo style.

The Wilbur, 252 Tremont St., Boston, 426-5827.
Built in 1914 by A.L. Wilbur and Messrs. Shubert, the building is one of the country's few theatres built in the London tradition. In 1969 it underwent a $250,000 renovation, its first. The Wilbur and the Colonial are under the same management. They release blocs of tickets to various subscription services. Tickets are available at the box office or through the mail-order forms published with advance ads.

RESIDENT PRODUCTIONS

Charles Playhouse, 76 Warrenton St., Boston.
Opening for the 1956-57 season and housed in an old intimate theatre, the Playhouse has attracted an enthusiastic following to its interesting productions drawn from both classical and modern repertories (emphasis on the latter, including new playwrights). Price range from $2.25-5. Student discounts available for certain performances. A popular Children's Theatre series is also scheduled on Saturday mornings.

Theatre Company of Boston, new location unavailable at press time. Check information.

A splendid, newer company producing avant-garde and classical plays and interested in encouraging and sponsoring other worthwhile dramatic ventures in the area. For instance, during both the 1968-9 and 1969-70 seasons it was joined in several productions by the **New African Company,** a workshop for young blacks formed in 1968. Regular subscription price range is from approximately $2-4 per ticket. Student discounts available for certain performances. A special free Monday night series of concerts, stage readings, etc. was inaugurated during 1969-70. There are also programs and special productions for children.

National Center of Afro-American Artists, 122 Elm Hill Ave., Roxbury, 442-8820.

Spanning the performing and visual arts, this new center was formed in 1968 to spread knowledge of black heritage and culture and to be a center for the expression of black creativity. At the heart of this center is the dynamic Elma Lewis, whose School of Fine Arts has for 20 years or so been offering classes to both children and adults in such fields as dance, music, theatre, and costuming. The School building is next door to the National Center offices and the new Museum, housed in what used to be a Jewish synagogue. The Talley Beatty Dance Co., a professional resident company formed in 1968, has joined with the National Center to become its dance arm. Future plans include creation of a professional orchestra and renovations in the synagogue to enlarge its small auditorium into a more suitable theatre. Summer activities of the Center have revolved around its "Playhouse in the Park," an outdoor theatre in Boston's Franklin Park. A variety of concerts and dance and dramatic offerings have appeared at the Playhouse and the Center's auditorium under National Center sponsorship.

Craft Experimental Theatre, 96 Brookline Ave., Boston (near Kenmore Sq.) Opened in 1968 to do just what it says.

The Proposition, 241 Hampshire St., Cambridge.

Improvisational, satirical revue "baked fresh daily" according to their ads. Weeknights you can meet the actors after the show.

Hub Theatre Center, 131 Cambridge Street, Boston (near Government Center). Opened in 1966.

Caravan Theatre, Harvard Epworth Methodist Church, 1555 Mass. Ave., Cambridge.

A very-much talked about company, presenting new theatre. Features sessions where the audience can talk with the actors. Very reasonable ticket prices. Both childrens' and adults workshops have been introduced. WOMEN'S LIB THEATRE... VERY GOOD!

UNIVERSITY THEATRES

Loeb Drama Center, Harvard University, 64 Brattle St., Cambridge.

Built in 1960, the Loeb is noted for its advanced facilities. Seats for regular plays are $1.50-2. Most of the Fall-Spring plays are produced by the Harvard Dramatic Club, drawing from the classical and modern theatre repertories. Special season touring presentations are also offered, including international and foreign language plays and visiting student productions. Experimental plays in the little theatre downstairs are free and advertised by posters around Harvard Square. A repertory company has been producing excellent plays in recent summer seasons. Free brochure available upon request.

Spingold Arts Center, Brandeis University, Waltham.

Opened in 1964 and worth seeing. Excellent schedule of plays including world premieres. The Dreitzer Art Gallery is located in this building. Free brochure available.

Boston University Theatre, 264 Huntington Ave., Boston.

The Theatre Division of B.U. School of Fine and Applied Arts produces a variety of theatrical experiences (new and old). Performances are in an old theatre, built in 1925, diagonally across from Symphony Hall. Information at box office, 353-3392.

There are also smaller, undergraduate groups in the area who do some interesting things. Lowell or Leverett House (Harvard) will often give an opera in their dining hall spring semester. There are shows by Harvard's Hasty Pudding Society and both MIT and Harvard's Gilbert and Sullivan Society. There have been 15th-century morality plays and modern poetic dramas performed by students in Cambridge churches. Watch for posters in Harvard Square shops, and consult the schedule of events for each institution for complete listings of theatrical productions.

DON'T MISS THE HASTY PUDDING THEATRICALS

OPERA AND DANCE

Boston Opera Association, 420 Boylston St., Boston, 536-2430.

This organization sponsors one week of performances by the New York Metropolitan Opera, at the John B. Hynes Auditorium. Tickets (by mail only) are hard to get and priced approximately from $3-20. Put your name on the mailing list for order form and brochure.

Opera Company of Boston, Inc., 172 Newbury St., Boston, 267-8050.

Directed by Sarah Caldwell, this company, formed in 1957, has been labeled by Life Magazine "the most exciting venture of its kind in the country." In spite of the enormous costs of producing opera in this country, this company is holding its head above water and fulfilling its promise of giving Boston outstanding resident opera, including premiere productions. The glorious-voiced Beverly Sills is a star member of the company. For the 1970 season, opera productions were staged in both MIT's Kresge Theatre and Boston's Savoy Theatre. Tickets, by subscription only, range from $8-15 per performance.

Boston Ballet Company, 577 Washington St., Boston, 426-6066.

Established in 1965, this company moved into the Savoy Theatre for its 1969-70 season, while continuing as well to perform in such places as the Loeb Drama Center (Cambridge) and the Music Hall (Boston). In addition to building its own talent, the Ballet Company draws upon the services of numerous world-celebrated guest artists. It has a growing repertoire of classical, modern, jazz and contemporary works. In mid-December the Company presents sell-out performances of The Nutcracker. Tickets for the season series range from approximately $3-7 per performance.

Music

Friday mornings during the season, the line at Symphony Hall begins to form before nine. Old ladies with folding stools and James Bond novels, students with chessboards balanced on their knees, and music-lovers of all ages with sandwiches in their pockets queue up for the $1 seats which go on sale at noon.

Boston's musical riches have no price tag. There are posh concert series, to be sure, but there are also surprisingly varied and lively concerts at moderate prices. Hundreds of programs offered each year by such venerable institutions as the New England Conservatory, the Gardner Museum, the Mason Music Foundation are free for the asking. Symphony is available on any budget. "Boston," says Globe critic Michael Steinberg, "hardly knows itself what it has."

This chapter surveys the musical scene, giving you addresses where ticket information may be obtained from specific organizations. Watch the Sunday newspapers and BAD for current music news. Check your local weekly newspaper for word of sing-ins and play-ins by amateur local groups. Opera information was given in the last chapter.

Boston Symphony Orchestra, Symphony Hall, 251 Huntington Ave., Boston 02115, 266-1492.

Formed in 1880, under the patronage and devoted care of Henry Higginson, the Boston Symphony Orchestra is one of the country's finest, performing in what many think is the country's finest concert hall, acoustically-speaking. Achieving musical eminence under the leadership of Serge Koussevitzky and the late Charles Munch, the Symphony is now under the musical direction of William Steinberg (succeeding Erich Leinsdorf) with Michael Tilson Thomas as assistant conductor. The Symphony management works hard to ensure enough flexibility to enable any resourceful person to attend BSO concerts at a price he can afford. Program brochures are available upon request.

MICHAEL TILSON THOMAS EVEN MAKES OLD CHESTNUTS SOUND GOOD

A number of **Season-Series** choices are offered to the public, for weekdays or weekends, at prices that range from approximately $2 to $10 a ticket. Also tickets for Thursday-night **Open Rehearsals** are offered at a series price of $2.50/ticket, individual tickets $3; seats are unreserved and the conductor runs through an entire program, usually the following Friday's, sometimes stopping to rework sections.

If one wishes to attend a **Single Concert** there are several alternatives in addition to advance box office purchase. A good way is to show up at the box office 30-45 minutes early and wait for a ticket resale. (Those who cannot attend a concert for which they have purchased tickets usually will phone their tickets in for resale; the original purchaser gets credit for a tax-deductible donation to the Symphony, and the income gained is used to reduce the Orchestra's deficit.) Also 150 seats at $1 each are available for each Friday afternoon and Saturday evening concert. These "rush line" seats go on sale two hours before the start of the concert, noon on Fridays and 6:30 p.m. on Saturdays. In addition, 10 minutes ahead of performance time students with identification cards may for $3 purchase any remaining available seat.

Each of the Friday afternoon and Saturday evening concerts are **Broadcast** direct from Symphony Hall by Boston station WGBH FM (Friday) and WCRB-AM and FM (Saturday). The Saturday evening concerts are also broadcast in four-channel stereo by WCRB-FM and WGBH-FM in collaboration. Selected Tuesday evening concerts are broadcast from WGBH-FM. Usually a half dozen or so concerts are televised live from Symphony Hall in color by WGBH (Channel 2). Watch the TV guides for details.

CONDUCT AT HOME WITH WGBH...

The New England Conservatory of Music, 290 Huntington Ave., Boston. For free monthly concert list phone 262-1120, ext. 217-8.

Gunthur Schuller, president, is a noted figure on the

Boston musical scene. This eminent music school presents its students and faculty in approximately 100-150 free concerts between October and May in Jordan Hall (30 Gainsborough St., Boston), Recital Hall (290 Huntington Ave.) and Brown Hall (294 Huntington Ave.). The variety of musical offerings is immense (orchestral and choral music, opera, vocal and instrumental soloists, chamber groups, etc.). Many of the student performances combine freshness with professional polish. The conservatory also offers a guest artist series to the public; performances are in Jordan Hall and the price range for individual tickets is from $2-4, less for the series. There are student discounts. All major concerts are listed in the newspapers.

Isabella Stewart Gardner Museum, 280 The Fenway, Boston. For free weekly musical calendar write Museum Office, 2 Palace Road, Boston 02115.

Free musical programs by conservatory students and established guest artists are held on Thursdays, Saturdays and Sundays at 3 p.m. and on the first Thursday of the month at 8:30 p.m. Arrive early for seats. The diversified programs feature instrumental, vocal and chamber music from classical, jazz, musical comedy and folk repertories. The museum concerts date back to 1925, just after the museum was opened to the public, and shortly after the death of Mrs. Gardner. They were in keeping with Mrs. Gardner's custom of inviting noted musicians to perform for informal gatherings of her friends. The Sunday afternoon concert is broadcast by WGBH-FM every Sunday at 10 p.m.

The Peabody-Mason Music Foundation, 59 Fayerweather St., Cambridge. Write for free program schedule.

For over 20 years this foundation has been sponsoring a series of superior concerts, free of charge. Held at Sanders Theatre, Harvard University, Cambridge, the concerts feature gifted European artists. Apply for tickets by mail ONLY by writing to the Foundation, 59 Fayerweather St. (the President's private residence), and enclosing a stamped, self-addressed envelope. Requests must be mailed no sooner than

THE CONSERVATORY WILL GRATEFULLY ACCEPT DONATIONS TO ALLEVIATE ITS PRESENT FINANCIAL STRESS

CHECK INDEX FOR OTHER "FREE" ITEMS

a month before each concert or they will be returned, unfilled, to the sender. A separate request must be sent for each two tickets desired. Usually a few additional tickets are available at the door. Non-ticket holders may occupy any seats remaining at 8:25 p.m. Children under 10 years of age are not admitted.

Boston Philharmonia, 416 Marlboro St., Boston 02115, 536-6311. Schedule available upon request.

With Harvard composer Leon Kirchner as principal conductor, this chamber orchestra, formed in 1966 and made up of talented and youthful free-lance musician-teachers, is emphasizing twentieth century works. It is a needed and popular addition to the Boston-Cambridge scene and is starting to carry its musical programs to the outlying suburbs. With present zeal and plans for the future, it is launched toward becoming a full-time orchestra. Tickets are moderately priced. Student discount.

Boston University Celebrity Series, 535 Boylston St., Boston, 536-6037.

This series, launched in 1937 by Aaron Richmond and continued today by his widow, presents top concert performers and promotes benefit performances for local groups. A sizable amount of each year's proceeds is donated to the Boston University School of Fine and Applied Arts for scholarship grants. Subscribers may choose 7 or 14 events each year from a list of approximately 25 events. Offerings range from symphonic music, dance, instrumental and vocal soloists, and chamber ensembles to special attractions such as the British Tournament and Tattoo. Tickets from $3 and up. Single tickets are sold at the box office 3 weeks ahead of performance.

Cambridge Society for Early Music, P.O. Box 336, Cambridge 02138, no phone. Iva Dee Hiatt, Musical Director.

THIS IS VERY GOOD

Founded in 1952, this group is devoted to performance of music from Renaissance, Baroque and early Classical periods. Within this range, a wide variety of concerts have

129

been presented, performed by vocal and instrumental ensembles appropriate to these periods. Noted performers of early music from all over the world have appeared in this series. The concerts have been held in Sanders Theatre. Tickets moderately priced. For further information, write the Society.

Camerata Concerts, Museum of Fine Arts, 456 Huntington Ave., Boston, 267-9300. Joel Cohen, Director.

Brochure describing the series upon request to the Musical Instrument Dept., MFA.

IF YOU DIG THE
VIOLA DA GAMBA,
THIS IS YOUR BAG.

Camerata is a Renaissance term for small chamber ensembles. Three concerts are held each year in the winter and spring. Early music is performed on antique instruments in the Leslie Lindsey Mason Collection. Concerts are given by gifted amateurs, often students selected by audition, and/or guest artists. Admission: $2.50/ticket or $6 for the series. Student discount.

Handel and Haydn Society, 25 Huntington Ave., Boston 02116, 536-2951. Thomas Dunn, Musical Director.

Formed in 1814, this oldest continuously active musical group in America offers some unusual programs, combining choral works with other art media such as ballet, opera, puppetry, films. Performing in recent seasons with the Society has been the Boston Philharmonia. The society also offers two traditional December performances in Symphony Hall of Handel's Messiah. Prices for Jordan Hall performances at $2.50 and up. Student discount.

Chorus Pro Musica, 645 Boylston St., Boston, 267-7442. For information on auditions, rehearsals and concerts phone. Alfred Nash, Founder and Musical Director.

This twenty-year old group gives quality performances from its expansive repertoire of secular and sacred music at a variety of locations, including Symphony Hall, Tanglewood, area churches, etc. It has recorded with the Boston Symphony and has radio and television appearances to its credit. During the 1969-70 season it combined with the BSO

130

in a special Beethoven Festival. The ticket cost varies, depending on the program and concert location.

The Cecilia Society, Office All Saints Church, 1773 Beacon St., Brookline. Donald Teeters, Conductor.

For information on auditions, rehearsals and concerts phone 277-4115 or 227-6289.

Approaching a century of existence, the Society, deliberately limited to 50 members, has helped to shape Boston's appreciation of oratorios. For those unfamiliar with the name, St. Cecilia is the patron saint of music. Rejuvenated in recent years and presently limited to 50 members, it performs chamber pieces, appropriate to its size, from Baroque through contemporary repertories. Three major concerts a year are performed, usually in Sanders Theatre. Prices are moderate. Student discount.

The Masterworks Chorale, Lexington. Schedule information, 861-0424, membership information, 861-0205. Allen Lannom, Conductor.

One of the finest of the suburban choral groups, the 30-year old Lexington Choral Society has recently changed to this name to indicate expanded membership and scope. It has a popular series of free Lexington concerts and one in-town concert for moderate prices. Also popular is its Christmas Messiah Sing, in which the audience and choir sing together. Bring your own music if you have it. Summer Sing sessions have also been introduced.

UNIVERSITY CONCERTS

All the universities in the area have musical programs of a wide variety—often open to the public and free. **Brandeis** holds chamber concerts in the Slosberg Music Center on the campus. **MIT** holds noon concerts in the **MIT** Chapel. **Harvard** has held organ concerts in the Memorial Church, and the University Choir presents an exalted Christmas Carol Service. Harvard Glee Club and band concerts, performing on the steps of Widener Library in Spring twilights, are delightful. Dunster House Music Society at Harvard also offers a multitude of esoteric musical experiences. Major concerts will be listed in newspapers. For complete listings consult the schedule of events for each institution. (See page 00 for where to write.)

BEAUTIFUL

ROCK

Locally where it's at is **The Boston Tea Party**, on Lansdowne Street behind Fenway Park's center-field wall. Smaller spots come and go; keep your eye on *Boston After Dark* for full coverage of happenings important to the now generation. In good weather there are rock concerts at the Cambridge Common, Boston Common, Back Bay Fens—all free Saturday and Sunday afternoons. You can usually find a bearded or pimply enthusiast willing to share a blanket on damp or dusty ground. Hard-core fans tell us WBCN-FM is out of sight, it's so intelligent and groovy on the rock scene. No question but what it's loud; it's Boston's most powerful stereo station.

SUMMER CONCERTS

Boston Pops Concerts at Symphony Hall

Arthur Fiedler, Conductor since 1930. Harry Ellis Dickson, associate conductor. Actually signalling the arrival of Spring, rather than Summer, these famous concerts by BSO members, begun in 1885, have evolved from a once rowdy and boisterous beer-hall atmosphere to their present sedate and decorous state. The music ranges from light classical to musical comedy and popular rock and folk music; the audiences are seated at tables downstairs sipping champagne and soft drinks. On any given night the audience is drawn largely from one or more institutional groups. More than 100 of these patiently wait their turn each spring to take a bloc of seats in the house. The general public may also purchase tickets at the box office on the evening of the concert or in advance from sponsoring groups. Cost range is $4-8. Concerts begin at the conclusion of the regular season and run nightly (except Sunday) through June.

ARTHUR FIEDLER CHASES FIRE ENGINES

Esplanade Concerts, The Hatch Shell on the Charles River banks, Storrow Drive, Boston.

In July, free outdoor evening concerts are given by the Boston Pops with Arthur Fiedler and Harry Ellis Dickson conducting. Bring a blanket and a sweater. Watch the newspaper for details, or inquire at Symphony Hall. Band concerts and other musical offerings also take place at the Hatch Shell during summer months.

Berkshire Music Festival, Tanglewood, Lenox, Mass.

The summer home of BSO is the 200-acre Tanglewood estate, former residence of Nathaniel Hawthorne. For 8 weeks in July and August, the orchestra performs Friday and Saturday evenings and Sunday afternoons. There is a Saturday morning open rehearsal. Tickets for seating inside the shed are expensive, general admission to the grounds less so, but still not cheap. Bring your blanket and picnic, or buy picnic baskets on the grounds and enjoy a pleasant evening

TANGLEWOOD IS ON A BOSKY HILL

133

under the stars. Write well ahead for shed tickets.

The Berkshire Music School holds its own concerts by students on weeknights; one price for everyone. Information at Symphony Hall.

Castle Hill Summer Festival, Crane Estate, Ipswich, Mass. (1-356-4351)

The Castle Hill Foundation, maintaining the former estate of Richard T. Crane, Jr., Chicago millionaire, holds a series of concerts on the Crane Estate in July and August. The grounds are open July 1 to September 9 for picnicking, viewing the sculptures, the Rose Garden, and the ocean. Crane Beach is nearby. For specific concert information watch the newspapers or write or phone the Foundation in Ipswich.

Boston's on-again, off-again **Summer Festivals** include a variety of concerts and other events. Watch the newspapers for details.

Museums

Of course the former "hub of the solar system" has a passion for the past. Bygone glories lurk on every corner. Yet Boston's museums are a surprisingly lively lot. Rembrandts, fish, outer space, Tin Lizzies, spinning wheels, paint-ins, movies, Japanese shields, Tintoretto and John Singer Sargent share the scene.

This chapter surveys the major museums and galleries in the city. The geographical bounds have been stretched a bit in the science section to include a few specialized technological museums outside the standard metropolitan area. Indispensable if you're interested in the subject, they're nice to know about if you're out for a drive.

For the avid culture-collector there are hundreds of possibilities beyond Boston. The State Department of Commerce and Development publishes a free "Guide to Massachusetts Museums" which lists local fire engines of historic interest as well as major institutions. Phone the Vacation-Travel Department (727-3201) for a copy. An annual free guide to "New England Museums and Historic Houses" is available from the New England Council office, 542-2580.

ART MUSEUMS

Museum of Fine Arts, 465 Huntington Ave., Boston, 267-9300,
Open Tues-Sun 10-5, closed Mondays and major holidays.
Open Tues evenings until 9 Oct-May.
Adults $1 except Sun 10-1 50¢, Tues 5-9 free
Children under 16 and members free

DON'T MISS
THE
BODHISATTVAS

The MFA was the first museum to be incorporated in the

United States—in 1870, when Bostonians were transforming the Back Bay tidal marsh into an elegant residential district. Among the treasures it inherited was a comprehensive collection of plaster casts of Greek and Roman statues. One of the Board's first problems was to decide for or against fig leaves. That the MFA has long since become one of the world's great museums tells something about the cosmopolitan spirit of the Back Bay Brahmins who were its first supporters. The museum's only contribution from public monies was a small grant of land in the newly prestigious Copley Square. In 1909 Edward Forbes and his fellow trustees braved Brahmin fury and moved the cramped collection to "the Fenway swamp," its present location.

Today the MFA stands second only to the Metropolitan in this country. Its Oriental galleries are said to be the best outside of Tokyo, its Egyptian collection the finest this side of Cairo. For lovers of early Americana, there are the Gilbert Stuart portraits, Paul Revere's own silver, and magnificent furniture displays. The excellent array of Impressionist painting testifies to the foresight of Boston's 19th century collectors. It has a superb art school and a busy schedule of gallery talks, lectures and films for the general public.

One of the few privately-financed museums in the world, it was finally forced, beginning in June, 1966, to charge admission. (Special exhibitions often have an extra admission fee.) One hour **Introductory Tours** are given by the voluntary ladies committee Tues-Sat at 11:30 a.m. Single **Memberships** are $20, family memberships $30. Among other things, members receive free admission, invitations to receptions and exhibit previews plus reduced rates on subscription events and art classes. For a **Monthly Calendar** send $2 to the Treasurer's Office. The quarterly publication "Bulletin" is available for a $4 subscription fee.

Isabella Stewart Gardner Museum, 280 The Fenway, Boston, 566-1401. Open Tues-Thurs-Sat 10-4, Sun 2-5, first Thurs of month 10-10 tour at 7:30.
Closed Mon-Wed-Fri except for tours at 11 and 2
Closed August except for weekday tours 11 and 2. Free.

The sober brick exterior of 280 The Fenway gives little clue to the artistic splendour within or to the sensation Fenway Court created in proper society when it was opened in 1903. Isabella Stewart Gardner (less reverently, "Mrs. Jack") lovingly superintended the construction of her Back Bay Venetian palace, even getting up on the scaffolding when necessary to show the painters a thing or two. At her death in 1925, she left it for "the education and enjoyment of the public forever"—as long as no one tried to change anything. Every detail of the museum, from the lush flower arrangements in the central court to the dim-lit eccentricity of some of the displays, is exactly as she left it. The collection itself is magnificent—Titian, Tintoretto, Rembrandt, Whistler, Corot, and Matisse are represented, along with Sargent portraits of Mrs. Gardner in surprising settings. With the Audio-Guide (75¢) you can discover the museum at your own pace.

F. MARIAN CRAWFORD WAS DEVOTED TO "MRS. JACK" FOR A TIME... HE WROTE NOVELS SUCH AS: "LOVE IN IDLENESS: A TALE OF BAR HARBOR; "THE WITCH OF PRAGUE; "DOCTOR CLAUDIUS; & 29 MORE!

De Cordova and Dana Museum and Park, Sandy Pond Road, Lincoln, 259-8355.
Open Tues-Sat 10-5, Sun 1:30-5
Adults 50¢, under 21 free

A small and lively community art center with a permanent and growing collection of paintings, prints, drawings, water colors and sculpture. Exhibits can be viewed in a short time, change often and frequently extend to sculpture on the lovely, spacious grounds. The De Cordova is also a center for performing arts and has an art school.

THE ISABELLA STEWART GARDNER MUSEUM 1903

137

Williams Hayes Fogg Art Museum, Harvard University, Quincy St., Cambridge.
Open Mon-Sat 9-5, Sun 2-5. Closed holidays. Closed weekends July through Labor Day. Free

The museum was endowed by Mrs. Elizabeth Fogg in 1895 in memory of her husband. The enlarged collections were moved into the present building in 1927. The arcaded motif of the Court (of Italian travertine) was copied from the facade of the presbytery of the Church of the Madonna di San Biagio at Montepulciano in Italy. The museum houses the School of Fine Arts and is a teaching museum; therefore, the exhibits change often. They are drawn from the University's extensive collection of Occidental and Oriental art, the richest collection of any university in the world.

Carpenter Center for the Visual Arts, Harvard University, Quincy St., Cambridge (next to the Fogg)
Open Mon-Sat 9-5 (building) Exhibit hours 1-6 Tues-Sun (also Thurs 'til 10 depending on exhibit). Free

The only LeCorbusier-designed building in this country was opened in the spring of 1963. Special exhibits are held from time to time in the upstairs Exhibition Hall. Students works are often on display in the lobby. Film and design studios are on the lower floor. **Film showings,** generally classics of their time, are scheduled for the general public.

Busch-Reisinger Museum, Harvard University, Corner Kirkland St. and Divinity Ave., Cambridge.
Open Mon-Sat 9-5
Free. No children without an adult.

Founded in 1902 for the study of Germanic culture. Moved to the present vaulted building in 1921. Collections emphasize sculpture, painting and decorative arts of Austria, Germany, the Low Countries, Scandinavia and Switzerland from the Middle Ages to Modern Times. Especially rich in modern German art, much from the Bauhaus School. Bring your own lunch and enjoy the pleasant, small sculpture garden with its lunch tables. Concerts are given occasionally on the famous baroque organ. Watch the Harvard Gazette. Membership brings certain advantages. Call for information.

138

SEE:
JEWETT ART GALLERY
ROSE ART MUSEUM
HAYDEN GALLERY, MIT
THE BUSCH-REISINGER

Jewett Art Gallery, Wellesley College (part of Jewett Art and Music Center), Wellesley.
Open during academic year Mon-Fri 8:30-4:30, Sat 8:30-12, 1-5, Sun 2:30-5:30.
Free

A teaching museum, housing one of the finest small college collections. Exhibits rotate from the permanent collection. Notice the sculpture gallery upstairs. The building itself was designed by Paul Rudolph and was opened in 1958. **Chamber Concerts** are held in the Music Center portion of the building.

Rose Art Museum, Brandeis University, Waltham.
Open Tues-Sun 1-5. Closed Mon. Closed in between exhibits. Free.

This excellent institution brings many special exhibits to the area during the year; the emphasis is often modern. During the summer months, its own rather catholic permanent collection is exhibited throughout the museum and in the Dreitzer Gallery in the Spingold Theatre (same exhibit hours).

Hayden Gallery, MIT, Library Building, Memorial Drive, Cambridge.
Open academic year Mon-Fri 10-5, Sat and Sun 1-5-

Contemporary paintings and sculpture are displayed in this small gallery in the Library, also technological exhibits on occasion. Exhibits change often. An outdoor work of art worth noticing is the giant Calder stabile, completed in 1966. It is in front of the Green Building between Hayden Library and Walker Memorial.

GALLERIES

If you like browsing in galleries or purchasing art originals, explore the numerous Newbury Street galleries, a number of which reflect well what is going on locally in art. **Ward-Nasse**, 118 Newbury, specializes in New England painting and sculpture. Other galleries with a contemporary outlook are **Alpha**, 121 Newbury; **Kanegis**, 123 Newbury; **Obelisk**, 130 Newbury; and **Harcus Krakow** at 167 Newbury. Look for primitive and ancient art at **Origins**, 134 Newbury, not at **Childs**, 169 Newbury, which specializes in 18th and 19th century English and American paintings. **Weeden Gallery**, 35 Lewis Wharf, has New Art in an anti-establishment setting. Most Newbury Street galleries are open Monday through Saturday 9-5. A few close on Monday. Since many close for awhile during July and August, phone before making a special trip.

SWEDISH PRINTMAKER RAGNHILD KARLSTRÖM'S WORK IS AT NIELSEN GALLERY (179 NEWBURY)

The galleries in and around Harvard Square are also worth a try. If you want to rent a picture to enliven your own art scene, be sure to drop in at the **Cambridge Art Association**, 23 Garden Street, Cambridge. **Roten Gallery**, 26 Dunster Street, Cambridge, is excellent for prints, as is **Retina Gallery**, 1169 Mass. Ave., Cambridge, which has good-looking frames as well. Don't miss the rental-sales gallery on the **Institute of Contemporary Art**, 1175 Soldiers Field Road, Brighton. The resurrected ICA, trying to provide a vital link between Boston artists and the public, is also sponsoring shows and bus tours around town and underwriting efforts of Boston artists.

WARD-NASSE
ALPHA
KANEGIS
OBELISK
HARCUS KRAKOW
ORIGINS
NIELSEN

WEEDEN GALLERY
CAMBRIDGE
ART ASSOCIATION
ROTEN GALLERY
RETINA
INSTITUTE OF
CONTEMPORARY ART

SCIENCE MUSEUMS

Museum of Science and Charles Hayden Planetarium, Science Park, Boston, overlooking the Charles River Basin, 742-1410. Open Mon-Sat 10-5, Sun 11-5, Fri nights until 10. Closed holidays.
Adults $1.50, children 5-16 50¢
After 5 p.m. Fri, adults $1, children 25¢
Planetarium: 50¢ extra for everyone; children under 5 not admitted.

See how life begins, observe the transparent woman, hear your own telephone voice, watch simulated waves in motion and the simulated motion of celestial bodies in space, plus hundreds of other fascinating exhibits from zoological, medical, scientific and technological fields. Various special courses and lectures in the fields of science and astronomy are offered for pre-schoolers through adults. A new west wing is under construction as of this writing.

Single **Memberships** are $4, family $15. Memberships give free admission and discounts on special programs.

The **Planetarium** programs change throughout the year, featuring both natural and man-made celestial phenomena of the past, present and future. Shows at 11 and 2:45 Mon-Sat, Fri nights at 8 and Sun 12:15 and 2:45. Extra performances scheduled during peak demand days.

The New England Aquarium, State St. and Atlantic Ave., Central Wharf, Boston
Open Mon-Fri 9-5, Sat 10-6, Sun 12-8. Closed holidays
Adults $1.50 children 5-14 75¢ children under 5 free

Boston's newest attraction on the museum scene, completely privately-financed and featuring a giant cylindrical ocean tank, a giant rectangular fresh water "tray," interesting architectural innovations, a small Children's Aquarium with a tidal pool, and a growing collection of world-wide sealife. Especially informative and educational written material is printed on the walls near each exhibit. **Membership:** $10 for individuals, $15 family.

THE CRANE OVER THE DOOR IS NON-FUNCTIONAL

University Museums, Harvard, Oxford St., Cambridge
Open daily except July 4th and Christmas 9-4:30, Sun 1-4:30
Free except the Ware Collection of Glass Flowers (adults 25¢)

This building contains not one but five separate teaching museums. They are all connected on the third floor, however, and it is no problem to wander from one to the other. The **Botanical** exhibits begin on the first floor, but most visitors head for the Ware collection of glass flower models on the third. On this floor you can enter the fascinating maze of the **Comparative Zoology** museum, which includes a 42-foot fossil "Sea Serpent" as well as a virtual zoo of stuffed specimens. In another wing is one of the world's finest **Mineralogical** collections. Nearby is a room devoted to **Geological** displays, mostly relief models. The **Peabody Museum of Archaeology and Ethnology** can be reached from the third floor of the main building or through its own entrance on Divinity Ave. It is worth a separate visit on its own, covering as it does five floors of totem poles, weapons, canoes, costumes, and other trappings of exotic cultures.

DON'T MISS THE ANNUAL ANTIQUE AUTO AUCTION IN MAY →

Antique Auto Museum, 15 Newton St., Brookline (Larz Anderson Park) Open Tues-Sun 1-5, Adults $1, children 6-13, 25¢

A collection illustrating the evolution of transportation since 1850. The carriages and antique cars are parked in a coach house built in 1888 modeled after a French chateau. Special days at the museum include the Duster's Meet, first Sunday in August, when costumed drivers arrive in their own antique autos. **Memberships,** $10, give free admission to museum and special events.

Francis Hart Nautical Museum, M.I.T., Entrance at 77 Mass. Ave., Cambridge, ask the guard. Open daily 9-9
Free

A small museum emphasizing marine engineering. Most notable is the large collection of ship models from 1000 AD to the present.

Peabody Museum of Salem, 161 Essex St., Salem, Mass. Open Mon-Sat 9-5, Sun and holidays 2-5. Closes at 4 Nov. 1-Mar. 1. Free

A national historic landmark. East India Marine Hall was built in 1824 to house the "natural and artificial curiosities" gathered by Salem clipper-ship captains. The museum today has outstanding collections in maritime history, ethnology, and local natural history. Of special interest—relics of Captain George Crowninshield's yacht "Cleopatra's Barge," and fascinating collections of utensils, dress, and weapons from the South Seas, Africa, and the Orient.

Merrimack Valley Textile Museum, Massachusetts Ave., North Andover, Open Tues-Sat 10-4, Sun 1-5 Free

First opened in 1964 and fast becoming an outstanding resource center. Imaginative exhibits trace the history of wool manufacture from sheep shearing to finished cloth. Textile equipment includes such gems as an antique shearing machine ca. 1800 and an automatic bobbin-changing dobbin loom ca. 1923. Guided tours and continuous demonstrations enliven Sunday afternoons.

Whaling Museum, 18 Johnny Cake Hill, New Bedford. Open Summer Mon-Sat 9-5, Sun 1-5; Oct 1-May 31, Tues-Sat 9-4, Sun 1-4
Adults $1, children 25¢

Devoted to the industry which made New Bedford famous. The exhibit of scrimshaw, ship crafts, and whaling gear is dominated by a half-scale model of the 1850 whaling vessel "Lagoda." After walking its decks you may want to visit the Seaman's Bethel next door immortalized in *Moby Dick* as "The Whaleman's Chapel."

And Other Attractions

CHANNEL TWO

For dial-flippers who haven't yet discovered it, Channel 2 is Boston's nonprofit educational television station. But "educational" is a stuffy word for such WGBH regulars as Maggie Lettvin, just as "exercise" hardly describes her show "Maggie and the Beautiful Machine." Channel 2 has its pedestrian documentaries, but its programming is more often innovative and exciting. Some of the best PBL and NET productions have originated with WGBH. Its viewers were among the first to see Frederick Wiseman's "Hospital." "Say Brother," by blacks, for blacks, has become a regular feature. "The Forsyte Saga" for months interrupted Boston social life every Sunday night at nine. "The Advocates," a new public debate series, invites audience response. For gourmets, Channel 2 offers Julia Child and Joyce Chen; for new parents "Dr. Turtle's Babies"; for preschoolers "Misterogers" and the widely acclaimed "Sesame Street." Local coverage has included school committee hearings, championship matches at the Longwood Cricket Club, and stereo broadcasts of the Boston Symphony.

WOULD-BE GREEN-THUMBERS, WATCH THALASSA CRUSO'S "MAKING THINGS GROW"

A contribution of $15 or more to WGBH, 125 Western Avenue, Boston 02134, brings a monthly program guide.

144

CLASSES AND LECTURES

University Extension Courses, 75 Mount Auburn St., Cambridge, 868-7600, ext. 4024.

An excellent program administered by Harvard and involving several other institutions in the Boston area. A majority of classes are taught by Harvard personnel; many are comparable to day-time classes. The basic tuition for these "erudite and particular courses" was set in the will of John Lowell, Jr., in 1836 at "the value of two bushels of wheat." Even with a few extra fees added, that comes out as the best educational value around. A Harvard degree, Bachelor of Arts in Extension Studies, is offered.

Boston Center for Adult Education, 5 Commonwealth Ave., 267-4430.

Cambridge Center for Adult Education, 42 Brattle St., 547-6789.

Non-credit classes offered in everything from dance to urban renewal. Phone for complete class lists and costs.

IT'S POSSIBLE TO TAKE CLASSES AT THE BOSTON ARCHITECTURAL CENTER ON NEWBURY ST.

Boston YWCA, 140 Clarendon St., Boston 02116. 536-7940.

A variety of courses for self-improvement or diversion. They also have a counseling and guidance service.

Radcliffe Institute for Independent Study, 78 Mount Auburn St., Cambridge.

Radcliffe has been a leader in providing opportunity for educated women to up-date their skills or resume work as family pressures allow. The Radcliffe Seminars (mostly non-credit) are intensive courses in a variety of topics. Courses are expensive, though some scholarships are available. Most classes meet one week-day morning a week.

DOCTORATES ARE HELPFUL HERE

The Prospect Union Educational Exchange, 18 Brattle St., Cambridge, 876-3080.

A center for information on adult education courses in all of the many colleges and universities in the Boston area.

Their annual catalogue listing all courses available will probably be in your library. It is available from Prospect Union for $2.50.

Ford Hall Forum, 80 Boylston St., Boston 02116

An autumn series of free lectures at Jordan Hall (30 Gainsborough St., Boston), Sunday nights at 8. Doors open at 7:45.

This venerable cultural institution, dating from 1907, encourages tolerance, diversity and audience discussion. Speakers are sometimes dull, sometimes expert, often famous. Lectures are rebroadcast on FM. Tax-deductible memberships are available for $3 (students) and $5 (adults), which assure early admission and, therefore, seats on crowded evenings.

Boston Globe Book Festival, Suffolk Downs, East Boston.

A recent phenomenon on the literary scene, the festival appears to be well on its way to becoming a successful tradition. Each fall for several days in succession, the public is treated, free, to a wide choice of lectures, films, discussions with authors, and exhibits featuring highlights of the next publishing season. Children's programs include story-telling, games and folksongs. Watch the **Boston Globe** for details.

UNIVERSITY LECTURES

There are all kinds of lectures open to the public at most schools. Some of the most important—involving public figures or visiting poets—are jammed, but often can be heard in the comfort of home over WGBH, Channel 2. If you want to be aware of the full range of free lectures open to the public, subscribe to the calendars of events at the various institutions. A good sampling of addresses is given below:

Boston University, Office of Public Information, 353-3665.

The B.U. newspaper, *Currents,* is published weekly and includes a complete listing of all university events. $3.50 per year. In addition, a free quarterly calendar of all art, music and theatre happenings on campus is available from the B.U. School of Fine and Applied Arts.

Brandeis University, Office of Public Affairs, Waltham. 894-6000.

Monthly free calendar listing art, music, theatricals and lectures.

Harvard University Gazette, University Hall, Cambridge, 868-7600.

A newspaper published weekly during the academic year by the University administration. Includes complete schedule of events, recent publications by Harvard University Press, appointments to the faculty. Expanded in 1969 to include campus news. $4, academic year; $2, term.

Massachusetts Institute Of Technology, Institute Calendar Office, Cambridge. 864-6900.

Weekly issue of M.I.T. happenings. $4 academic year, $2, term.

Wellesley College, Information Bureau, Wellesley. 235-0320.

Weekly bulletin of all events on campus. $1, academic year.

LIBRARIES

For scholars Boston has such gems as the new Francis Countway Library of Medicine, with its instant computerized bibliographies, or the famous Athenaeum, whose colonial treasures include George Washington's library. The Air Force Cambridge Research Library at Hanscom Field specializes in geophysics and cartography; the Babson Institute in Wellesley has Sir Isaac Newton's library housed in a replica of the library in his London town house. The institutions listed below have facilities more readily available to the general student or exhibits of interest to the public.

Boston Public Library, Main Branch, Copley Square. Open Mon-Fri 9-9, Sat 9-6, Sun 2-6.

Lectures, children's story hours, film programs, recorded music, current foreign language books, and interesting exhibits are specific features of this oldest public library in the United States. Non-residents may use materials in the building; special borrowing privileges are available. Monthly calendars at the information desk.

Massachusetts Historical Society, 1154 Boylston St., Boston. Open Mon-Fri 9-4:45.

The oldest historical society in the country founded in 1791.

Massachusetts State Archives And State Library, State House Open Mon-Fri 9-5.

Library on third floor, archives museum in basement.

New England Historic Genealogical Society, 101 Newbury Street, Open Mon-Fri 9-4:45.

Specializing in family history and genealogy.

Society For The Preservation Of New England Antiquities, Harrison Gray Otis House, 141 Cambridge St., Boston, Open Tues-Sat 10-4. Admission $1

148

"O MY BROTHERS, GOD EXISTS."
—RALPH WALDO EMERSON

RELIGIOUS SERVICES

The city that once banished Quakers, burned convents, and paid its only Jew to settle elsewhere is today a center of religious diversity. Boston's Roman Catholic archdiocese is the second largest in the United States; Back Bay's First Church of Christ, Scientist is world headquarters of that denomination. Local congregations of Unitarians, Swedenborgians, and Latter-day Saints had their beginnings in the religious experimentation of 19th century New England; historic congregations of Jews, Armenians, Albanians, Greeks, and Chinese have their roots in the immigrations which begin to change the character of the city at the same time.

We have listed here a few Boston and Cambridge churches, chosen for their architectural or historical interest and accessibility. Services are on Sunday unless otherwise indicated.

Arlington Street Church, Unitarian, 355 Boylston St., Back Bay. Church school 10:30, service 11.

History—and social conscience.

Associated Synagogues Of Massachusetts, 177 Tremont St. Services Mon-Thurs 1:15 and 4:30; Fri 1:15.

Across from the Common.

Christ Church, Episcopal, Zero Garden St., Cambridge
Morning prayer and sermon, 11
George and Martha Washington worshipped here.

Church Of Jesus Christ Of Latter-Day Saints (Mormon), 2
Longfellow Park (near Harvard Square). Sunday school 9:30,
sacrament meeting 3.
The authors of this guide worship here.

Church Of The New Jerusalem, Swedenborgian, 140
Bowdoin St., Beacon Hill. Worship service 11.
Among the earliest residents of the Hill.

First Baptist Church of Boston, Commonwealth Ave at
Clarendon, Back Bay. Sermon 11.
Founded in 1665, the building designed by H.H. Richard-
son in 1872.

First Church of Christ, Scientist, Falmouth and Norway
Streets, Back Bay. Services 10:45 and 7:30.
The Mother Church.

Friends Meeting, 5 Longfellow Park, Cambridge (near Harvard Square). Worship at 9:30 and 11.
Off Brattle Street, in the shadow of Longfellow's House.

King's Chapel, Unitarian, Tremont and School Streets,
Downtown. Morning prayer and sermon 11.
The first Church of England in the Bay Colony, the first
Unitarian Church in America.

M.I.T. Chapel, Massachusetts Institute of Technology,
Memorial Drive, Cambridge. Catholic Masses, 9:15, 12:15,
4:45; Protestant service 11, Jewish services Fri and Sat.
Striking non-denominational chapel designed by Eero
Saarinen.

Old North Church, Episcopal, 193 Salem St., North End. Morning prayer and sermon 11.

CHARLES WESLEY PREACHED IN THE OLD NORTH CHURCH IN SEPT., 1736.

Paul Revere's.

Old West Church, Methodist, 131 Cambridge St., Boston, Beacon Hill. Sermon 11.

Asher Benjamin church, built in 1806.

St. Stephen's, Roman Catholic, 401 Hanover St., North End. Lovely Bulfinch church—across the mall from the Old North.

Temple Israel, 260 Riverway, Back Bay. Boston's second oldest Jewish congregation, founded in 1854.

Trinity Church, Episcopal, Copley Square, Back Bay. Morning prayer and sermon 11.

H. H. Richardson's masterpiece.

TRINITY CHURCH

Nature

Millions of years ago a great ice mass swept over the mountains of what is now New England, grinding them down, gouging out the land, filling in the valleys, and leaving behind great stretches of glacial moraine, lake-pockets left by melting ice, and rocky outcroppings ignored by the passing glacier. Forests later covered the rocky land, building up a thin layer of topsoil. Today, because of this glacial action, Boston and its surrounding countryside have many areas ideally suited to outdoor recreation. Rock-ridged hills, never very high, give way to low-lying marshes where many species of birds may be seen. Lakes and ponds, ideal for swimming, fishing, and boating, dot the landscape and, along the coast, rocky headlands or smooth dunes line the shore.

Despite assaults on the land by industrialization and increased population, much of this natural beauty remains. It does so partly because Massachusetts was blessed in the nineteenth century with groups and individuals who not only loved the countryside but had the will and the means to preserve it. This chapter describes some of those groups and the lands they preserved. It closes with a list of contemporary organizations who are urging us to act now to save this wealth for the future.

CITY PARKS

When the first settlers arrived, Boston was a rocky peninsula "bare of wood" and free from "the three great annoyances of woolves, Rattle-snakes and Musketoes." Surrounded on three sides by water, it made a natural fortress against the terrors of the wilderness behind. As the population increased and the colony grew stronger, Boston began to transform its landscape, literally cutting down the hills to fill the coves. The oldest of Boston's "parks," the Common, was the Puritan pasture, but the park system as such dates from the 19th-century when the greatest topographical changes occurred. It was based on the plan of Frederick Law Olmstead, veteran conservationist and designer of New York's Central Park, for an "emerald necklace" stretching from the Common through the Back Bay to the rapidly growing suburb of Roxbury. Today the necklace is broken in several places, but important areas remain. **The Public Garden** is a sedate city park, more formal than the Common, which it adjoins, and best known for the Swan Boats. **The Fenway**, though much diminished, was Olmstead's solution to draining the marshy lowlands of the Muddy River. It winds past the Museum of Fine Arts through Longwood to Jamaica Plain, a peaceful oasis for the many apartment dwellers who live along it. In winter children skate on the little ponds and in summer feed the ducks or try to catch minnows. Walkers enjoy the changing contours of the land and the arched bridges of native stone. City-bound gardeners enjoy the chance to plant and dig in the Fenway Gardens, off Westland Ave. not far from Symphony station. These little plots originated as "Victory Gardens" during World War II and added so much charm to the area they were kept. Gardeners lucky enough to get space can plant anything they want— radishes, tulips, even peanuts—as long as they keep their patches weeded. The Fenway Garden Society, a private group authorized by the Park Department, assigns the plots. The current president is Mr. Richard Parker, 1 Peterborough St., Boston, 266-2775.

The **Arboretum** is discussed later in the chapter. **Franklin Park**, the largest park in Olmstead's plan, has a tired look from heavy use but has received a new burst of energy from Elma Lewis' Playhouse-in-the-Park and concerts sponsored by "Summerthing." The possibility of turning the rag-taggle zoo over to a private group has been discussed recently.

THE TRASH CANS ON THE COMMON LOOK LIKE SICK TREE STUMPS.

Each city or town in greater Boston has areas set aside for open space and outdoor recreation. **Fresh Pond Park** (off Fresh Pond Parkway and Huron Ave., Cambridge) is a Cambridge city park with a small playground, grassy area for picnics, and great slopes for rolling. The bicycle path around the pond is especially nice in autumn when the leaves are reflected in the water. There are no sanitary facilities in the park.

Larz Anderson Park in Brookline has a pretty duck-feeding area, picnic tables and fireplaces, and grassy hills for kite flying or sledding. The Antique Auto Museum is located here. Entrances are on Goddard Ave. and Newton St. in Brookline.

Menotomy Rocks in Arlington is a pleasant city park at the foot of the rocks on Arlington Heights. A small pond, grassy space for games, rocks for climbing, and woods to walk in make it a favorite place to picnic. Fires are allowed with a permit, but there are no restrooms. Reach it from Jason St., off Massachusetts Ave. above Arlington Center. Call 643-6700 for more information.

Prospect Hill, Waltham, (Winter St. exit west off 128) is a steep unspoiled wooded area close to Boston. The road winds up to the picnic areas, where you may build a fire if you have a permit. In the winter a rope tow provides good skiing for beginners. In August families have been known to pick enough blueberries for pancakes or muffins. The fire tower at the top of the hill is often closed, but the view from the hill itself is worth the climb to the top. There are rest rooms and water. Ski tow fees are less for Waltham residents. For a complete schedule of fees and times open call 893-2206.

Lynn Woods (Penny Brook Road off Rt. 129, Lynn) has 2,000 acres of wild natural beauty crisscrossed by dirt or wood roads with connecting paths. It is said that before the American Revolution these woods were a favorite hiding place for pirates who came up the Saugus River in small boats. Automobiles aren't allowed, picnickers are, and fireplaces are provided.

"I PERCEIVE NO MOSQUITOES NOW."

THOREAU

DON'T FORGET LYDIA PINKHAM!

156

MDC RESERVATIONS

The Metropolitan District Commission is a regional confederation of greater Boston towns and cities to provide water, sewage, and recreational facilities. Anyone planning outdoor recreation should call the MDC Parks Division, 20 Somerset St., Boston, 727-5250, and ask for the free booklet, *Recreational Facilities,* describing all MDC offerings. In addition, the Parks Division will answer your specific questions—"Where can I go to build a fire outside a fireplace?" "Can I reserve a ballfield?" There are six major reservations maintained by the MDC.

The Blue Hills, off Routes 3, 28, 128, and 138 south of Boston, has some of the oldest and highest hills along the Atlantic Coast. The reservation comprises 5,700 acres of lakes, ponds, streams, and woodlands with a network of hiking and bridle trails. These are patrolled by the MDC mounted police—fun for the kids to see. Parking, bathing, and picnic facilities are located at Houghton's Pond. There are riding stables with horses to rent, a golf course, three flood-lit ski slopes, natural and artificial ice skating, athletic fields, children's playgrounds, and pond and brook fishing. The Trailside Museum has live animals, trails, and exhibits showing the natural history of the Blue Hills. Admission is 25¢ for adults, 10¢ for children under 12. For more information about the museum call 333-0690. For information about the reservation itself call 698-5840. For ski rates and hours and current snow condition, phone 828-5070. The ski school is at 828-5090.

Middlesex Fells, Malden, Medford, Melrose, Stoneham, Winchester, (off Route 28 and 93) is 2,063 acres of rough woodlands, granite outcroppings, scenic ponds and meadows traversed by wood roads, bridle paths and foot trails. There are numerous picnic areas, a swimming pool, pond fishing, natural and artificial ice skating, horses for hire in a nearby stable, and an excellent zoo that has recently been renovated. For more information call 396-0100.

Breakheart, Saugus and Wakefield, (off Lynn Fells Parkway near Route 1) is 560 acres of beautiful ponds, rocky ridges and woodlands which make for good hiking. There is a bathing beach on the lower lake, fishing, artificial and rink skating, and picnicking. There is a deep ravine, or flume, between lakes. MDC has maps of the reservation. Phone 396-0100.

Stony Brook, West Roxbury, Hyde Park, (off Washington St.) is a beautiful rugged area with lots of rocks, boulders, woods and a brook. Here the sounds of the city are shut out, and it is peaceful to hike and climb among the rocks and tall trees. Surprisingly this area does not seem to be worn down or heavily used. You can picnic, fish, skate and play baseball here. Phone is 698-5840.

Beaver Brook, Belmont and Waltham, (Route 60) is a well worn, small reservation of 58 acres. There are two ponds and a brook that runs the length of the reservation. There are picnic areas, baseball fields, tennis courts, a coasting hill, playgrounds and a very crowded popular wading pool. Don't miss the trail leading around the duck pond into the woods. The children will be delighted to spy a small waterfall. Phone 484-0200.

Georges Island, Boston Harbor, is an old military fort that has been used in the defense of Boston Harbor in all U. S. wars. During the Civil War, it was used as a prison for Confederate military and civilian personnel. There are picnic facilities and a playground. The Island can only be reached by boat. Excursion boats from Boston are available. Open May 30-Oct 15, 10-7 p.m. Phone 925-0054.

158

Polluted it may be, but the **Charles River** is still one of Boston's greatest natural assets. The MDC maintains many facilities along it. The lower basin is filled with sailboats from April to November and on busy summer days, when pleasure craft wind downstream toward the bay, it is fun to watch the operation of the **locks** near the Museum of Science. The Esplanade off Storrow Drive near Back Bay is the scene of summer concerts and the starting point for canopied **excursion boats,** which embark about every half hour 1-9 daily between June and Labor Day. (Adults 75¢, children 50¢) A **bicycle path,** at sunset filled with joggers, runs along both sides of the river between Eliot Bridge and Science Park. There is a small playground on the Boston side of the upper basin and a large play area with wading pool and picnic grounds off Soldier's Field Road in Brighton. At the Newton-Watertown line the river is lost to industry, emerging again at **Norumbega,** off Rt. 30 near 128. In good weather the parking lot here is busy and the ducks choosy about what they will eat. A river path and a road lead from the duck area to Norumbega Tower, the monument erected to the "lost city of the Vikings" by Eben Norton Horsford, a professor at Harvard, but not of history. Near Rt. 16 we can again follow the course of the river, this time along Quinobequin Rd. to the small MDC reservation at **Echo Bridge,** once known as Hemlock Gorge. Further upstream between Newton and Dedham, the MDC owns a major stretch of riverbank, now undeveloped, called **Newton-Brookline Waterlands.** One entrance is from Kendrick St. near the Needham Industrial Center. (The berry-picking has been greatly restricted here by the construction of additional industry on the Newton side.) The second entrance is in Dedham, opposite St. Susanna's Church on Needham St. Neither entrance is marked. This reservation is swampy and may be most easily explored by canoe.

159

STATE PARKS AND FORESTS

The State of Massachusetts has many parks and forests open daily throughout the year for hiking, riding, skiing, and other snow sports. Camping and day-use areas are open May 1-Oct 15 from 10-8. A fee of $1 covers parking and facilities. Season passes are $10. Campsites, usually in state forests rather than state parks, are on a first come-first served basis. They are close together and become very crowded in summer. For an excellent booklet listing all Massachusetts recreational facilities, camping areas, and rates and regulations governing parks and forests, call or write: Dept. of Natural Resources, Forests and Parks Division, 100 Cambridge St., Boston, 727-3184. We have included here a partial list of the best state facilities closest to Boston.

THERE ARE 735 DIFFERANT KINDS OF OAK GALLS

Willard Brook State Forest, Townsend-Ashby, (access Route 119) has beach, bath house and picnic sites located near Damon pond. An excellent place to see pink and white mountain laurel in June. Fishing, picnicking, swimming, hiking, snowmobiling and camping.

Harold Parker State Forest, North Andover, (access from Routes 125 and 114) has swimming, fishing, picnicking, snowmobiling, camping and hiking through hardwood and pine forest. Its ponds, woods, birds and wildflowers entice walkers in all seasons.

Salisbury Beach State Reservation, Salisbury, (Routes 95, 110, 1 and 1A) Four miles of fine ocean beach, modern bath houses, extensive lifeguard and safety facilities, play equipment for children, camping, boat launch ramp, picnicking and barbecueing.

Myles Standish State Forest, Plymouth-Carver, (access Routes 3, 3A, 58 and 44) contains several beautiful spring-fed fresh water ponds with sandy beaches. There are picnicking, swimming, and camping facilities. Snowmobiles allowed.

Ashland State Park, Ashland (access Route 135) has swimming and picnicking around a beautifully wooded lake. Snowmobiles allowed.

160

Cochituate State Park, Natick (access Route 30) features a boat launch for powered and sail boats, swimming, and a children's wading pool. Snowmobiles allowed.

Hopkinton State Park, Hopkinton, (access Route 85 south of Route 9) has swimming, fishing and picnicking.

Bradley W. Palmer State Park, Topsfield (access off Route 1) is a beautiful park with unusual trees and shrubs set amid the estates of Essex County. The Ipswich River runs through the park. A children's wading pool, bridle trails, hiking, and picnicking facilities are some of the other features.

THE WHITE PINE HAS 5 NEEDLES IN A CLUSTER

Additional open spaces are operated by the State Fish and Game Division primarily for hunting. These **Wildlife Management Areas** may also be used for fishing, hiking, birdwatching and nature walks. But don't go during hunting season unless you wish to hunt or be hunted. Massachusetts hunting and fishing regulations and locations of these areas can be acquired from the Mass. Fisheries and Games Division, 100 Cambridge St., Boston, 727-3151.

NATIONAL WILDLIFE REFUGES

Massachusetts is in the path of the Atlantic flyway. To protect migrating birds, the federal government has set aside National Wildlife Refuges. Two closest to Boston are described below.

The Parker River National Wildlife Refuge, Newburyport, is located on Plum Island between Newburyport and Ipswich. From Interstate 93, take the Newburyport exit and follow the signs to the refuge. On the way be sure to drive down the main street of Newburyport to see the old clippership homes. The beach at Plum Island (in the refuge) is one of the most beautiful and isolated around the Boston area. It is also one of the best surf-fishing areas in New England. During the summer there are lifeguards. The water is great for experienced swimmers. For children it is suitable for wading but not for swimming because of the undertow. You can

THE ENGRAVER BEETLE WORKS ON DEAD WOOD!

picnic or barbeque on the beach. There are sanitary facilities but no bathhouses. In summer, the entrance fee is $1 per car. Only the first 500 cars are admitted on busy days.

Behind the beach are sandy dunes covered with low vegetation. Between the dunes and the mainland are fresh and salt water marshes where most of the birds are found. During March and October there are concentrations of up to 25,000 ducks and 6,000 Canadian Geese. You can walk for miles along the beach or on trails through the dunes and marshes. Children love to slide down the dunes—but watch for poison ivy. After August 31, the beach plums are ripe and may be picked.

Great Meadows National Wildlife Refuge, Concord, is land along the Concord River set aside for bird migration. It is undeveloped and there are no facilities, but you can take a pleasant walk along the river to look for ducks and water animals and to watch for birds. It is reached from Route 62 in Concord and from Rt. 117 and Sudbury Rd.

AUDUBON SANCTUARIES

DID YOU KNOW THAT MOST BIRD COLORS ARE REFRACTED LIGHT?

The Massachusetts Audubon Society is the world's oldest Audubon Society and the largest conservation organization in the Commonwealth. It owns and maintains some of the loveliest natural areas in the state. All sanctuaries and nature centers are open every day from sunrise to sun down. There is a parking fee of $1.50 for nonmembers on weekends. Picnicking is not allowed at any sanctuary, except in the case of organized groups, who may be given special permission at some locations.

Drumlin Farm, Lincoln (Rt. 117 and South Great Road) is headquarters for the society. The farm has wild and domestic animals, fields to run through, woods to hide in, ponds with ducks, and a chicken house where you can see the hens laying eggs. Most of the farm animals are kept inside during the winter and early spring, so be sure to arrive before the buildings close at 4:30. The gift shop has nature books,

162

natural history supplies, and a comprehensive collection of approved bird feeders. It is open Mon-Sat 10-5 and Sun 1-5, phone 259-9500, ex. 47.

Ipswich River Sanctuary, Topsfield, Hamilton, and Wenham (US 1, east on State 97, 1/2 mile to Perkins Row on left) is a natural arboretum of 2,300 acres, rivaling the Arnold Arboretum in Boston for springtime beauty. The azaleas and rhododendrons in the woods and the wildflowers in the rockery around the pond are brilliantly colored in late spring. The Ipswich River runs through the sanctuary, which includes forests, open fields, swamps, eskers, and an island. There is a trailside museum and many miles of marked trails. Maps are available at the registration station.

Moose Hill Sanctuary, Sharon (US 1 and 140) has 310 acres with marked hiking trails through hilly woods, marsh and meadow, and around a small pond. There is a wildflower and fern trail—May is the best month to see this—and a small museum. It is fun to hike up to the firetower to see the view.

Stony Brook Sanctuary, Norfolk (access Route 140) is made up primarily of wetlands. There is a boardwalk through the marsh area where in summer you can observe frogs, turtles, fresh water birds, and other water animals and plants.

Eastern Point Sanctuary, Gloucester, (at the end of Eastern Pt. Blvd. by the Yacht Club) is a real New England beauty spot. It is a rocky headland with marsh, woods, and tidal pools. This is an excellent place for marine study. The high season here is summer but it should also be visited in September and October when the monarch butterflies migrate to the seaside goldenrods. Trails are not marked. Watch out for poison ivy.

Marblehead Neck, Marblehead, and **Nahant Thicket,** Nahant, are areas where the bird lover can watch the spring and fall migrations. The Audubon Society maintains other sanctuaries throughout Massachusetts. Call them for further information.

In addition to operating these open spaces, the Audubon Society runs a Conservation Services Center which produces educational and promotional materials for conservation-oriented groups. The **Hathaway School of Adult Education** offers courses during fall and spring in natural history, ecology, conservation, geology and nature study. The fee for each course is $22.50 for non-members, $17.50 for members. Elizabeth K. Darlington is an excellent instructor. For more information about the school, call 259-9500, ex. 67.

The **Voice of Audubon** (a taped report on birds) is heard by dialing 259-8805.

BOSTON HAS A GROWING SEASON OF 195 DAYS! ...BUT DON'T PLANT YOUR TOMATOES BEFORE JUNE FIRST...

PROPERTIES OF THE TRUSTEES OF RESERVATIONS

The Trustees of Reservations is a unique organization formed in the nineteenth century by public spirited men concerned about the loss of wilderness areas and historic sites. They have purchased privately owned lands and opened them to the public. A descriptive pamphlet explaining locations, developments and fees will be sent on request from their headquarters at 224 Adams St., Milton, Mass. 02186, 698-2066. We have listed here some excellent reservations close to Boston.

At **Rocky Woods,** Medfield, you can hike to an observation tower where you can see as far away as Mt. Wachusett, then walk past an old quarry and across a wooden bridge, where you can see lilies floating on the pond. In winter there is ice skating on a natural pond, skiing and snowmobiling. In summer there is hiking, boating, (no swimming), fishing (for members only), and picnicking. The entrance is at Route 109 and Hartford St. It is open 10 a.m. to sunset every day

164

except Monday. Parking fees are 50¢ per car Tuesday through Friday and $1 on Sat., Sun., and holidays. Fireplace and table use are 50¢ for two hours with wood provided. Skiing is 75¢ on weekdays, $1 Saturdays and $1.50 on Sundays and holidays. Snowmobiles rent for $5 per day.

World's End, Hingham (Route 3 through Hingham, left to Nantasket, left on Martin's Lane) is a peninsula on Hingham bay with dramatic topography and magnificent landscaping designed in 1890 by Frederick Law Olmstead. There is a splendid view of the Boston skyline and the South Shore. Two drumlins (low oblong hills left by the glacier) are connected by a low grassy neck almost at water level, where you can observe ocean life. There is a four-mile trail around the peninsula. Open 10-sunset. There are no restrooms or picnicking. The parking lot is only open on weekends and there is a fee. On weekdays, parking is difficult.

Whitney and Thayer Woods, Cohasset and Hingham (entrance on Route 3A opposite Sohier St. in Cohasset) has gently rolling woodlands with some marshy areas. The forest is traversed by wood roads which make pleasant walking. In the spring, broadleafed evergreens bloom on Milliken Memorial Path. Turkey Hill (187 feet) looks out over Cohasset Harbor and the tall spire of Minot's Light. The woods are open all year from sunup to sunset. There are picnic tables and restrooms.

Mt. Ann Park, West Gloucester, (access from Route 128 immediately west of Exit 4) is the table top of Thompson Mountain, 270 feet above sea level, and the highest land on Cape Ann. From its summit you can see sweeping views from Mt. Agementicus near York, Me., to the Blue Hills. There is also a glen with huge hemlocks and boulders. Picnic tables are provided. Open sunrise to sunset daily.

Richard T. Crane Memorial Reservation, Ipswich (Route 3 at Ipswich South Green) includes Crane's Beach and Castle Hill, the magnificent mansion and estate of the plumbing millionaire. The beach is of fine white sand with extremely clear water where you can find small hermit crabs, snails, and tiny fish. The water is gentle with very small waves, ideal for

165

children and for others who like swimming in a calm ocean. The reservation also includes pitchpine woodlands, salt marsh, and steep upland stretches. You may walk around the Castle grounds and see the deer, but the house is open only for private social events and concerts (see the music chapter). Bring mosquito repellent for evening. At the beach there is a bath house and refreshment stand. Open 9-sunset, May 30—Labor Day, weekends only from May 1-30. Parking Mon-Fri $1.50 per car, Sat, Sun, and holidays $2.75 per car. Steep Hill Beach is $3.75 per car.

BOTANICAL AREAS

Arnold Arboretum, Arborway, Jamaica Plain, one of the great collections of trees and shrubs in the world, welcomes all but picnickers, delights all but hayfever sufferers. Spring and fall field classes, which are helpful to those interested in horticulture or landscaping, are conducted by the Arboretum. Plant propagation classes are held in the spring, and occasionally in the fall. The Boston newspapers let you know when the lilacs, forsythia, magnolias, etc. are performing at their best, usually from mid-May to mid-June. Open sunrise-sunset every day. No charge for admission. Phone 524-1717.

Mount Auburn Cemetery, Mt. Auburn St., Cambridge, burying place of the Boston Brahmins and Mary Baker Eddy, is also the first garden cemetery in the country, a haven for birdwatchers and naturalists. From spring through fall the cemetery is abloom with a thousand varieties of shrubs, flowers and trees. The gates are open from 8-5: A map showing locations of famous graves is available at the gatehouse. Phone 547-7105.

THERE IS A STONE TOWER NEAR-BY WHICH GIVES A NICE VIEW, DEPEND-ING ON YOUR VERTIGO...

May and June are the best months to see the native American plants and wildflowers in their natural setting at the **Will C. Curtis Garden of the Woods**, Framingham (Route 20 to Sudbury, left on Raymond Rd., right on Hemenway Rd.). The New England Wildflower Preservation Society has its headquarters at the garden. In their building is a natural history library and a gift shop with conservation materials, books on nature, and gifts for outdoorsmen. The Society also has excellent classes for children and adults on nature, ecology, garden design, and wildflower gardening. The Garden is open April 15-Nov 15, 8-5, closed Sundays. Non-members 50¢, members free. The Gift Shop is open 9-4:30 on weekdays. Phone 877-6754.

There are woods, wildflowers and ferns at the new **Guernsey Sanctuary** in Wellesley (Dover Rd. in Wellesley to Livingston Rd. for one mile.) This nature preserve is administered by the Wellesley Conservation Council. It is loveliest in late May when the ladyslippers are in bloom but is also interesting in winter when you can see animal tracks in the snow or discover early skunk cabbage coming up. There are small rustic bridges over wet areas. It is open dawn to dusk. A helpful book put out by the Council has maps of the trail and points of interest along the way and also descriptions of the plant life to be seen. The booklet costs $1.25, is in all Wellesley book stores or available by mail from Mrs. Franklin Sanders, 32 Skyline Dr., Wellesley, Mass. 02181, 237-0147.

The Case Estate, 135 Wellesley St., Weston, is maintained as the nursery and experimental planting area of the

Arboretum and has a well known collection of woody plants and ground cover. It is most beautiful in spring and fall. Open April 15 through Sept. from 9-6. No picnicking, no cars allowed outside of parking area. Phone 524-1717.

Ashumet Holly Reservation, East Falmouth, (Route 151 between Routes 28-130) is famed for its 2000 holly trees, some of them winter-hardy varieties developed by the late Alfred Wheeler. There are also native and ornamental trees and shrubs, wildflowers, an herb garden, a demonstration tree nursery, a collection of heath and heather, and ponds and trails. Open dawn to dusk, $1.50 parking for nonmembers on weekends, and no picnicking. For more information phone the Audubon Society at 259-9500.

ENVIRONMENTAL GROUPS

Those interested in the state of our environment should contact any of the following groups. Information is plentiful. Volunteers are needed.

Sierra Club, Eastern New England Group, p.o. Box 32, West Somerville, Mass., 02144. Roger Marshall, chairman, phone 864-5003.
Boston Area Ecology Action, 925 Mass. Ave., Cambridge, Mass. 02139 Alan Berube, chairman, 876-7085.

Massachusetts Audubon Society, South Great Rd., Lincoln, Mass. 01773, phone the volunteer department, 259-9500.

Committee for a Better Environment, P.O. Box 490, Cambridge, Mass. 02139, Sam Fogel 354-0182 or Laura McMurry 625-1263

Boston Environment, Inc., 14 Beacon St., Room 803A, Boston, 02108, 227-2669. John Putnam, Executive officer.

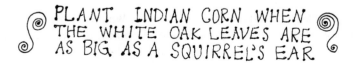

PLANT INDIAN CORN WHEN THE WHITE OAK LEAVES ARE AS BIG AS A SQUIRREL'S EAR

Environment, Inc. has been educating the public recently in the art of complaining. Their list of phone numbers is reprinted here with Mr. Putnam's permission:

Air Pollution—(smoke, odors, burning dumps) Massachusetts Department of Public Health Metropolitan Air Pollution Control. Frank Reinhardt, 727-5194 (motor vehicles) 727-3185.

Noise—From airplanes. Massachusetts Port Authority, Thomas P. Callaghan, 482-2930

From Motor vehicles. Registry of Motor Vehicles, J. L. Hourihan, Vehicle Inspection Section, 160 North Washington St., Boston. License number, color and make of vehicle. Written complaints only. Other noises. Local police department.

Water and/or Oil Pollution—Massachusetts Department of Natural Resources, Water Pollution Control, Thomas McMahon, 727-3855.

Pollution and Contamination from Pesticides—Massachusetts Department of Public Health, Pesticides Board, Lewis F. Wells, 727-2670.

Litter and Rubbish—City of Boston, Public Works Department, Sanitary Division, 536-7150; City of Boston, Parks and Recreation (Re litter in parks), 722-4100; Other cities and towns, local police or local city halls.

Wetlands (Filling in Ponds and Marshes)—Massachusetts Department of Natural Resources, Division of Conservation Services, George R. Sprague, 727-3170.

Sports

At high noon on Patroit's Day, more than a thousand runners
from all over the world compete in the famous Boston
Marathon. The race begins in Hopkinton, follows Commonwealth Ave. into the city, and ends approximately two hours
and 26 miles later at the Prudential Center. Anybody over 18
can enter. The Japanese National Team has run, so have
clerks, Harvard students, and at least one woman. In a recent
year an assistant professor at a local university lost tenure
because he spent more time training for the race than
publishing. The prize? A bowl of stew for those who finish.

In Boston, all sorts of "minor" sports get major atten-
tion. You can play squash or attend the dog races, see a
demolition derby or watch a crew race from the banks of the
Charles River. A professional soccer league is just getting
LET'S NOT established. Curling has become the rage at some suburban
FORGET THE country clubs. At Franklin Park in May the Committee For
REMARKABLE The Better Use of Air sponsors the annual Greater Boston
FRISBEE Kite-Flying Contest.

This chapter describes the most popular individual and
spectator sports. As you migh expect, "water" and "winter"
are common settings. If you are interested in bicycling,
snowmobiling, fishing, hunting, riding, or camping, check the
Index for references to these activities in other chapters. If
you haven't discovered a public golf course, tennis court, or
ball field nearby, try the MDC recreational booklet men-
tioned in the last chapter or phone the Parks Division at
727-5250.

BOATING

If you want to master **sailing**, consider membership in the Community Boat House, 21 Embankment Road off Storrow Drive in Boston. They have an especially outstanding program for "juniors", age 11-17. A membership fee of $1 per season gives young people the use of boats, lessons and guest privileges. They must have parents' permission and proof of swimming ability. The adult sailing season is from April 1-Nov 1. The cost is $15 a month or $45 a season. The Boat House is a non-profit leased MDC facility.

SMALL CRAFT

GALE

STORM

HURRICANE

If you are an experienced sailor, you'll find Marblehead Harbor worth your attention. Marblehead Boat Rental on Front St. on the harbor has several classes of sailboats for rent May-November. Phone 631-2259 to reserve one.

There are **rowboats** for rent at many of the state parks listed in the last chapter. The Jamaica Pond Boat House, Boston, rents them for $1 an hour from mid-April to October. Phone 524-9691.

At **Walden Pond State Reservation**, in Concord off Rt. 126, fishing is allowed and boats are rented to anyone over 16 for 50¢ an hour with a $2 deposit. Four persons are allowed in a boat, and if you do not bring your own lifejackets you must pay $1 deposit per person. If you do happen to make it to the bottom of the pond, you can check to see if it is still the same depth as when Thoreau measured it "with a cod-line and a stone . . . . exactly one hundred and two feet." Picnic tables are available. The bathhouse and restrooms are open after April 19. When the water level is high enough there is free swimming. The telephone number of the caretaker is 369-3254.

Canoeing is pleasant on the Concord-Sudbury River. The South Bridge Boat House on Rt. 62, Concord, rents canoes by the hour. The Needham YMCA has a boat house on the Charles River at 58 Fisher St., Needham. It is open after April 18, daily 10-6. Canoes rent for $1.25 an hour, $6 a day. Young people 10-16 must have parents' permission and proof they can swim. Phone 444-5321.

Owners of boats should watch for the Boston *Globe* annual "Cruising Guide" published in mid-April, which gives a complete list of launching ramps in New England. Fishermen should send for the free "Salt Water Fishing Guide" published by the State Department of Commerce and Development. Write them at Box 1775, Boston 02105.

To add romance to your boating, join one of the trips of the **Harbor Ramblers**, a loosely-knit group led by Edward Rowe Snow, snowy-haired Santa Claus of the lighthouses and chronicler of Boston Harbor. Since 1928 Mr. Snow has been leading harbor excursions. The regular charge per trip is $3 a person. Sometimes a taste of steamed clams is included, but you should bring your lunch. Annual dues of $2.50 entitle you to a monthly notice of trips. For more information, write Mr. Snow, 550 Summer St., Marshfield, 02050, or phone 472-7000 between 8 and 10 a.m. weekdays and ask for his office.

There are many **excursion boats.** The Charles River sightseeing boat was described on page 159. The Massachusetts Bay Line has a "Lunch Boat" leaving Rowe's Wharf in Boston Mon-Fri at 12:15 and 1:15 in good weather. It costs 75¢ for the half-hour ride. They also have longer harbor tours June through Labor Day three times daily and regular trips to George's Island and Nantasket. Schedules change, so it's a good idea to phone them at 542-8000.

The Windjammer Spray leaves from Long Wharf twice daily in good weather. Adults $3.75, children $2.50. Phone them at 742-5707 to check the sailing time, as charters can cancel a regular trip.

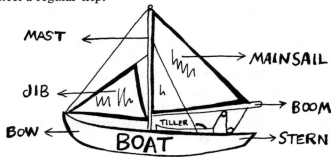

HIKING

To newcomers from the Rockies, hiking in Massachusetts' old, worndown hills may seem tame. But whatever these trails lack in drama they make up for in the abundance of plant and bird life. While many hiking areas are a few minutes walk from paved parking lots and major highways, the density of the woods cuts out the world. Along the coast there are dramatic changes in ecology over the span of a few feet. If you are a serious hiker you may know about the activities of the Appalachian Mountain Club. Their Massachusetts Trail Guide is available from the Club for $4.50 and contains a complete listing of trails in the state with maps and detailed instructions about how to find and follow them. The Appalachian Club also sponsors a full schedule of outdoor events all year round. Summer camps, Scout training programs, organized hiking, skiing, mountain climbing and snowshoeing are included in their calendar. Call 523-0636 or write to 5 Joy Street, Boston, 02108 for the Mass. Trail guide and schedule of events. The office is open Mon-Fri 9-5, and has a large map and photographic collection and a mountaineering library. There are dozens of nearby areas for the hiker, as a reading of the "Nature" chapter will show.

WIND CHILL TABLE

TEMP.	WIND SPEED			
	10	20	30	40
+50°	40	32	28	26
+30°	18	4	-2	-6
+20°	4	-10	-18	-21
+10°	-9	-25	-33	-37
0°	-21	-30	-48	-53
-10°	-33	-53	-63	-69
-20°	-46	-67	-79	-85

SKATING

New England winters can be long, dark, and cold. Spring does not come until May—if at all. In self-defense learn to enjoy snow and ice. Look for supervised ponds and tennis courts in your neighborhood and get out and skate. There is natural ice much of the winter at the Public Garden, the Common, the Fenway, and in many of the reservations described in the last chapter.

The new rink at the Prudential Center is open Dec-March every day until 11 p.m. Adults $1.50, children 75¢.

The MDC maintains more than a dozen rinks. There is sure to be one near you. They are open Nov 15-March 15 for three sessions daily: 9-12, 2-4:40, and 7-10. Adults 50¢, children 10¢ except for evening sessions and afternoons on weekends and holidays when admission is 25¢. There is often instruction available. Skates rent for around 75¢ when they have them. Look for used skates at clothing exchanges or the Dover Country Store (see "Bargains.")

SKIING

Pep up winter by getting out among the snowcovered trees, fields, and mountains. During most winters, there is enough snow to begin skiing by the Christmas holidays. The season usually ends in April. Some say spring skiing is among the best.

Skiing in New England is different from that in the West. It is more expensive. For a large hill you might expect to pay from $6-10 per person per day for lifts, for smaller hills from $3-6. The **snow conditions** here are variable since the weather is constantly changing. There are somtimes thaws or rains during the winter which create icy patches on the slopes or melt the snow. Many areas have snowmaking machines to maintain uniform conditions. Occasionally there is a snowfall of over two feet, in which case the slopes must be packed before they can be skiied. Before you head for the hills, get information on conditions. Most recorded ski reports are overly optimistic. If they rate the snow good, it is probably fair. An easy way to find out about conditions is to call the local operator of the town where you are going. These reports are usually more reliable, and they are also free. The best information is at the Ellis Ski Information Center, phone 482-0690. They have the latest snow reports and any other information you may need to know about an area.

Most areas are more crowded than in the West. If you wish to stay overnight, most have adequate lodging. Some have local organizations that will help you find a place to stay within your price range. Smaller areas cater to families and are not as expensive. Most have nurseries for small children, rent equipment for the whole family, and operate

THERE IS
A TYPOGRAPH-
ICAL ERROR
ON THIS PAGE
– CAN YOU
FIND IT?

174

ski schools with private and group lessons. The Boston Globe runs a ski school at Boston Hill in North Andover during Christmas vacation.

One of the easiest ways to get **information** and make reservations for lodging is to look in the Yellow Pages under "Ski Centers", where there is a large listing of accommodations in the most popular areas of Massachusetts, Maine, New Hampshire, and Vermont. The New Hampshire Vacation Center (426-9818) has information. Ski 93 Reservations (603-745-8101) makes reservations as does the Vermont Development Department, Montpelier, Vermont 05602.

There are several **areas** within an hour's drive of Boston ideal for beginners or families. These hills usually have small vertical drops with open slopes and trails. Many have snow machines. Call the Department of Natural Resources, 727-3180, for an excellent pamphlet, *Ski Mass.* It has descriptions, prices and locations of most ski areas in Massachusetts. Those areas nearest to Boston are: Blue Hill Ski Area, Canton; Prospect Hill Ski Area, Waltham; Mt. Towanda, Woburn; Boston Hill, North Andover; Rocky Woods, Medfield; Neshoba Valley, Westford; and Mt. Wachusset, Princeton-Westminster.

If you like longer trails and more challenging slopes and are willing to drive 2 1/2 to 4 hours, Vermont, Maine, New Hampshire and western Massachusetts might be for you. Excellent areas in New Hampshire are at Franconia Notch (2 1/2 hours) where you can ski Cannon Mt., Mittersill, Waterville Valley and Loon Mt. Also recommended are Cranmore at North Conway and Wildcat at Pinkham Notch. Sunday River in Maine is also in the same general area. In Southern Vermont it's Mt. Snow near Wilmington (2 1/2 hours) or if you want to travel 4 hours to northern Vermont you can ski at Stowe, Mad River Glen, or Sugarbush. Sugarloaf in Kingfield, Maine is 3 1/2 hours away.

If the lift lines are long and you really want to get out into the white wilderness call the Appalachian Mountain Club for information about their snowshoeing and cross country skiing trips.

SWIMMING

Bostonians believe in starting **swimming instruction** early. The Boston YWCA, 536-7940, 140 Clarendon St., starts lessons for three-month-old children. For "oldsters" there are year-round classes in various certification levels. The YMCA, 536-7800, 316 Huntington Ave., offers private lessons in the evenings and classes when sufficient requests are received. There are no regularly scheduled lessons at the YMCA.

The Boys Club of Boston, 242-1775, 923 Park Square Building, offers instruction, competition teams and co-ed splash parties. The Girls Clubs of Boston, 242-2560, 15 Green, Charlestown, gives lessons at the Boys Club facilities. American Red Cross courses are taught at the Y's and at the Boys Club during the winter months. Courses are offered at pools and beaches during the summer.

There is plenty of water to choose from. Many of the state parks and reservations listed in the last chapter have **fresh-water ponds.** Those at Breakheart, Harold Parker, Cochituate, Hopkinton, and the Blue Hills are popular. Many towns have their own ponds and pools. The MDC maintains Sandy Beach at the Mystic Lakes in Winchester. There are lifeguards and picnicking facilities. The Beach gets very crowded.

Salt-water swimming is bracing in New England. Hardy swimmers like it that way. Some people say North Shore beaches are coldest, Cape Cod beaches warmest. Others insist they are all refreshingly brisk, and they like them that way.

176

Boston's city beaches are well-used by nearby residents but they draw few outside fans. The **South Boston lagoon** near Castle Island is nice for sunning. There are band concerts on Sunday afternoons. **Winthrop Beach** is pleasant and not too far away. If you want, you can sit on the jetty and cast for fish. **Revere Beach** is crowded and dirty with a carnival atmosphere, though there is some talk of resurfacing the beach and putting in new sand. It has the advantage of being accessible by MBTA and is much more pleasant north of the amusements at Point of Pines. Between Point of Pines and Revere is Oak Island Beach, a quiet, sandy area with a pavilion shelter.

Two MDC beaches which can be reached by public transportation from Boston are **Nahant**, north of Boston in Lynn, and **Nantasket** on the South Shore. Nahant is a narrow neck reaching out into the ocean, ideal for swimming, with small breakers and shallow surfing. There are fireplaces and a playground area. The swimming at Nantasket is similar. It is a clean, big crowded beach with an amusement park. In summer it can be reached by boat from Rowe's Wharf. (see "Boating" above)

Some of the most scenic beaches are on the North Shore. **Crane's Beach**, discussed under Trustees of Reservations in the last chapter, is beautiful and calm, almost like a swimming pool. The miles of white sand make it outstanding. **Plum Island** is less well known. It faces the open ocean, has big breakers and a strong undertow. It is more fully discussed in the last chapter under "Parker River Wildlife Refuge."

A winding road leads to **Wingaersheek** in Gloucester, a popular, pleasant, and fairly small beach which gets quite crowded on warm days. At low tide, there are long sandbars with warm little tidal pools for wading. The parking fee is $1 weekdays, $2 weekends and holidays.

There are many small and lovely town beaches on the North Shore, but unless you can display a resident sticker on your car you are not admitted. Make friends in Manchester as Singing Beach there really sings.

On the South Shore, **Wollaston Beach** is operated by the MDC. It is a pebbly, shallow beach with broad clam flats.

"ON MARCH 17, 1776 THE BRITISH FLEET...DROPPED DOWN TO NANTASKET ROADS, AND THENCEFORTH BOSTON WAS FREE!"

Other good South Shore beaches open to visitors include **Humarock, Fieldstone,** and **Ocean Bluff.** The beach on the **Duxbury** peninsula is excellent. Further down at the head of the Cape at **Scusset Beach** you can see the boats on Cape Cod canal; they look like they are sailing from the ocean through dry land. All these beaches are large enough to be listed on a good road map. Expect a parking fee, especially on summer weekends.

Cape Cod is famous for beaches. **Nauset Beach** in the National Seashore Park is first class for swimming and beaching and one of the few Eastern spots for surfing. **Craigville** is a popular beach midway on the Cape. **Falmouth** is well known, but probably better for making acquaintances than anything else. **Old** or **New Silver Beach** present a lovely sweeping expanse. For more on Cape swimming, see chapter ten.

WATCHING

With all the colleges and universities in the area, there is a wealth of spectator sports. Even **high school games** are taken seriously. There have been riots in Harvard Square after the annual Thanksgiving Day game in Harvard Stadium between Boston Latin and Boston English. The older high schools have been playing "grudge games" on Thanksgiving since before the turn of the century. Schoolboy basketball and schoolboy hockey can be exciting during the Eastern Massachusetts tournaments in March.

For a dollar you can get admission to the grounds at the Longwood Cricket Club during the **U. S. Lawn Tennis Association National Doubles** competition each summer. For championship matches later in the week or for better seats in the grandstands, you'll pay more. The gates usually open at 1:00.

Boston's big league teams are legendary. The **Boston Red Sox** have been an American League powerhouse from the beginning. The fans simply ignore the bad years. They have won 7 pennants and 5 World Championships. In 1903 they beat Pittsburgh in the very first World Series. Fourteen Red Sox have been elected to baseball's Hall of Fame, including Ted Williams, Jimmy Foxx (the extra "x" belongs), Joe Cronin, and Babe Ruth. All home games are at Fenway Park, corner of Jersey St. and Brookline Ave. For further information call 267-2525.

Some of the greatest names in basketball have worn **Boston Celtics** Green: Bob Cousy, Bill Russell, "Easy Ed" Macauley, and "The Jones Boys," to mention just a few. Arnold "Red" Auerbach coached them to eight straight World Championships, a feat never equaled, nor even approached, by any other team in basketball or any other professional major league sport. Home games are at the Boston Garden, above the North Station at 150 Causeway St.

The Boston Bruins, of the National Hockey League, are known for a team of all-time greats, Eddie Shore, Bill Cowley, Milt Schmidt, and Dit Clapper. They have finished high the last two years, though any year they play a slam-bang game of hockey. "Standing Room Only" is the order of the day with the Bruins, so get tickets early. Phone Boston Garden, 227-3200.

The Boston Patriots, a charter member and one of the most exciting American Football League teams, almost left Boston for want of a stadium. The suburb of Foxboro, south of Boston, has invited them to stay. At this writing, plans for the next two seasons are incomplete.

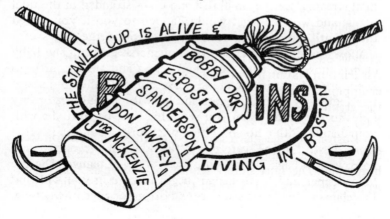

179

Three Ways To Have A Clambake

DIG YOUR OWN

At low tide near Crane's Beach in Ipswich you will see miles of mud flats. Upon closer inspection you will see people with forks, like hay forks, raking over the flats and pulling up clams. These are the famous Ipswich clams which are so tasty to eat. The small clams are the steamers which we enjoy at clambakes. The bigger size are Cherry Stones and Little Necks, which are eaten on the half shell; and the biggest ones are Quahogs, which usually find their way into chowder.

Clamming is possible on any shallow beach. Each town has its own shellfish regulations, so before you begin, get a permit from the town hall. They will give you a metal ring used to measure clams. Only those too big to pass through it may be kept. Consult your local tide table and when the tide is lowest walk out on the beach. It is fun to wade across the tidal streams, see the small fish and crabs stranded in the tidal pools, and wonder what would happen to you if you stayed there until the tide came back in. Around the edges of a shallow ocean grow varied types of marsh grasses. The baby clams, those that slip through the ring and are too little to keep, are usually in the grass. Move out onto the sand about five feet away from the grass and look for air bubbles or tiny holes in the sand. When you see a big one, begin to dig with your hands, with a hoe or with a pitchfork. Your hands often work best, but be careful of the long, white, sharp and narrow razorback clam shells. They are well named. Dig the hole deeper and as the edges begin to cave in you will find the clams in the loose sand at the bottom or edge of the hole.

Keep digging deeper and wider. You should find more clams. As you pick them up, wash them off in salt water, test them on your ring to see if they are big enough to keep, and put them in your bucket which has sea water in it. In digging you will also find long fat sea worms, excellent for ocean fishing, and big snails which feed on the clams. That is why you will also find some empty clam shells in the hole. When you can find no more clams, look for more air bubbles and begin digging again. You should be able to get enough clams for a meal in an hour. You'll find they taste much better when you dig them yourself; perhaps it's because you had to work so hard to get them.

If your clamming expedition fails, you can buy steamers at a good fish market. Beginners should know how to tell a dead clam from a live one. If its neck is poking out, touch it and it should withdraw. If it doesn't, don't cook it—throw it out. Good fresh fish doesn't smell fishy and should only be bought at reputable places.

Once you have captured some clams, wash the shells, put them in about half an inch of water in a big pot and put on a lid. Steam until they are fully open. Serve them in the shell, dunking the body in hot, melted butter. Put the broth from the steaming in cups and drink this (the sand is supposed to settle to the bottom). Corn, salad, potato chips and whatever fixings you want come next. Then lobster. Get a good lively one. If you can't cook it for an hour or two, leave it in the bag it comes in. Lobsters "drown" in fresh water. When you're ready to begin boil a big pot of water to which you have added at least a quarter of a cup of salt and some seaweed, if you have it. Drop in the live lobster and cook at a rolling boil for about 15 minutes. Remove from the pot, open it down the center, drain and serve with a wedge of lemon and hot butter. If you find some small red stuff, this is roe or eggs and indicates a female. Some say it's delicious. The green in the inside is liver and also edible. The only non-edible part is the digestive sac under the eyes.

If you can boil water you can have a clambake on your own!

AMBROSIA!

181

INVITE 100 PEOPLE

When you get to be an expert, perhaps you'd like to try a clambake on a big scale. The authentic way to do this is as follows: Arrive at the beach with all supplies early in the morning. Build a roaring fire, collect rocks along the beach, bury the huge barrels in the sand and when the rocks are hot proceed as follows: seaweed, hot rocks, lobster, hot rocks, seaweed, potatoes, hot rocks, seaweed, corn, repeating hot rocks and seaweed between each layer, ending up with clams. Then put heavy parchment over the top and leave it for 4-5 hours until the clams on top are steamed and all is ready. This is truly the most delicious method.

But from the standpoint of time and children at the beach, there is a more efficient way. The morning of the clambake, dash over to Atlantic Ave. to the wholesale houses and pick up a bushel of clams, as many lobsters as have been ordered plus six extra. Go back to Haymarket Square for salad greens and native corn, then a deep breath. Don't forget hot dogs for the children. Stop and get dry ice for punch, then go over to H. P. Hood's in Chelsea for ice cream. Ward's or some of the other big bakeries will deliver your frankfurt rolls right to your church or collecting point. The night before, buy all the condiments at any big super market—this means lots of butter. Figure three paper cups per person, plus napkins, hot butter cups, plastic forks for salad, hot cups for clam broth, and two plates. These can also be picked up in the wholesale region. Then load all the supplies in a rental trailer and head for the beach. Get a fire going underneath a metal grating. Place large new trash cans and big open wash tubs over this to which are added water. When the water is boiling, put corn, clams, frankfurts, and lobster in individual pots. Be sure you water-check all your trash cans for leaks before you leave for the beach—or disaster!

You can eat one hour after the fire is going. Take a big cutting board to split the lobster. Sit down to pick and chew. Bring a ball and net for some games; later sit around the campfire with a good singing leader. And that is a real fine clambake!

LET A PROFESSIONAL DO IT.

It is much easier to let a professional do it. The **Bass River Fish and Gun Club** in West Dennis on the Cape has two big clambakes each summer using the seaweed method. They serve lobster, clams, sweet and white potatoes, hot dog, sausage, onions, corn and watermelon. The price last year was $5.50. But prices and dates vary. Write them c/o Stuart Ellis, Cove Rd., W. Dennis 02670.

On the North Shore, **C. C. Roberts and Son**, 11 Atlantic St., Gloucester, will produce an old-fashioned clambake in a portable pit with no damage to your grounds. The meal per person is around $5 and includes lobster or chicken, clams, corn, frankfurter, pickles and watermelon. They have a children's menu.

George's Island, an MDC park on a Boston harbor island, is a good site for a clambake, professional or not. There are cooking and playing facilities and large old Fort Warren to wander through. If you want to go and cook your own food you must first call Captain Booth at 925-0054 and get permission. But if you want a professional to cook it, call the "Surf" in Nantasket (925-1600) who will bring your clambake to you for $6 a person. You will need to arrange transportation with the Massachusetts Bay Line, unless you have your own boat. They run regular trips from Rowe's Wharf to George's Island and also to Nantasket June through September. Other times, you can charter one of their boats. The cost per person is $3.50 adults, $2.50 children with every tenth person called a chaperone going free. Call them at 542-8000 for the current schedule.

However you do it, don't let summer pass without a clambake!

SCRUB CLAMS.
COOK IN WATER JUST
UNTIL SHELLS OPEN

· · EAT · ·   ENJOY!

Browsing

Browsing is a respected pursuit in Boston. In very few places will salesclerks shepherd your stroll through a store. This is true even in department stores, as long as you carefully avoid appliance departments. Here are three especially green fields for browsers, places where it's often as much fun to look at the shoppers as at the goods. For converted suburbanites we have added a footnote on the major shopping plazas.

DOWNTOWN

According to Cleveland Amory, a truly proper Bostonian never shops on Washington Street. Brahmin neglect hasn't hurt business any. The Summer-Winter Street corner where **Filene's** conveniently faces **Jordan Marsh**, is always mobbed. During the pre-Christmas crush mounted policemen are called in to protect street traffic from the hordes of pedestrians. There are dozens of department stores and specialty shops in the narrow, crooked streets. Filene's is famous for its basement. Jordan Marsh is Boston's biggest; you can get in and out of the subway through its Great Basement Store and spend an entire day browsing without ever getting out in the rain. The little red telephones near the escalators are to help you navigate through the Main Store, New Store, and Annex Store for Homes, but plan to get lost. Seamstresses will want to check the **Windsor Button Shop** behind Jordan's on Chauncy Street and then take a short walk along Chauncy and Harrison via Chinatown to the Kneeland Street textile area.

There are many dealers in books, old prints, and coins in the small streets off Washington. On Bromfield Street is the **Old Corner Book Store**, modern descendant of the famous 19th century shop. Across the street is the **Massachusetts Bible Society** which has Bibles in 300 languages, plus commentaries, atlases, and related volumes. The books at **Williams**, 18 Province St., **Brattle Book Store**, 5 West Street, or **Goodspeeds**, 2 Milk Street are "used." At the other Goodspeeds shop, 18 Beacon Street, they are more precisely "rare."

Devotees of The Sundae will find **Bailey's** on Temple Place, another good browsing street. Small children enjoy visiting **Ludlow's Pet Shop** or looking at forbidden pocket knives and swords at **Stoddard's Cutlery**. **Melvin & Badger**, apothecaries since 1831, still carry herbs and spices, lavender water and cologne under their own label. At the corner of Temple Place, facing the Common and The Hill, is **R. H. Stearns**, in perfect taste since 1847, having made no concessions to escalators or bargain-basements. Creative Playthings' inventions enliven the toy department upstairs.

BACK BAY

In the Back Bay shopping area bounded by Newbury and Boylston Streets, proper Boston, artistic Boston, and sophisticated Boston meet. They do not necessarily speak.

Disciples of Julia Child get their fondue sets at **The Pot Shop**, 405 Boylston, recently graduated from a basement across the street. Proper Boston ladies who still pour tea get their pots at **Shreve, Crump & Low,** jewelers to the city's first families since 1800. Other venerable institutions nearby are **Walpole Brothers**, 400 Boylston, linens since 1766, and **Cooley's, Inc.**, 34 Newbury, where the same family has dealt in china and glassware for more than 100 years. **John Lewis**, 337a Newbury, has been making interesting and affordable handcrafted jewelry since the 1960's.

Newbury Street is known for art galleries—and hair. Even **Pappagallo**, which ordinarily specializes in shoes, now dresses heads in its Loft. It is difficult to get by with less than $10 at any of the salons on the street. Try **Salon Boccaccio,** 161 Newbury near Copley Square, for a superlative cut.

Along Newbury, basement galleries and here-and-now boutiques neighbor such bastions as **Bonwit Teller,** elegantly housed in the old building of the Boston Society of Natural History. **Traynor Flowers** at 47 Newbury keeps the Boston Social Register handy for your convenience. **Brooks Brothers** is across the street; **F.A.O. Schwarz** is nearby. On Boylston look for **Book Clearing House,** where in good weather you can browse through the book bargains in the sidewalk stalls.

With the completion of the Prudential complex, Back Bay browsing extends beyond Copley. **Lord & Taylor**'s new department store is at 750 Boylston just past the public library; their Bird Cage Restaurant is open for lunch and tea. Changing displays and events add to the interest at the Pru. In the winter there is skating south of the tower; in July and August band concerts on Wednesday evenings. **Brentano's,** Booksellers to the World, is the most notable of the shops within the plaza itself. A branch of **Saks Fifth Avenue** is soon to come.

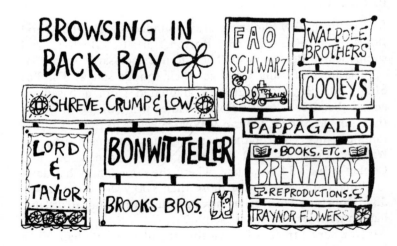

HARVARD SQUARE

Harvard Square is an area formed by the junction of Brattle Street—once Tory Row—and Massachusetts Avenue, the rebel-road of 1775. It is jammed with Ivies and hippies, ladies on bicycles, babies in back-packs, students, shoppers, commuters, luminaries of the Establishment and heroes of the underground press. In a car you can take 20 minutes to cover a block even when there's not a fire-engine blocking Brattle, and when there is, you might see a fire-sale sign posted before the traffic clears.

The local products are innovation and erudition. The biggest store, the Harvard **Coop**, is most notable for its three-story book annex on Palmer Street; the most interesting, **Design Research**, is provocatively ensconced in a new glass house. Harvard Square rewards the browser with the unexpected, like an art display in the windows of Charley Chin's Laundry or the labyrinth of **Truc** in the cellar of the Brattle Theatre. Other dealers in truck come and go. You might have your gift selection sealed in a can at one Brattle Street shop or find antique jewelry at another. Along Boylston Street toward the river you can shop for shaggies and leather at the **Antartex Sheepskin Shop**, with more famous purveyors of sheepskins nearby.

Books, of course, are big. Try **Schoenhof's** for foreign language books and art prints, **Mandrake's** for imports direct from Britain, **Paperback Booksmith** for a big selection of paperbacks day and night. Visit **Phillips'** new quarters in Holyoke Center or leaf through dusty old books at **Starr Bookshop** in the Lampoon Building on Plympton Street. The new **Reading International** has a xeroxing service as well as a good collection of international periodicals and children's foreign language books. Don't miss the kiosk in the center of the Square which probably has your hometown paper.

The flavor of Harvard Square has extended along Massachusetts Avenue in both directions. The **Coffee, Tea & Spice House** near Porter Square toward Sears, has an interesting clutter of trifles as well as edibles. One of its more

CAMBRIDGE COFFEE, TEA & SPICE HOUSES ARE APPEARING IN SUBURBIA...

outstanding neighbors is **Fabrications**, where you can buy clothes or a variety of cloth. Contemporary tableware and accessories are sold at the **Upper Story**, which recently bestowed its expensive stability on Putnam Square at the other end of Mass. Ave. An increasing number of tiny shops make good browsing in this neighborhood.

If you don't have time for a meal at one of the places listed in our restaurant chapter, stop in at **Bailey's** or **Brighams** for lunch or a sundae. The **Window Shop** serves tea from three to five. **Cardullo's** dispenses sandwiches from their meat counter.

SUBURBAN SHOPPING CENTERS

Chestnut Hill Shopping Center is a small but attractive complex on Route 9 in Brookline, near the Newton line. The major stores are Filene's, R. H. Stearns, and Franklin Simon. Much further out Route 9 are **Natick Mall**, with branches of Sears and Filene's, and **Shopper's World**, with Jordan Marsh. This Natick-Framingham stretch of Route 9 is a jumble of shopping centers, bargain barns, and hamburger stands, a lot of good shopping unpleasantly arranged. Route 1 both north and south of the city has the same kind of hit-or-miss development. Sears and Bradlees are the major stores at the **Dedham Mall** on Route 1. Child World, Lechmere and Raymond's are not far down the road.

Somewhat better integrated are the **North Shore Plaza** in Peabody, which has branches of Jordan's and Filene's, and the **South Shore Plaza** in Quincy, which has an R. H. Stearns as well. The newest of the suburban centers is the big **Burlington Mall**, which has the major Sears store in the area plus branches of the downtown department stores and an attractive collection of small shops in an enclosed mall. There are grocery stores and movie theatres at most of the suburban centers. Many feature special events at Christmas and Easter. Brigham's and Friendly's are often in the mall; McDonald's and Howdyburgers are never far away.

Bargains

This chapter is dedicated to Yankee Thrift and to that rugged, penny-stalking creature—The Bargain Hunter. But for beginners, a few words of caution. If you are the kind who decides that today is the day to buy yourself a pair of shoes (purple pigskin with crimson linings) then sets off in pursuit not to return home until you find them, you won't enjoy Boston bargain hunting. Hence, Rule number one: Be Flexible. You can never be sure what you will find in any of the places listed below. Rule number two: Don't Take Husbands or Children. Either can be tolerated if absolutely necessary, but bargain hunting requires patience and neither are noted for it. Rule number three: When Returning Empty-Handed, Smile. Remember, in any safari the hunt is as much a part of the game as the kill. Now for the bargains.

CLOTHING—NEW

Filene's Automatic Bargain Basement, 426 Washington St., downtown. Open 9:30-5:30 daily, Mon. and Wed. 'til 9.

Upstairs, Filene's is one of Boston's better department stores. Downstairs it's the scene of some of Boston's liveliest, if not most historic, battles. Go to see the spectacle of women fighting over the same dress or trying on clothes in the aisles. The famous bargains include merchandise "automatically" priced according to number of selling days as well as surplus lots and seconds from stores as widely separated as

" WHAT AN INFINITE BUSTLE!"

THOREAU

191

Neiman-Marcus and Montgomery Ward. All kinds of clothing—from diapers to wedding dresses. Also linens, giftware, toys, and occasional book bonanzas.

Jordan Marsh Basement, 450 Washington St., downtown. Hours same as Filene's.

New England's biggest department store. The basement includes rugs, unpainted furniture, housewares as well as clothing. (Enter "Annex Store for Homes" basement on Chauncy St.) Not as famous—or as crowded—as Filene's.

Gilchrist's Basement, Porter Square, Cambridge. Open 10-10 Mon-Sat (the downtown basement has a lesser following).

Good buys in children's clothing, toys, housewares. Especially good for shoes if you know brands. (For fabrics, see below.)

Bargain Center, Davis Square, 220 Elm St., Somerville. Open Tues-Wed-Sat 9-6; Mon-Thurs-Fri 9-9.

Has everything from railroad-salvaged furniture to fire-sale clothing. Good browsing.

Calvert's Department Store, 938 Highland Ave., Needham (easy to find on a road map—just off Route 128) Open Mon-Fri 9 a.m.-10 p.m.; Sat 9-5:30.

Across the street from the Carter Underwear Factory, they carry seconds on famous Carter's children's clothing as well as samples and "imperfect" lots from other manufacturers. Adult as well as children's clothing. Prices and stock vary. End of season specials are outstanding. (You might combine this with a trip to Dover Country Store.)

Goodwill Store, Morgan Memorial Main Store, 93 Berkeley St., Boston, Open 9-5.

Almost all of their things are used, but often they have Carter's children's pajamas and clothing which are new, but damaged, miss-sized, or soiled, and not fit for Calvert's. If you go when a shipment has come in you can get some surprisingly good clothing for 50¢ or so.

Decelle of West Roxbury, 1870 Centre, West Roxbury, Open daily 9-10, Sat 9-6.

Like Calverts, carries seconds of Carter's and other manufacturers. Especially good for toddler and baby clothes.

Hit Or Miss, Mt. Auburn St., Watertown (under Star Market), Open 10-9:30, Sat 10-6; and Center St., Newton Centre, Open 9:30-9, Sat 9:30-6.

Popular with mods as well as matrons. Women's brand-name clothing at discount prices.

Loehmann's, Rt. 9, Natick, Open daily 9:30-5:30, Wed 10-9:30.

New York originals, expensive mark-downs as well as good quality clothes at moderate prices.

Marshall's, 160 Great Road, Bedford, and Rt. 1 West Roxbury. Open Mon-Sat 9-10.

Seconds and close-outs of various manufacturers. If you can recognize brands, you can get some excellent buys.

OTHER BARGAIN PLACES REMAIN KNOWN ONLY TO THOSE WHO WOULDN'T TELL US ABOUT THEM!

Quincy Bargain Barn, Rt. 3A, Weymouth, Open 9:30-5:30; Fri 9:30-9; CLOSED Wed at 12:30.

A suburban "Filene's Basement" with furniture and appliances as well as clothing. One informant on a recent trip to the barn bought $1 jeans and a $100 bracelet, both shrewd buys she tells us.

Sear's Catalogue Surplus Stores, 401 Park Dr., Boston. Open 10-9 weekdays; 9-5 Sat; and 240 Moody Street, Waltham, Open daily 9-5:30; Wed and Fri until 9.

Catalogue merchandise at less than mail-order prices. Clothing, toys, housewares, linens, appliances, hardware, and furniture.

Twin Kee Factory, 720 Park St., Stoughton, Mass. Open Mon-Fri 'til 9, Sat 'til 6.

Raincoats. You can see into the factory, be waited on by the owners. The bargains are men's, women's, and children's

193

raincoats made from the same material as those famous ones you pay a premium for.

Revere Knitting Mills, 108 Ferry St., Malden. Open Mon-Tues-Wed-Sat 9-5:30; Thurs-Fri 9-9.
Knitwear—also all types of yarn at reduced prices. They take mail and phone orders.

Westarknits, Rt. 9 near Carlings Brewery. Open 9:30-9:30.
As they advertise, 50,000 sweaters to choose from.

New Hampshire Mills
Some of the best knit bargains are in New Hampshire. We have grouped our favorites in a separate section for your convenience in planning a bargain excursion. See page 208.

CLOTHING—USED

PTA Clothing Exchanges
The wife of one not-to-be-mentioned executive buys all his suits at the "Ritzy Vu," a euphemism for the **Weeks Jr. High School Clothing Exchange,** 7 Hereward Road, Newton Center. Open every Wed 10-3 during the school year. Buying used clothing is a respectable local custom. Most towns have an exchange or two, often sponsored by the PTA. Check your local newspaper.

Bargain Box, 117 Newbury St., Boston, Open 9:30-4:30 Tues-Sat.
A clothing exchange run by the Boston Junior League. More fashionable address; higher prices.

Joe Keezer's Harvard Community Exchange, 1094 Massachusetts Ave., Open Mon-Sat 8:30-5:30.
It is rumored that some Harvard men buy their sport coats here.

SHOES

The Barn, Republic Co., 25 Kempton Pl., West Newton (off Washington St., watch for sign) Open Mon-Fri 9:30-9:30; Sat 8:30-6.

Good quality shoes for men, women, and children at much less than regular prices. They do a good job of fitting children. Sneakers and overshoes cheap.

Hanlon's, 762 and 705 Centre St., Jamaica Plain. Open 9-9, Sat 9-6. (also 27 Cottage Ave., Quincy; 325 Main St., Malden, and Mass. Ave., Lexington)

Huge selection of famous brand shoes at good prices.

THERE IS A
CAPEZIO
FACTORY STORE
ON HALL ST. IN
MEDFORD.
OPEN:
TU-THUR, 12-4
SAT, 9-1

Hoffman's Shoes, 1245 Commonwealth Ave., Allston, Mon-Thurs-Fri 9-8:30; Tues-Wed-Sat 9-6.

Cancellations of better shoes. Hoffman's is conveniently located next door to another cancellation store and across the street from a third; a lot of shopping on the spot. (Near the intersection of Harvard Ave. and Commonwealth.)

Touraine's, 38 Brattle St., Cambridge. Open Mon-Wed-Sat 9-6; Thurs-Fri 9-9.

Very lovely women's shoes are marked down drastically for sales.

Corcoran's Basement, 615 Mass. Ave., Central Sq., Cambridge. Open Mon-Wed-Sat 9:30-5:45; Thurs-Fri 9:30-9.

Shoe specials for women and children in basement store (Harvard Square Store which closes at 5:45 every night does not have shoes.)

Hyde Athletic Shoe Factory, Outlet, 535 Windsor St., Cambridge, open Mon-Sat 9-5.

Footwear—including skates.

The Shed, 2304 Washington St., Newton (Rt. 16 just across 128). Open daily 9-5:20.

Good for sneakers and all sorts of rubber footwear.

French Shriner, Route 9, Natick and also Rt. 1 on the North Shore. Open Mon-Fri 9:30-8:45; Sat 9:30-5:30.

Factory outlet of a Boston manufacturer. Excellent buys; all sizes in men's shoes.

Bostonian Factory Store, Commonwealth Shoe and Leather Co., Marble St., Whitman, Mass. Take S.E. Expressway to highway 18. Follow signs to Whitman; they are not large and you have to keep alert. Open Mon-Thurs 9-4:25; Fri 9-8:25; Sat 9-4:55.

Worth the drive to get famous Bostonian men's shoes for close to half. They also have women's loafers. Brockton, nearby, has many shoe factories. If you feel like exploring, cross the railroad tracks to the non-factory side, and look for shoe outlets on side streets off the main shopping street.

Webster's, Hudson
Diamond Shoe Store, Marlborough

For those who live west of Boston it is worth a drive to check out shoe bargains at these two stores. In the main shopping areas of small towns; easy to find.

FABRICS, TRIMMINGS

Kneeland Street (walk from Boylston St. MBTA stop to Stuart, which becomes Kneeland after a block or two; or walk down Washington St. from the department store area.)

This is Boston's center for fabrics, especially locally produced woolens of excellent quality. (It also adjoins Chinatown.) You enter dark stores overcrowded with bolts and rolls of fabric. "How much is this piece?" Standard reply, "How much do you want?" This means he is willing to bargain, but it might also mean: 1. "there's not much on the bolt," or 2. "are you really interested?" 3. "life is hard and dealing with women all day is not the best way I know to make a living." Which is to say that Kneeland St. shopping is more fun and less predictable than department store shopping. One of the bigger shops, **Eastern Textile**, see below, recently moved nearer the big department stores, but enough of the textile outlets remain to make Kneeland St. worth exploring. Don't miss the side streets nearby. **Fainart's**, 61 Kneeland, Open 9-5 Mon-Sat has almost any drapery fabric you could want—hardware, too. **Chas. Slesinger**, next door, packs a lot of bargains into a little space. Open 9-5 Mon-Sat, "but I'm usually here earlier." Saturdays in July and early August most of the smaller stores are closed.

General Textile, 47 Temple Pl., Boston. Open daily 8:30-6, Mon and Wed 'til 9.

Formerly on Kneeland St., the main floor has quality fabrics at standard prices. Discount prices on selected materials upstairs and down.

Windsor Button Shop, 36 Chauncy St. (behind Jordan Marsh) Open daily 9-5:30, Mon and Wed 'til 8:30.

Delightfully jammed with buttons, sequins, braids, trims, novelties, and notions! They also have unbleached muslin, felt linings, and quilt batting.

Fabrications, 1724 Mass. Ave., Cambridge. Open Mon-Wed 10-6. Thurs-Fri 10-8, Sat 10-5; 1337 Beacon St., Brookline, Open 10-6, Thurs 10-9, Sat 10-5.

Marvelous for knits. A new store with a following.

Fabric Village, 543 Boylston St., Boston. Open Mon-Sat 10-5:30.

Up-to-date prints at discount prices. Stop in on a Newbury St. jaunt.

Kroll Hammond Design Workshop, 1122 Mass. Ave., Cambridge. Open 9-10 Mon-Sat.

Berserk—but interesting. African prints, velvet, silks.

Ralph Jordan's, 332 Washington St., Brighton, Open 9:30-5:30, Tues and Fri 'til 8:30.

Ralph has moved into a bigger store; he has an even better selection of yard goods, notions, trims, and patterns.

Eastern Mills, Rosenblatt Brothers, 170 Third St., Chelsea. Open Mon-Fri 9-12, 1-5. Closed Sat.

Our famous felt-man sells it by the pound. Choose your own pieces from a huge selection. Much, much cheaper than buying it by the yard in a regular store.

Mill Outlet Store, Railroad Ave., Chelsea. Open 9:30-5:30 Mon-Sat.
Lillian's Fabrics, 119 Ferry St., Malden. Open Mon-Thur-Sat 9:30-6; Tues-Fri 9:30-9.
Stevens Mills, North Andover, Rt. 93 to Haverhill exit. Open Mon-Sat 8:30-5:30.

The three favorite spots of our shrewd Somerville seamstress. Try them if you're north of Boston.

Fabric Fair, 765 Revere Beach Parkway. Open 9-5, Thurs 9-8:30, Sat 10-4:30.

Discovered on the way home from the beach. Lots of exciting cloth! They even sell Belding Corticelli thread at a discount.

Natick Mills, 64 Main St., Natick. Open 9-5 Mon-Sat.
Especially good for draperies.

Sportswear, Inc., 136 Howard St., Framingham. Open 9-5,
Thurs-Fri 9-9.
Seamstresses west of Boston say this is the place to go.
Fabrics, trims, drapery materials.

L. T. Moulton Company, 10 Corey St., Melrose. Open 8-5
Mon-Sat.
Custom draperies. Excellent work at excellent prices.
Sales are at the factory.

Gilchrist's Basement (listed above) usually has such things as
quilted nylon, cotton knits, or other specialty fabrics at very
low prices. They also have 9¢ zippers if you dare trust them.

Zayre Department Store, 160 Alewife Brook Parkway,
Cambridge (and lots of other locations) Open 10-10 Mon-Sat.
Typical discount department store. Fabrics aren't too
bad. Good yarn buys on sale.

King's Department Store, 171 Watertown St., Newton. Open
10-10 Mon-Sat.
Good for cheap but gay prints. Zayre's and King's fabrics
are often unmarked seconds.

FOR FABRICS TRY: RALPH JORDAN TEXTILES

FOOD

Public Market, Haymarket Sq. On Fri and Sat find the street vendors calling their wares: "Hey dearie, want some pork chops?" Or "Not a bone, not a stone, these dates are pitted!" The wary shopper can come home laden with bags of beautiful fruit and vegetables at half supermarket prices—but the gullible gal will soon find the rotten oranges and frozen string beans in the bottom of her bag. Haymarket rules: Be alert, take plenty of shopping bags with heavy handles; don't be afraid to sass back; double up on transportation as parking is scarce.

Farm Produce Stands can be found on country roads not far from Boston. Route 2 and 2A toward Lexington and Concord have many stands piled high with pumpkins and cider jugs in the Fall. Closer in is DeVincent Farms, 378 Beaver St., Waltham. They pick corn while you wait.

Kay's Market, 594 Mt. Auburn St., Watertown. Open 8-6 Mon-Fri. Fresh fruit, vegetables, assorted nuts, Syrian and Armenian products.

DiMare Bros., 493 C St., Boston. Open Mon-Fri 8-4.
Nuts in bulk for squirrel lovers and other eager consumers of peanuts, pistachios, almonds, walnuts, and pecans.

Tip: The thriftiest woman we know buys all her fruits and vegetables by the bushel at the end of the day when the produce man wants to get rid of them. She spends a lot of time sorting, but says it's worth it. A friend of hers climbs fences. When she sees pears or apples falling to the ground she runs around and rings doorbells and offers to pick them. When you find a better deal, don't tell.

JULIA CHILD BUYS MEAT AT SAVENOR'S, 92 KIRKLAND IN CAMBRIDGE

Waltham Supermarket, 836 Main St., Waltham. Open Mon 9-6, Tues-Wed-Thurs 8:30-9, Fri 8-10, Sat 8-6.
Besides having the most variable store hours in the city, they have good bargains on meat. Women who know cuts and quality do better than average.

Salett's, 65 Salem St., Boston. Open daily 8-6, Fri 8-9.
Reliable meat; good prices. There are many meat markets in the Haymarket-Faneuil Hall area. You have to be an expert and a skeptic to survive some of them. There are good ones, however, and Salett's (across the freeway from Haymarket) is one of the best. Mostly wholesale, their biggest retail business is on Fridays.

George A. Field Co., 22 North St. (Haymarket area) Mon-Thurs 7-6, Fri 7-9, Sat 6:30-6.
A dependable place to guy GOOD meat. Prices comparable to supermarkets.

Pepperidge Farm Thrift, Trapelo Road, beyond Cushing Square towards Waverly, Belmont. Open 10-6 daily, 10-5 Sat.
Good day-old bread. If you have a freezer or neighbors to split it with, buy a case of bread, usually available on Tues-Wed-Thurs. Bargains by the loaf are available every day.

Kasanof's Bakery, 219 Blue Hill Ave., Roxbury. Open 7-4.
Good buys on Jewish bread and rolls.

Arnold Thrift Store, 493 Common St., Belmont. Open Mon-Sat 10-6.
Surplus and day-old products. Cheaper by the case.

201

Morton's Commissary Store, Boylston St., Brookline. Open Mon-Sat 7-6, Sun 8-1 p.m.

A small self-service store is attached to the bakery which makes all the goodies for Morton's Store, FRESH as well as day-old bargains. Free samples, too.

Tip: Get to know a route man. It's fresher off the truck than at the day-old stores.

These firms will deal with churches if buying in large amounts for dinners, etc. They might sell to individuals if they are buying $30-50 worth at a time.

Suffolk Grocery Co., Inc., 460 E St., Boston. Open 8:30-4:30 weekdays, until 12 on Sat.

Kyes Supply Co., (meat) 25 Foodmart Rd., South Boston. No set hours but they're there by 7; closed Sat.

FURNITURE AND HOUSEWARES

Design Research, Warehouse: 237 Putnam Ave., Cambridge. Design Research hardly belongs in a chapter on bargains. It is expensive and snooty and great fun for browsing. But occasionally colorful flags will fly on Putnam Ave. announcing a warehouse sale. Furniture, Marimekko dresses and fabrics, pottery, glass and wood products will be marked down. Signs announcing the sale will be posted at the store on Brattle St. a week or so before.

Harbor Design, 63 Long Wharf, Boston. Open Mon-Wed-Fri 10-9; Tues-Thurs 10-5:30.

Scandinavian furniture—some say for less. An inspection trip to the wharf is fun.

Building 19 Sales Company, Hingham Industrial Center Rt. 3A, Hingham, Mass. Open two days only: Sat 9-5, Mon 9-9.

The outstanding buys are carpeting and appliances. Also clothing, housewares, and furniture.

Don's Contract Sales, 259 Lowell St., Somerville. Open daily 9-5; Sat 'til 1, Wed 'til 9.

Furniture show room in a mattress factory. They make dormitory bedding for many colleges in the area. Sleep like a Harvard man.

THERE IS A
GREAT SUB
SHOP JUST
DOWN THE
STREET...

Don't Forget The Quincy Bargain Barn.

Furniture-In-Parts (also called the Door Store), 42 Boylston St., Cambridge. Open Mon-Tues-Wed-Fri 10-7; Thurs 10-9; Sat 10-6.

Just what it says. They sell tops and legs and backs and sides and cushions. You can certainly buy lumber cheaper if you want to track it down in the suburbs. But they do sell some things that are hard to get elsewhere. They are convenient and popular with students.

Commonwealth Builder's Supply, 375 Boylston St., Brookline. Open 8:30-6 daily; 8:30-1 Sat.

Commonwealth has moved their desks and shipping boxes to a new store on Rt. 9. Small appliances are on display, but for major items the most they can show you is a brochure—and a decidedly lower price. Do your looking elsewhere.

Raymond's, 518 Washington St., Boston. Open Mon and Wed 9:30-9. Tues-Thurs-Fri-Sat 9-5:30.

Ignore Uncle Eph but not the rug department. Watch the ads for outstanding broadloom buys—even better at warehouse sales. If you know what you're looking for you can even discover some Oriental gems among their special shipments.

National Foam and Rubber Company, Inc., 394-396 Atlantic Ave., Boston. Open Mon-Fri 9-5; Sat 9-12.

All kinds of foam cut to order. The kids can watch the boats in the harbor while you look over the remnants upstairs. TIP: Watch Paul Simon's mother gluing scraps of latex together for tractor seats. Idea? (Near So. Station, not far from Harbor Design.)

Moe Black's Shack, 140 Lexington St., Waltham. Open Mon-Fri 9-9; Sat 9-6.

Plumbing supplies, sporting equipment, toys and miscellaneous—with the emphasis on miscellaneous.

J. B. Green and Co., 314 Arsenal St., Watertown. Open Mon-Fri 7:30-5; Sat 7:30-11:45.

Bricks: they'll sell you 1 or 1,000. Some people use them to build book cases. One impoverished graduate student used them to elevate his furniture several feet to take advantage of the warm air closer to the ceiling.

Cross Imports Inc., 210 Hanover St., Boston. Open 8:30-5:30.

A reader writes: "It has the most fascinating window display of all sorts of imports—practical and impractical." Inside the prices are O.K. too.

China Fair, 1638 Beacon St., Brookline. Open 10-6, Thurs-Fri 10-9.

A poor man's pot shop. Pots, stainless, housewares, imports. Even seconds of Vera tablecloths.

Newton Pottery, 1021 Boylston St., Newton (Rt. 9) Open 9-5:30.

Pottery, imported and local. Cookware, woodenware, stainless steel, seconds of Arabia dinnerware, all for less.

The Upper Story Warehouse, 171 Huron Ave. Open daily 10-5:30.

A limited selection of mark-downs from their big store on Mass. Ave. Dishes, accessories, furniture.

FURNITURE—USED

Morgan Memorial—Goodwill Stores, main store 93 Berkeley St., Boston. Open 9-5.

Variety of old furniture most with a coat of Goodwill's own inimitable varnish.

St. Vincent De Paul, 1280 Washington St., Boston. Open 8-4:30 daily; 8-12 Sat.

The Catholic charity. They supposedly price according to how needy you look.

Salvation Army, 718 Mass. Ave (and lots of other locations: see phone directory) Open 9-4 (closed for lunch 12-1); 9-3:30 Sat.

Like Goodwill and St. Vincent De Paul, they have occasional gems among the salvage.

Back Bay Movers, 188 Brighton Ave., Allston. Open 8-5:30 Mon-Sat.

Friendly and cheap.

Dover Country Store, Dover, Mass. 128 to Needham or follow Centre St., through Newton; past Rt. 9. It becomes Highland Ave. and leads you directly into Needham Centre. Turn right on Great Plain Ave., then left one block later at the sign pointing to Dover. Follow a delightful country road until you see a small green with a war-memorial monument. Bear right and you'll see the country store.

A truck full of used furniture comes in every day anytime between 2 and 4. There is always a small crowd of potential buyers who watch the unloading greedily, then pounce on their favorite when the last piece is out of the truck. Amazing bargains at prices much below city stores. Each day's bargains vary and not much is left over from one day to the next, so try to make it about unloading time. There is penny candy to help pass the time.

Albany Carpet Cleaning, Rugg Road, Allston. Open 7:30-5 Mon-Sat.
A full department of used rugs.

Person-to-person Sales
You can eliminate the middle man by scouring the ads in local papers, checking bulletin boards at the supermarket or at such places as Holden Green (take Holden St. off Kirkland, Cambridge), Peabody Terrace (Harvard married student housing) and Westgate (MIT married housing). An excellent lead is a small weekly sheet called the **Want Ad-Vertizer**, readily available at the supermarket or corner drugstore.

Trash Day
Spring is a good time to make an after-dark trip to the rubbish cans behind your building (you'll probably meet the neighbors). Or pick up bargains on the street. One enterprising girl made slipcovers out of bunting found outside of Symphony Hall; another used wine box dividers found behind a French restaurant for spice shelves. For the serious collector, there are more substantial rewards. Last season was tops for antique beds.

Auctions

There are all kinds of auctions. Professional dealers specialize in antiques; churches, firemen, and local clubs sponsor benefit auctions where you might discover anything from a broken washing machine to a piece of Tiffany glass—more often a broken washing machine. The newspaper classified sections list many. For country auctions look for posters in store windows and notices in local newspapers. If you are serious about buying, attend the preview, usually a couple of hours or a day before.

WATCH THE CHANNEL TWO AUCTION ON JUNE FIRST

For sleuths: a Lincoln mother of seven suggests calling auctioneers (listed in yellow pages) and asking for names of their outlets for clothing and surplus merchandise.

PRINTS, BOOKS, SCHOOL SUPPLIES

Harvard Coop, Inc., 1400 Mass. Ave., Harvard Sq., Cambridge. Tech Store at MIT; Medical Coop, Longwood Ave. Open 8:50-5:30 Mon-Sat.

With a Coop card ($1 for students, employees and alums of Harvard or MIT) you get a dividend at year end, sometimes amounting to 10% of your purchases. Three stories of books in the Harvard Coop Annex—also good buys on records and prints.

Harvard Book Store, 1248 Mass. Ave., Cambridge (with branches at Northeastern and Tufts). Open daily 9-10.

A big selection of art prints, unframed, for $1. Also travel posters, framed prints.

Schoenhof's, 1280 Mass. Ave., Cambridge. Open 9-6 six days.

A very fine print and framing section in the back part of a foreign book store. They have quite a few inexpensive prints, travel and kindergarten posters.

Marlboro Barber Shop, Marlboro and Mass. Ave., Boston.

In the back room they have 15, 25, and 50¢ used picture frames.

New England Mobile Book Fair, 70 Needham Street, Newton. Open Mon-Sat 8:30-5:45.

20% off on most books. Good sale on art books. Fun warehouse browsing.

Used Book Sales

There are many around—rummage sales, secondhand stores, used bookstores. Watch for annual book sales by Wellesley College and other schools in the area. Brandeis holds one near Christmas in an empty store downtown.

Hubley Auctioneers Co., 364 Broadway, Cambridge, holds a week-long sale each year between Christmas and New Years. Years.

J. L. Hammett Company, 48 Canal St. (Haymarket Area) LA 3-5778, open 9-5:30, Sat 9-5.

School supplies, blackboards, maps. Even chair caning.

NEW HAMPSHIRE BARGAINS

Organize yourself for an excursion to Manchester, New Hampshire. Bargain hunters say it's worth the trip; combine it with a color tour in the Fall or sugaring in the Spring.

M.K.M. Knitting Mills, North Commercial St., Manchester.

Carries "Darling" brand sweaters, swim suits, skirts.

Phillips Manufactures, Commercial St., Manchester.

Yarn, brooms, brushes, mops, gifts.

Kimrick Mills and Factory, Turner and Foundry St. Sportswear.

Bee and Bee Shoe Manf., 4 North Bedford St., Manchester. Shoes for people.

Pandora Sweater Factory, Canal St., Manchester. Open 9-5:30; Thurs. 9-9.

PLANTS, FLOWERS, DECORATIONS

Wholesale Flower Market

Now located in a section around 500 Tremont St., Boston. It will move as soon as a new market is completed adjacent to the S.E. Expressway and Albany St. in the South End. There are many wholesale (and some retail) florists in this area. You need a florist's card to buy cut flowers in some stores, but most will sell supplies—bolts of ribbon, bags of ornaments, boxes of candles, styrofoam shapes by the dozen—to individuals. If you use enough to buy in quantity you will save a great deal. This is a wonderful place to go just before Christmas when they have many types of balls, artificial fruits, tree lights, as well as elegant ribbon. **Robinson's** opens at 5 a.m. Most close at noon on Sat.

JOHN D. LYONS IN CAMBRIDGE IS A GOOD GARDEN CENTER THALASSA CRUSO HAS BEEN SEEN THERE.

Lexington Gardens

From Lexington Centre, turn right at Minute Man statue, right at Hancock St., keep going until 93 Hancock, there it is. Hours 8-5, closed Sundays. Employees are very helpful and generous with their information. Good sales.

Arrowhead Gardens, 115 Boston Post Road, Wayland (Rt. 20) Open Mon-Sat 9-5:30.
   Great nursery, bug free plants.

A & P Markets have garden fertilizers, which one bargain hunter with a green thumb says give you the most for the least. **Stop & Shop** has excellent plant specials.

Farm Bureau, 158 Lexington St., Waltham, 893-3570.
   Here you can rent many types of gardening equipment from roto-tillers to wheelbarrows to lawn mowers.

209

An Erratic Directory
of Local Delights

Beanpots. Saturday supper begins at U.S. Fixture & Equipment, 31 Boylston St., Brookline. Pots in all sizes start around $1.50.

Bon Bons. A South Carolina chocolate-lover told us about Stowaway Sweets, 154 Atlantic Avenue, Marblehead, a Yankee paradise.

Cacti. A desert in a greenhouse at Carter's Cactus, Route 38, Tewksbury. Suppliers to dime stores, florists, and window-sill collectors.

Chambered Nautili, cross-sectioned and for sale at the gift shop, University Museums, Harvard.

Christmas Trees. The Chief Forester will tell you where you can cut your own. After December 1, phone the State Department of Natural Resources, Forest and Parks Division, 727-3180.

Cider. Best at Lawson's Mill, Rt. 2, Lincoln; easily identified by the lines of parked cars and the really-truly llama.

Cod Tongues and Cheeks. The Chinese Traveler ate them at the Parker House; you might try the Fisherman's Grotto—across from the famous ones—on Fish Pier.

Cranberry-Blueberry Preserves. Write for a list of cranberry yummies or stop in at the Ocean Spray Cranberry House, Rt. 6, Wareham.

Fish. Legal Seafoods, 237 Hampshire St., Cambridge, will tell you what it is and how to cook it. In the North End try Giuffre's, 50 Salem St. In Belmont, Greer's, 353 Trapelo Road.

Flags. The Flag Center, 1865 Massachusetts Ave., Cambridge. For Viet Cong flags try Boston Common.

Forefathers. Find out if they really came on the Mayflower or track down the family skeletons at the New England Historic Genealogical Society, 101 Newbury Street. Goodspeeds, at 18 Beacon, buys and sells family histories.

Harpsichords. Frank Hubbard, 185A Lyman St., Waltham, is king. Get around the five-year waiting list with his do-it-yourself kit. Eighteenth century French replicas start at $595.

Homemade Bagels, soft and lopsided, can be found at Lederman's Bakeries. If you insist on the factory-perfect ones, they've got those too. Also chale, biales, hamantashen, cissel and hot bubke soon after they open at 7. In Brookline at 406a Harvard Street and 1655 Beacon. In Newton Center at 1223 Centre Street.

Honey Health Bread. Four years on our list hasn't spoiled Henry's Bakery, 279 Belmont St., Belmont. They still have the best homemade bread and rolls around.

Jacob's Cattle Beans. Biblical baked beans in cans at the gift shop, Old Sturbridge Village.

Kilns. Everything for the serious potter at Newton Potters Supply, 96 Rumford Ave., near the city incinerator. Dabblers and kids like their self-hardening clay.

Lamejun. Watertown is the spot for things Armenian. Try Aintab Lahmejune, 569 Mt. Auburn St., for fila to make your own baklava. Across the border in Belmont, the Eastern Lamejun Bakers, 145 Belmont St., are open Fridays until 8:30.

Laughing Gas and 25 other comedy-classics of yesteryear. Plan an old-time movie show with Norman Kay, Box 98, Newton Highlands. For a small fee, he will show films from his fascinating personal collection, full-length silent features as well as one and two-reelers. Cheer the hero! Hiss the villian!

Left-Handed Scissors. Stoddard's Cutlery, 50 Temple Place, Boston, has got them. Also swords, magnifying lenses, fly-tying equipment, and stainless-steel thermos bottles starting at $19.95.

DELICIOUS COOKIES & CHOCOLATES, Too.

Macaroons. Constantin makes the pastry and candy at the New Paris, 10 Cypress St., Brookline. Good for a Gallic orgy.

Maple Syrup I. You can't get a better deal than at the Bernardston Auto Exchange, Bernardston, Mass. (just north of Greenfield). Quart, half-gallon, and gallon tins, Grade A and Fancy. Gas-up out front. Check the tractor prices out back. Get your syrup and groceries inside. Top it off with the best 15¢ ice cream cone in the state.

Maple Syrup II. Write Coombs Sugar House, Jacksonville, Vermont, for a brochure describing all kinds of maple delights. They mail gift packs.

Macrobiotic Toothpaste. The Erewhon Trading Company, 303 B Newbury St., Boston, is a faddist's bazaar.

MY FRIEND

Old-Time Uniforms. Recollections, 700 Washington St., Brookline, has them, also old postcards, mounted elk heads, and a resident potter.

212

Oriental Rugs I. Arthur Gregorian, 2284 Washington St., Newton, specializes in Persian lore and exotic display. He deals in cash only, lots of it.

Oriental Rugs II. Treasures may lie beneath the disorder at the Brookline Oriental Rug Co., 1475 Beacon St. It helps if you speak Arabic. Look for extremely fair prices at the Rug Galleries, 1680 Beacon.

THE NICEST RUG MAN IN TOWN IS MR. ZULALIAN AT 1680 BEACON ST.

Papaya Strips and English Gooseberries. Cardullo's, 6 Brattle St., Cambridge, is good for homesickness; canned goods you can't get elsewhere.

Quail Eggs. A quarter a dozen at the ag-school dairy bar, housed in a Richardsonesque railroad station at the University of New Hampshire, Durham. Hard-boil them for small eaters.

Ravioli Cutters. For imaginative cooks and Italian mamas. Cross Hardware Co., 210 Hanover St., has got it all.

Sharksfins, dried mushrooms, bean thread, and other oriental ingredients can be purchased at Sun Sun Company, 24a Oxford St., Boston, or at nearby Chinese import companies.

Six-Foot Recorders. Friedrich von Huene, 59 Boylston St., Brookline, maker and importer of historical woodwinds, has a recorder taller than he is.

Six-Foot Sandwiches. For parties or big appetites, King Caterers, 379 Cambridge St., Brighton, makes submarines six-feet long. They need three days' notice.

Squirrel Traps. If you have visitors in your attic, call the Massachusetts Society for the Prevention of Cruelty to Animals. They will help you solve your problem non-violently.

Titmice Satellites and other enticements for birders and birds are sold at the Audubon Society gift shop, Drumlin Farm, Lincoln.

Tramways. Soar between trees with the greatest of ease with backyard equipment from Child-Life Play Specialties, 1640 Washington St., Holliston. They'll mail a catalogue.

Wallace Beery Undershirts. Be hip from the inside out. Shop Snyder's Army Navy Store, 601 Washington St., Boston.

Whale Steak. Try Clements Market, 223 North Harvard St., Allston.

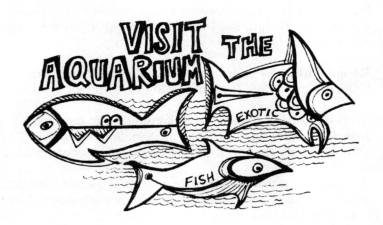

John D. Peters

Indians

SUSA

This chapter is devoted to children, to places they like and things they like to do. Most of the offerings included are described in full. A few entries are simply reminders from a child's point of view of well-known museum and historic sites. If you don't find all you need to know about them in this chapter, check the index for other references in the book.

A is for action . . . Push computer buttons, turn a clothes wringer, weigh yourself with cans of soup, giggle at the funny mirrors, crank the stereopticon, taste Indian pemmican, try on a pro basketball player's shoes—or do whatever else is new at the **Children's Museum**, 57 Eliot St., Jamaica Plain, where learning about the world is fun. Membership in the museum admits you free and brings a newsletter telling about current events and happenings. Call the "What's Up" number, 522-5454, for the daily program. Open weekday afternoons 1-5, Sat-Sun 10-5. Adults $1.25, Children 75¢.

B is for battleship . . . Children who like climbing over the cannons on Old Ironsides might enjoy taking on "Big Mamie," the mammoth World War II battleship, **U.S.S. Massachusetts**, docked at State Pier, Fall River, 45 miles southeast of Boston. Plan on about two hours once you're aboard. Open year round 9-sunset. Adults $1, children 50¢.

B is for boats . . . The sedate and old-fashioned Swan Boats in the Boston Public Garden are pedaled, not paddled, by a young man seated in the "swan" at the end. They are still operated by descendants of the inventor, "Admiral" Paget. Bring along some bread to feed Mr. and Mrs. Mallard and their brood, then when you get home read about them in Robert McCloskey's *Make Way For Ducklings*. The Swan Boats are afloat Easter through September. Adults 25¢, children under twelve 15¢. There are lots more boats in Chapter 17 - the sports chapter.

C is for circus . . . The big show comes to town in May. Watch for announcements in the papers and on telephone poles. Jordan Marsh has a free animated circus in July. The Circus Room at the Sudbury Country Store near the Wayside Inn is open in summer, 25¢.

P. T. Barnum was once a trustee of Tufts University in Medford. His memorabilia, including the stuffed skin of his mascot elephant Jumbo, are in the **Barnum Museum** on campus. Open during the academic year Mon-Fri 8-4:30, Sat 9-12 and 2-5, Sun 2-5.

217

D is for dinosaur . . . Look for the small case of dinosaur eggs in the corridor between the botanical exhibits and the gift shop at Harvard's **University Museum**. The pre-historic skeletons are in the room to your left; the musk ox, boa constrictor, rhinoceros, anteater, giraffe, Galapagos tortoise, all safely stuffed and glass encased, are in adjoining rooms. Harvard's natural history museums are free and popular with children. "Perambulators are not permitted." Open Mon-Sat 9-4:30, Sun 1-4:30.

E is for easel . . . Crafts, painting, treasure hunts, films and other artistic activities are free at the **Children's Room**, Boston Museum of Fine Arts. But you must pick up a ticket at the Fenway entrance to the Museum 15 minutes before class time, as each class is limited to 35. Grades 1-2 are welcome on Tuesday from 3-4:30; grades 3-4 on Wednesday 3-4:30; and all grades on Fridays 3-4:30 and on Saturdays 10:15 and 1:30.

THE BROOKLINE ARTS CENTER, 86 MONMOUTH, ALSO HAS GOOD CHILDREN'S PROGRAMS.

The **Children's Art Center**, 36 Rutland St., has free classes Saturday mornings and after school. Open 9-5 weekdays, Saturday 9-11:30, September through June.

The **DeCordova and Dana Museum and Park**, Sandy Pond Road, Lincoln has art, dance and dramatic classes for children. Phone 259-8355 for information. The Museum itself is fun for a family art outing. If the current exhibit inside doesn't appeal to you, you can explore the grounds, discovering sculpture among the trees. Open Tues-Sat 10-5, Sun 1:30-5. Adults 50¢, children free.

F is for footlights . . . Energetic performances in an intimate theatre make for lively interplay between actor and audience at the **Charles Playhouse Musical Theatre for Children,** 76 Warrenton St. Children need little encouragement to join the actors on stage afterwards to ask for autographs or question them on details of the story. October-April there are plays at 11 and 2 Saturdays, and on weekdays during school vacations. All seats are $1.50. The series of 5 is $4.80. Phone 338-9393 for reservations.

The Boston Children's Theatre produces excellent plays with kids as actors October-May at New England Life Hall and on Stagemobile Tours in July and August. For tickets write to 263 Commonwealth Ave. or phone 536-3324.

The Cambridge Opera Workshop stages productions for children at First Church Congregational, Saturdays December through May. Phone 876-5829 or 259-8937 for schedules and ticket information.

Other theatre companies in the area schedule occasional performances for children. Watch the newspapers for details.

G is for globe . . . There is a 25-ton revolving globe in the courtyard outside the map building at **Babson Institute,** Babson Park, Wellesley (Rt. 16 to Abbott Rd. to Forest St.). Inside the building is the world's largest relief map of the United States. The Coleman May Building is open daily 2-9. You can see the Globe anytime.

Get inside the world at the **Mapparium,** Christian Science Publishing Company, 1 Norway St., Boston. Once you step onto the transparent bridge, you are completely surrounded by an illuminated world globe. Open Mon-Fri 8-4:15, Sat 8:15-4. Free

H is for houses . . . Children get a mimeographed "see what you can find" game when they enter the **Adams Birthplaces** in Quincy. **John F. Kennedy Birthplace** in Brookline may be even more interesting to those born in the Kennedy era. The guides at **Longfellow House** in Cambridge will point out the portraits of "grave Alice, and laughing Allegra, and Edith with golden hair."

The **Whittier house** in Haverhill (north of Lowell) is notable as the setting for "Snowbound"—and for the bedroom built over a rock too big to move. The house is on Amesbury Road, Route 110, Open Tues-Sat 9-6, Sun 1-6, adults 50¢, children 25¢.

In Sudbury there is proof that an even better-known literary masterpiece was based on fact. The **Little Red Schoolhouse** which Mary's Lamb once attended has been moved to a spot near the Wayside Inn and is open afternoons in summer free.

The **Jackson Homestead**, 527 Washington St., Newton, was once a station on the Underground Railroad. It is a busy community center with after school classes in fireplace cookery, candle-dipping, weaving, handling of guns. Visitors are welcome Mon-Fri 2-4 unless classes are in session. Phone 332-3920 to be sure.

220

I is for instrument . . . Children's concerts of the **Boston Symphony Orchestra** are geared especially to those fifth grade and older, but younger children are welcome if they can sit still for an hour. There are three concerts each month, Saturday mornings in November, January, and March. The $6 series tickets admit the holder to one concert each of the three months. But they sell out early. Phone 266-1492 for information.

Newton, Brookline, Belmont and many other suburban towns have local children's programs. These are often a more convenient and less expensive introduction to concert going. Local groups often sponsor performances by the **Boston Youth Symphony Orchestra** under the direction of the School of Fine Arts at Boston University. Watch your local newspaper or look for posters in store windows.

For children who want to play as well as listen there is **instruction** available at the two branches of the Community Music Center, 32 Rutland St. and 251 Commonwealth Ave., both open to non-residents. The All-Newton Music School, 321 Chestnut St., West Newton, has group and individual lessons for adults and children.

The Longy School of Music in Cambridge and the New England Conservatory are professional music schools offering instruction for children. The Conservatory has suburban branches. Those interested in the Yamaha Music Course for children should contact the Williams Piano Shop, 123 Harvard St., Brookline. For residents of Belmont, instrumental lessons sponsored by the Belmont Music Committee are an excellent value. Pick up a brochure at the Belmont Library or phone Mrs. Powers, 484-2714.

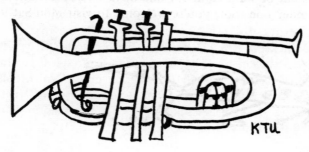

J is for jitney . . . Look for one at the **Antique Auto Museum** at Larz Anderson Park in Brookline. If you don't have the admission price in your pocket, peek over the fence at the parked cars gathered for the annual Duster's Meeting, the second Sunday in August.

You may see an antique auto or two along the turnpike any summer Sunday. **The Sturbridge Auto Museum**, a mile west of the Village, is open 10:30-9:30 daily April to December. Adults 75¢, children 25¢.

K is for kitten . . . Adopt a foundling kitten or dog at the Animal Rescue League, 10 Chandler St., Boston, (open Mon-Fri 10-4, Sat 9-11:30) or at the Adoption Ward of Angell Memorial Hospital, 180 Longwood Ave., Boston, (Mon-Sat 10:30-3:30).

Ellen M. Gifford Sheltering Home, 30 Undine Road, Brighton, 254-2962, is just for cats—150 of them. If you have an extra cat or want to adopt one or just can't imagine that many under one roof, you're welcome to visit Mon-Sat 9-5.

L is for locomotive . . . Ride behind a real steam locomotive at **Edaville,** in South Carver, Massachusetts, 40 miles south of Boston. After a six mile ride through the cranberry bogs, eat barbecued chicken and cranberry sauce under the pines. Then visit the recreated 19th-century village with its drug store, barber shop and horsedrawn fire engine. At Christmas time, the heated train takes you past brightly lit Christmas scenes. From June 19-Labor Day, Edaville is open 10-5 daily, Sun 12-5. Also Sundays 1-5 in May, September, and October. The Christmas Festival in December is open weekdays, 4-9, weekends, 2-9. The train ride is $1.25 for adults, 60¢ for children; the museum, adults 35¢, children 15¢. The combination ticket is adults $1.50, children 70¢.

Red-blooded New England children get that way by eating cranberries raw. After a trip to Edaville to see how they grow, grind them into relish with mother's help or dump a box full into a pan of water. Throw out those that sink. Cook the rest with sugar and water until they pop.

M is for mummies . . . Find them downstairs in the Egyptian collection at the Museum of Fine Arts. Friendly guards will point the way and suggest other areas of the museum children may enjoy.

Well-behaved musicians eight and older may handle some of the instruments in the antique collection. (see Camerata Concerts)

N is for nature . . . A Thornton Burgess story, complete with juice break and visit with one of the characters, has been a Sunday afternoon feature at **Drumlin Farm**, South Lincoln. But the program for children varies. It might be sheep shearing, bird banding, or a hayride. Saturday and Sunday afternoon activities start at 3 and are listed in the weekend newspapers. Open daily until sunset. Buildings close at 5 pm. Free except for $1.50 parking charge on Sat and Sun which also admits you to afternoon activities.

In summer the Audubon Society sponsors four two-week **day camp** sessions at Drumlin Farm and at Mill Pond in Sudbury. Campers from grade three and up spend mornings in the field studying pondlife, flowering plants, birds, mammals and forestry. Older campers may learn dying, weaving, and building shelters. For information write or phone the Day Camp Registrar, Drumlin Farm, Lincoln 01773. (259-9500, ex. 65)

The Will C. Curtis Garden in the woods, Hemenway Rd., Framingham, also has nature courses for children. Phone 877-6754.

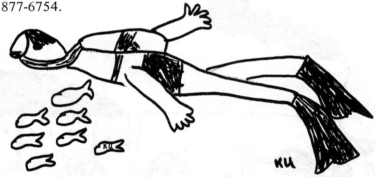

O is for ocean . . . Your explorations of the rocky New England shore may take on new dimensions after a visit to the **New England Aquarium**. Seals, porpoises, sharks, otters, penguins, all kinds of turtles, and an eery octopus are among the inhabitants on display. At the special pool on the third level children can sit on the floor and handle the starfish. Strollers are allowed. Open Mon-Fri 9-5, Sat 10-6, Sun 12-5. Adults $1.50, children 75¢.

Nate

P is for parade . . . At Easter time, Grover Cronin's in Waltham draws children from miles around to an Easter Bunny Parade. The Easter Bunny, joined by story book and TV characters parades down Lexington St. to Main, past the Common, then down Moody St. to the store. It's on a Sunday, three weeks before Easter at 2:30 p.m. Start out early as the streets will be packed.

Flower-covered floats and girls in bathing suits are foreign to New England. Bands, baton twirlers, dignitaries in open cars, and marching military companies ("Ancient and Honorable" as well as contemporary) are the main features of Boston parades on the 4th of July, Bunker Hill Day, Evacuation Day (which is also St. Patrick's Day), Memorial Day and all the other days dear to marchers and kids. The newspaper will give the time and place closest to you.

Q is for quack . . . which is what your feathered friends will do if you're kind enough to feed them. Boston Public Garden ducks are famous but their country cousins are just as hungry. Look for them at Larz Anderson Park in Brookline, Norumbega Tower in Newton, Beaver Brook in Belmont and at dozens of tiny ponds in the towns around Boston.

10...9...8...7...6...5...4...3...2...1
LIFT OFF!

R is for rocket . . . See lifesize Mercury and Apollo capsules at the **Museum of Science.** Then visit the Planetarium to get an idea of where they've been. When you're through exploring outer space, take a look at inner space. The Transparent Woman is a marvelous discovery for children interested in the mystery of "What's inside us." You won't exhaust the wonder in many visits to this family-oriented museum. Special programs and classes are offered for children four years and up. Call the Education Department (742-1410) for a list of courses and registration information. There are fee reductions for members. Open Mon-Sat 10-5, Sun 11-5, Fri eve until 10. Adults $1.50, children 5-16 50¢. After 5 p.m. Fri, adults $1.00, children 50¢.

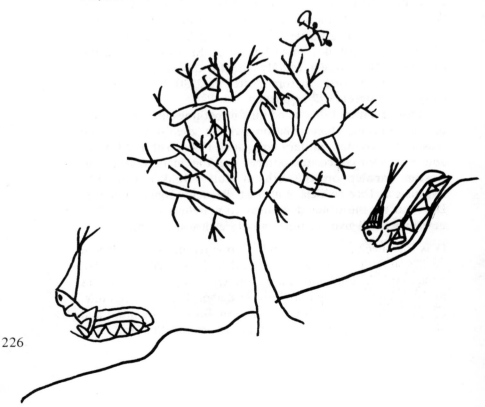

S is for snow ... one of New England's nicest and most abundant natural resources—if you **ski**. In New England children start young. There are beginner's ski hills at the Blue Hills and at Prospect Hill Park in Waltham. The Boston Globe ski clinic, for anyone under 19 is free. The papers will announce the time and place at least two weeks in advance.

One of the delights of snow for children is the way it tangles up traffic, forcing schools to close—day after day after day some winters. When everybody has cabin fever, you may like to try this recipe handed down by a New England grandmother and taste-tested by lots of children. **Snow Cream**: When snow is fresh and clean, get a bowlful. Stir in some sugar, maybe 4 teaspoonsful. Add a little milk and stir until the consistency is a bit like sherbet. Add more snow or more milk as needed, then 1/2 teaspoon of vanilla. Serve at once.

Or get out your can of real maple syrup, pack snow firmly into individual bowls, boil syrup until a bit dropped on snow forms a waxy glob. Get out the pickles and you've got a real sugaring-off party.

T is for trolley ... Underground at Park St. get on the Riverside Trolley. After a short subway ride you'll emerge just beyond Kenmore Station for a lovely view of the Fenway. Stay on for the half hour ride past backyards, through thick woods and busy neighborhoods and parks. You may see a poultry farm not far from proper Chestnut Hill Shopping Center or a tall gray farmhouse looking down on a cluster of newish "ranch houses." In autumn you'll get a refreshing color tour close to home. In winter, through trees bent low with snow, you'll see children skating on frozen Crystal Lake. The trip costs 50¢ each way for adults, children 5-11 20¢. The bounce is free.

Or take the "El" rapid transit from Washington Street to Forest Hills, for a rooftop tour of the South End and Roxbury.

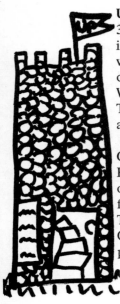

U is for up . . . For a New Boston vantage point, take the 32-second ride to the top of the Prudential Tower. The view is spectacular but the excess energy burned is not as great as when you climb the Bunker Hill Monument in Charlestown, or scramble up the rocks to the top of Prospect Hill in Waltham for a longing look at the ranger's tower. Norumbega Tower in Newton is less strenuous, but the crumbling rock and romantic lore make it an adventure.

You can see the activities of the harbor below from the Custom House Tower off India St. Park in the garage on Kilby St., and watch your car go up on the elevator. Whether or not you're meeting someone, it's fun to watch the planes from the observation deck at Logan International Airport. The Pilgrim Monument in Provincetown at the tip of the Cape has an inclined plane instead of stairs but you'll still puff getting to the top.

V is for village . . . Jordan Marsh's Christmas season greeting to the children of New England is the animated Enchanted Village of St. Nicholas. Quaint figures in windows downstairs beckon to children to come inside where markers direct them through the brightly decorated store to the wonderland at the top. Santa is usually close by.

W is for wharves . . . Boston's **Fish Pier** has none of the tourist gaiety of San Francisco's Fisherman's Wharf, but it has a faded, workmanlike charm of its own. On a weekday morning you might see fish being unloaded; even on a Saturday you can smell them. Take the Northern Avenue Bridge to the wharf area, then get out and walk. See if you can see an ocean liner from the parking lot of Anthony's Pier 4 Restaurant. Some let visitors on board; watch the newspaper for notice.

There is a new waterfront development in **East Boston**. Take the Callahan Tunnel, then turn right immediately after the toll booth. The pseudo-Americana of the shops may be less interesting than the activities of the harbor. Even on slow days you'll see a boat or two. On a Saturday, when Daddy is feeling brave, drive closer for a look at the ramshackle piers, where you'll see huge freight elevators, loading chutes, and lots of pre-pack cargo.

One of the best views of Boston Harbor is from Castle Island in **South Boston**, adjoining Marine Park. Climb up onto Old Fort Independence, rechristened by Sam Adams after the Revolution. From the water side of the hill you can see boats in the harbor and airplanes taking off from Logan Airport directly across the water. Sit on a park bench and watch the unloading of ships at the modern terminal.

X is for x - ing . . . . Boston's new pedestrian safety program insists upon common sense rules. Cross only in cross walks; obey traffic signals and police officers. But there is one way to cross a Boston street that every Beginner should experience. If you don't have at least five children in the family, borrow several of your neighbor's. You can then enjoy having a good Boston Irish policeman stop traffic for you, and wave you across as he booms: "God Bless You, God Bless You!"

Y is for yummy . . . Watch the Hill family and their helpers stirring, cooking, dipping, cutting, and wrapping endless batches of delectable sweets at Hebert's Candy Mansion, Route 20 in Shrewsbury. Mothers are impressed with the Italian marble and carved wood of the old house. All the kids care about are the goodies. The mansion is open every day 8-8. How much you see of the house depends on what's cooking.

PWP

Z is for zoo . . . Children can see, touch, and even feed the animals at the **Franklin Park Children's Zoo**. During the animal ring, (at 11, 2 and 4) a zoo attendant tells about some of the unusual animals. At feeding time, a half hour later, children may help. Familiar animals such as the rabbit and guinea pig are kept along with more exotic ones, like the fennex fox and the gibbon. The main attraction of the bird flight is the stork. Children's Zoo admission is 25¢ for children, 50¢ for adults, open 10-5 daily, Summer, Sundays and holidays, 10-6. Closed Nov to the end of April.

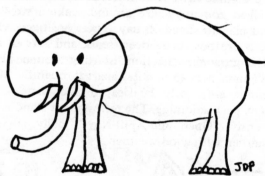

JDP

The main zoo at Franklin Park is rundown, but improvements are planned. Now it isn't unpleasant on a warm day to push a stroller from outdoor cage to outdoor cage. Let the children climb the huge puddingstone boulders or roll on the grass. Don't miss the "toilet trained" elephants, a good sight for impressionable two-year olds.

231

A smaller, but very pleasant zoo is the **Middlesex Fells Reservation** in Stoneham, renovated in 1966. It is off highway 93, at the end of Spot Pond, near the New England Sanitarium. In summer the zoo is open 8-7 (buildings 10-4:50). In winter the zoo is open 8-5 (buildings 10-4:30)

Trailside Museum, Blue Hills Reservation, has animals native to the Blue Hills, in addition to other natural history displays. Children are fascinated with the otter, deer, foxes, raccoons, pheasants, and other animals. Museum admission is children, 10¢, adults 25¢. There are many free animal exhibits out of doors. Open daily, except Mondays 10-5, Sundays 1-5. Closed Mon-Wed, October through April. The museum is at 1904 Canton Avenue, Milton, Route 138.

Benson's Wild Animal Farm, Hudson, New Hampshire, is worth the 45-mile drive from Boston. It's the closest thing to a full-fledged zoo anywhere around. Take a stroller and a picnic and plan to spend all day. There are tigers, elephants, baboons, cockatoos, baby deer, seals, and lots of monkeys among the growing collection. Starting around 11:30 a.m. there are animal acts 45 minutes apart through the afternoon. The grounds are nicely landscaped and there is a small amusement park adjoining. The refreshment stand is crowded and expensive. Open mid-April-Nov 1 daily 10-5. Closing hours lengthen with good weather.

233

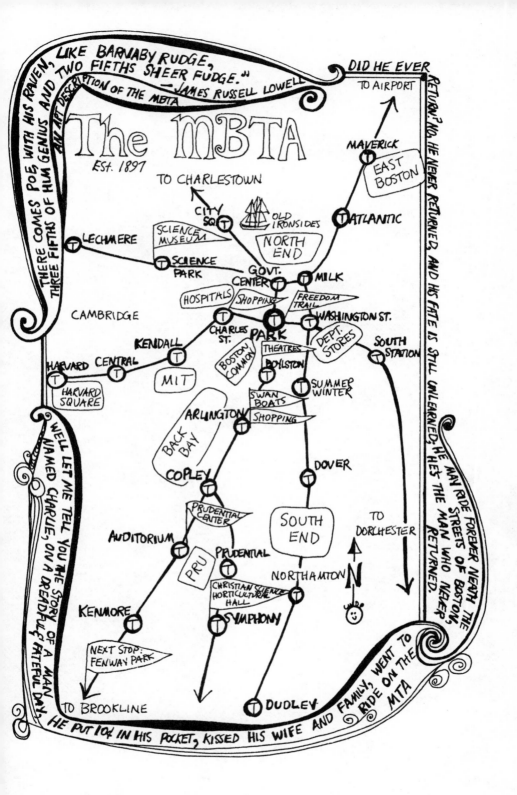

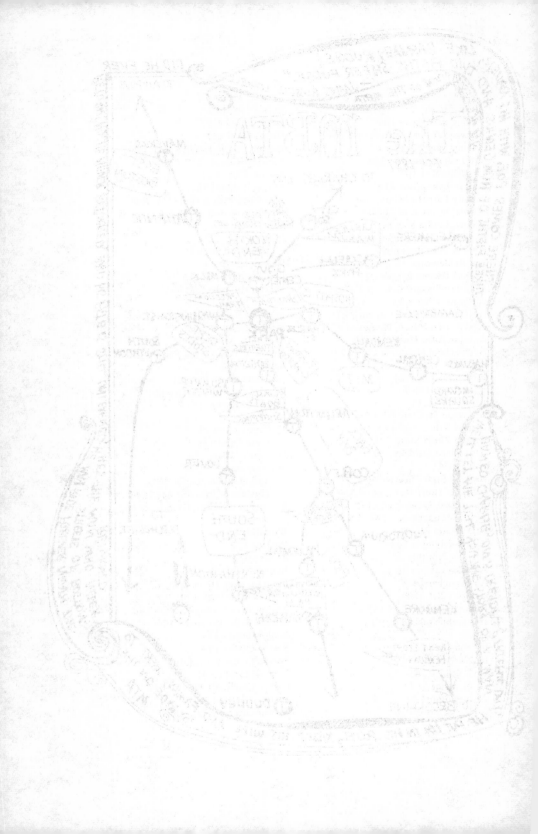

Index

HERE IT IS!

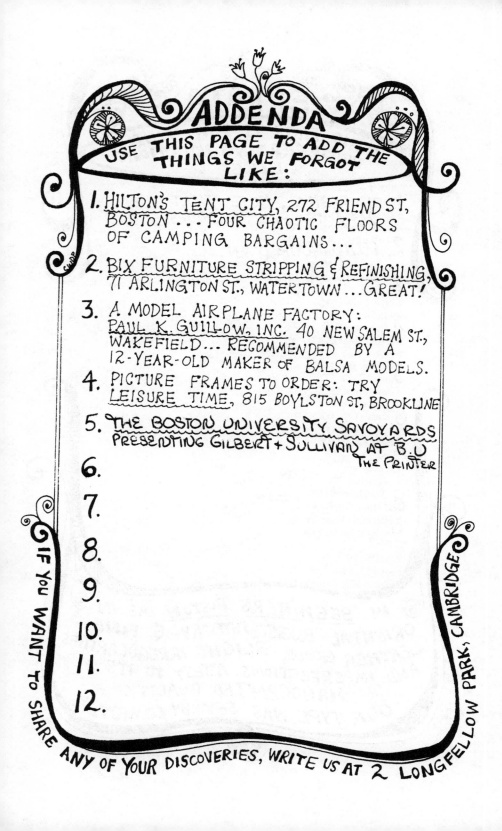

ADDENDA

USE THIS PAGE TO ADD THE THINGS WE FORGOT LIKE:

1. HILTON'S TENT CITY, 272 FRIEND ST, BOSTON ... FOUR CHAOTIC FLOORS OF CAMPING BARGAINS ...

2. BIX FURNITURE STRIPPING & REFINISHING, 71 ARLINGTON ST, WATERTOWN ... GREAT!

3. A MODEL AIRPLANE FACTORY: PAUL K. GUILLOW, INC. 40 NEW SALEM ST., WAKEFIELD ... RECOMMENDED BY A 12-YEAR-OLD MAKER OF BALSA MODELS.

4. PICTURE FRAMES TO ORDER: TRY LEISURE TIME, 815 BOYLSTON ST, BROOKLINE

5. THE BOSTON UNIVERSITY SAVOYARDS PRESENTING GILBERT + SULLIVAN AT B.U
THE PRINTER

6.

7.

8.

9.

10.

11.

12.

IF YOU WANT TO SHARE ANY OF YOUR DISCOVERIES, WRITE US AT 2 LONGFELLOW PARK, CAMBRIDGE

ERRATA

THIS PAGE IS FOR YOUR PROOFREADING NOTATIONS LIKE:

1. ON PAGE 2, NOTE THAT THE MFA IS OPEN FREE TUES. 5 TO 9.

2. FIND YOUR OWN...

3.

4.

5.

6.

7.

8.

9.

IN BEGINNER'S BOSTON, AS IN ORIENTAL RUGS, POTTERY, & FINE LEATHER GOODS, SLIGHT IRREGULARITIES AND IMPERFECTIONS ATTEST TO ITS HANDCRAFTED QUALITY.
OUR TYPE WAS SET BY COMPUTER.